NO DAY SHALL ERASE YOU

THE STORY OF 9/11

as told at the

NATIONAL SEPTEMBER 11 MEMORIAL MUSEUM

Foreword by Michael R. Bloomberg

Edited by Alice M. Greenwald, Museum Director

9/11
MEMORIAL

Skira *Rizzoli*
NEW YORK

This book is dedicated to the 2,983 men, women, and children taken from us
in the terrorist attacks of September 11, 2001 and February 26, 1993;
to the thousands of rescue and recovery workers whose determined efforts paved
the way for healing and rebuilding;
and to everyone who has contributed to the creation of the 9/11 Memorial Museum
so that—through remembrance and education—
we can honor them all and affirm an unwavering commitment to the
fundamental value of human life.

Throughout this book, names in blue signify individuals killed as a result
of the terrorist attacks of September 11, 2001 and February 26, 1993.

CONTENTS

FOREWORD

BY MICHAEL R. BLOOMBERG

Chairman of the Board and 108th Mayor of the City of New York

September 11, 2001, was a day unlike any other in history, and it was clear from the beginning that the 9/11 Memorial Museum would be an institution unlike any other in the world. No memorial or museum of its size has ever been constructed so soon after, and at the same site as, the events out of which it arose. Because of that, the Museum preserves history that is still being shaped. It is a place where people come to heal, but also learn about the past in order to better understand the present and future.

When our Administration entered City Hall on January 1, 2002, cleanup and recovery operations at the World Trade Center site were still underway. We vowed to do everything possible to help create a fitting memorial and museum to honor those who had died, and to teach future generations about what happened.

It wasn't an easy road. With so much riding on every decision and so many different people weighing in, key facets of the project moved slowly, costs swelled, and people began to lose hope that a memorial and museum would ever be built. By 2006, it became clear that the project needed renewed focus, direction, and clarity. That's why, when I agreed to serve as Chairman of the 9/11 Memorial and Museum, our first overarching goal was to open the Memorial in time for the 10th anniversary of the attacks. To reach that goal, we rallied public and philanthropic support, and we worked hard to build consensus around various design considerations.

When family members entered the Memorial Plaza for the first time in 2011 and saw the names of their loved ones inscribed in bronze around two beautiful memorial pools, it was a deeply gratifying day, and also a major milestone. But our work was not over—the 9/11 Memorial Museum was not yet finished.

The rebuilding of the World Trade Center site was one of the most complicated construction projects in the history of the world, involving the governments of two states, the federal government, and the public and private sectors. At the same time the Memorial and Museum were being planned, multiple skyscrapers were being built on the site, including the hemisphere's tallest building, One World Trade Center—as well as two major transit centers with two working railroads running through them. The site had to be refortified against the Hudson River and protected against any future security threats.

Work on the design and content of the Museum had progressed largely in parallel to the work on the Memorial. However, the intricacies of construction and negotiations over long-term governance meant that the Museum would have to open later. Our team, led by 9/11 Memorial President Joe Daniels and Museum Director Alice Greenwald, took advantage of the time to refine the Museum's design, content, and use of technology. We aimed to set a new standard for public engagement and historical interpretation.

Because the attacks of 9/11 are still so recent, the Museum can and does incorporate, perhaps more than any other historical institution, the firsthand accounts of people living today. It also includes real-time recordings—from television, radio, the Internet, and other mediums—on a scale that has never been attempted before, giving visitors a sense of how people around the world experienced 9/11. For those who lived through the day, and those too young to remember it, the Museum strives to make sure that the lessons we learned, and the people we lost, are never forgotten.

The collection of objects and artifacts, many of which are featured in the photos and essays in this book for the first time, is the heart of the institution. It is the result of painstakingly hard work that has been supported by people throughout America and around the world. Friends and family members who lost loved ones on 9/11 donated objects of immeasurable personal value. First responders, elected officials, and people from all backgrounds and walks of life contributed artifacts or oral histories to the Museum to help shine a light on our nation's darkest moment.

Choosing what to display and how to organize the Museum's exhibits required hours of thought, care, and debate. So many people have deeply personal connections to the Museum site and the history it contains. Many more have strong feelings about what the Museum should represent, and how that could be best achieved. There were no simple answers.

My own feeling has always been that in order to best honor those we lost, the Museum had to present the whole and unfiltered story of 9/11. That meant not being afraid to confront information that causes discomfort—or even controversy. When there was disagreement, we listened to every viewpoint and tried to find the best solution. The Museum's goal has always been to present the truth, no matter how difficult, without overwhelming visitors.

Now, the National September 11 Memorial and Museum stand as a powerful testament to what can be achieved when people work together towards a common goal, and we owe a debt of gratitude to everyone who helped bring it to life. In addition to those who donated artifacts or lent their voice to exhibits, civic-minded companies and organizations provided crucial financial support. Architects, designers, contractors, and construction workers created a beautiful structure worthy of the site and its history. The Memorial and Museum's board of directors worked hard to keep the Museum moving along and open it to the public, as did elected officials at every level of government. We also owe a special thanks to the entire Memorial and Museum staff.

In just two years since its opening, the Museum has been honored to welcome millions of visitors of all ages and from every corner of the world. No two people experienced 9/11 in the same way, and each person's visit to the Memorial and Museum has been different. By giving readers a glimpse into the Museum, this book will help more people learn, reflect, and remember—and in doing so, help the Museum achieve its ultimate goal of building a more peaceful future.

CHAIRMAN OF THE BOARD MICHAEL R. BLOOMBERG AT THE 9/11 MEMORIAL, SEPTEMBER 2012
Photograph by Jin S. Lee

INTRODUCTION

BY JOE DANIELS

President and Chief Executive Officer

September 11, 2001, felt like an absolutely incomprehensible moment in history. For those who witnessed the events of that tragic morning unfold—whether in person or, like billions around the world, on television—devastating images of that day are seared into our memories. We remember what we were doing, we remember those we were with, and we will never forget that moment when we understood the magnitude of what was happening.

These memories are visceral. For so many, they are associated with a sense that the world had been irreparably torn. Yet from the very first days following the attacks, the widespread instinct was to respond to this unimaginable tragedy with enormous levels of love and support. Spontaneous memorials sprang up across the United States and around the world. Union Square in New York City was filled with candles, mementos, and photographs within a day. People from all walks of life placed flowers and tributes at U.S. embassies overseas and held candlelight vigils in city streets in places as far apart as Beijing, London, Panama City, and Tehran.

As the months went on, the impulse toward compassionate response transformed into a commitment to preserve the memory of each individual killed in the attacks at the World Trade Center, the Pentagon, and near Shanksville, Pennsylvania. Missing posters that had plastered the surfaces of New York City immediately after the attacks as family members searched for loved ones soon became some of the most iconic and heartfelt memorials to those who were killed. Although the vast majority of people did not know a victim personally, there developed a unifying effort—perhaps as a way to channel the powerful impulse to contribute in the aftermath—to make sure the memory of nearly 3,000 men, women, and children would not fade. The overwhelming shock of such a dramatic loss created an emotional void that needed to be filled. In every sense, those who died that day represented who we are: mothers, fathers, sisters, and brothers, simply waking up and going to work.

This is why we built the National September 11 Memorial at the World Trade Center site, which was designed by architect Michael Arad and landscape architect Peter Walker and dedicated on the 10th anniversary of the attacks with thousands of 9/11 family members in attendance. It is a place to remember and honor the thousands who were killed in the attacks of February 26, 1993 and September 11, 2001; a place made sacred through tragic loss; and a place that recognizes the endurance of those who survived, the courage of those who risked their lives to save others, and the compassion of all who supported us in our darkest hours.

The purpose of the Memorial's companion, the Museum, was aligned with this mission, yet distinct. The attacks that occurred on this site and the history surrounding them were of such magnitude and had such far-reaching implications it quickly became clear that a museum adding depth of understanding and context was not only important, it was necessary. And more than that, visitors would need to know to whom the names etched into the bronze parapets of the Memorial reflecting pools belonged; to learn who these individuals were, to learn about the rich lives that each possessed.

To that end, we envisioned a place that would be the global focal point for telling the story of what happened on 9/11, what led up to it, and its aftermath. It would also be a place to honor and remember each of the individuals killed through the lives they lived, rather than the deaths they died, and to preserve the countless stories of compassion, bravery, and sacrifice on 9/11 and in the days following. One of the reasons 9/11 continues to resonate so many years later is that just as we see ourselves in the faces of those who died, events are unfolding in the news with shocking regularity that parallel that horrific day. In spite of these realities, though, the Museum reminds future generations about the positive legacy of 9/11: how we come together with limitless compassion when the times require.

The process of creating the Museum was a collaborative one, involving staff, members of the 9/11 Memorial Board of Directors, representatives from the 9/11 community (including family members, survivors, and rescue and recovery workers), architects, designers, landmark preservationists, academic advisers, and others with an interest in the story that is told here. Through hundreds of meetings and community forums, together we worked through some of the most challenging questions presented by this difficult history and translated a myriad of personal experiences of the attacks into exhibitions.

The Museum was dedicated on May 15, 2014, in a ceremony led by U.S. President Barack Obama and Memorial Chairman Michael R. Bloomberg. Over the subsequent week, we held special previews of the Museum for more than forty thousand 9/11 community members, including victims' family members, first responders, 9/11 rescue and recovery workers, survivors of 9/11, and lower Manhattan residents, before opening to the public on May 21, 2014. In only four quick months, one million people visited the Museum, and in just more than two years after opening nearly six million people from all 50 states and more than 150 countries have walked through its doors to learn what happened here, honor the memories of all those who were killed, and witness how the world came together on an individual and societal level.

Among those who have visited are thousands of teachers, students (many of whom were not even born at the time of the attacks), and future leaders. Our attendance also includes thousands of men and women at the beginning of their careers as law enforcement officers, intelligence analysts, and rescue workers. For them, the histories recounted here are deeply intertwined with their own, lending a particular power as they learn about one of their profession's most difficult periods of time and reaffirm the values that inspired them to follow such a noble path of service. Within the first 18 months of operations, world leaders ranging from Pope Francis to German Chancellor Angela Merkel to former Prime Minister of the United Kingdom Tony Blair to Indian Prime Minister Narendra Modi made a point of visiting the Museum, a strong demonstration of the continued international significance of the events of 9/11.

The powerful response we have seen from our visitors is a testament to the importance of the story we tell here and the significance of the place where we tell it. Located at bedrock of the World Trade Center site, seven stories below the Memorial, the Museum's core exhibitions allow visitors to learn about the history where it happened, at the very foundation of where the Twin Towers once stood. There are two core exhibition spaces. *In Memoriam*, the memorial exhibition, commemorates the victims of the attacks of September 11, 2001 and February 26, 1993. The historical exhibition, *September 11, 2001*, tells the story of what happened on 9/11 at all three attack sites and explores what led up to the attacks and their continued implications. The following chapters will bring you on a tour through these spaces, down the ramp to bedrock, between the remnants of the steel box columns that once supported the iconic Twin Towers, and through these exhibitions. You will also get an insider's view into some of the most challenging issues faced in the development of the Museum and how they were ultimately resolved.

At the 9/11 Memorial Museum, there is a strong emotional connection between the living and those who were killed—people just like us who simply got up that morning and went to work or boarded an airplane for a business trip or for pleasure. Tragically, there is a connection, too, between current events and the lessons of the past. The Museum does not avoid the hard truths of 9/11 but provides a lens through which to examine them. Despite all of the horrors of 9/11, our city, our country, and our way of life stayed strong. Despite the loss of thousands of family members, friends, and colleagues, recovery workers stayed on burning piles of rubble for weeks and months on end to enable us to rebuild.

Despite the continued existence of terrorism in this world, we can find hope and healing in the strength and resilience forever preserved in this sacred space.

THROUGH THE LENS OF MEMORY
Creating the 9/11 Memorial Museum

BY ALICE M. GREENWALD

Memorial Museum Director

. . . this sacred place of healing and of hope.

—U.S. President Barack Obama,
at the dedication of the National September 11 Memorial Museum

Millions of people from all over the world have experienced the National September 11 Memorial Museum since it opened in May 2014. They continue to come, many staying three hours or more, to remember, to encounter, and to approach an understanding of the unimaginable.

Time and again, visitors will ask what the process was like to create this museum; how we approached its many challenges and how we navigated the diverse and, at times, competing expectations for what it should be. What follows is a view into that planning process, highlighting a few of the critical issues and key choices made in realizing the 9/11 Memorial Museum.

ENVISIONING THE MUSEUM

In its earliest planning phases, those of us charged with the responsibility of envisioning this museum understood the project to be as much sacred as cultural. With work starting barely five years after the attacks, the planning team—museum leaders and advisers; curators, educators, and historians; designers and architects—recognized that the Memorial Museum had to provide a means for processing the experience of 9/11 and for facilitating the grief we all had to go through, as individuals, as citizens of this city and nation, and as members of a world community.

There were certain key assumptions that guided our approach. The 9/11 Memorial Museum had to be about remembering the victims, honoring those who went to their rescue, recognizing the survivors, and paying tribute to those who responded with selfless dedication during the recovery. It needed to communicate the absolute illegitimacy of indiscriminate murder. And it would have to attest emphatically to the unacceptability of terrorism as a response to any grievance, political or otherwise.

We recognized that there was a sense in which the 9/11 story was about great buildings that had been destroyed; that we were mourning their loss as well. But we knew that *our* story could not primarily be about buildings, except insofar as the towers themselves had come to represent something iconic or culturally specific, something inherently symbolic.

WORLD TRADE CENTER TRIDENT COLUMNS IN MUSEUM ENTRANCE PAVILION

With great humility, we acknowledged that our job—for the moment, at least—could not be to attempt to graft historical "meaning" onto the events. To be sure, the attacks would have to be placed in historical context within this museum; 9/11, after all, did not happen in a vacuum. But we instinctively understood that we could not produce a museum that would present this history as a conclusive lesson of some kind. The story of 9/11 was, and is still, evolving, its repercussions still unfolding; there is no "ending" as yet to this story. It would have been presumptuous to be prescriptive or didactic about the historical "lessons" of 9/11. It was simply way too soon.

And so we followed a different path. The character of a visit to this memorial museum would be, for the foreseeable future, an individual experience of meaning-making within a communal setting, a process informed by each person's particular associations with the events. Anticipating that a vast majority of our visitors had lived through an event estimated to have been witnessed by two billion people—one-third of the world's population in 2001—we knew that many would bring their own memories of that day to the Museum. We recognized that one of the great opportunities of this museum would be its ability to become a place where those memories could be affirmed, preserved, and integrated into the larger narrative it would contain.

The process of planning the Museum began in the spring of 2006. Because we were still so close to the events of 9/11, we believed that the Museum had to capture a certain kind of tension: the friction between the ambiguity and unfinished business of loss and the finality and permanence of death. We believed that the Museum could enable visitors to traverse the space between cognitive understanding and emotional intelligence; the space where memory resides. It would provide a lens into the void left in the wake of the attacks and focus, too, on the generosity of spirit that sought to fill it. As we experienced or re-experienced that void and were reminded of our own capacity for constructive response to it, we could, each and together, find a way to move forward.

More than any other aspect, we had to factor in the impact of the Museum being located at what had once been Ground Zero. Planned for the World Trade Center site, the 9/11 Memorial Museum would sit at the nexus of the void, at a site of memory. We knew from the start that this placement would intensify our visitors' encounter with authenticity; they would explore this history in the very space once occupied by the Twin Towers. Our aspiration was ambitious: within that authentic, archaeological context, might memory be harnessed to evoke a sense of common purpose that—if delivered well—could affirm our shared humanity? What a privilege to take on this project!

Not all history museums are situated at the very site where history was made. The specificity of our location required that we focus intently on what happened *here*, and also at the Pentagon, in the sky above us, and in Somerset County, Pennsylvania, on that terrible day in late summer 2001. At the heart of our program would be commemoration, the fundamental commitment to remember those who were killed as a result of the 9/11 attacks and also in the World Trade Center bombing on February 26, 1993.

Already by 2006, politics figured prominently in the many rebuilding projects at the World Trade Center site. This was a history whose ownership was at once singular and universal; whose thousands of constituents would argue for the primacy of their own points of view. We knew from the start that there was a fair chance we might fail; not because building this memorial museum was not worth doing, but because there would be so many forces with legitimate if not necessarily compatible perspectives about the "right" way to tell *this* story at *this* place.

We had to remind ourselves continually that this project was about memory, so that through the act of remembering, we might each confront something immutable and authentic. In the work to create the 9/11 Memorial Museum, we consciously applied the idea that an emotionally safe encounter with difficult history, experienced through the lens of memory, had the potential to inspire and change the way people see the world and the possibility of their own lives. We thus understood our charge: to deliver a memorial museum that could be an agent of resolve, demanding that each of us, individually, nationally, and globally, place a value on every human life.

We would do all of this inside a space that is essentially an urban archaeological site. Set within the remnant foundations of the World Trade Center, this would be a museum containing artifacts that would itself be housed *within* an artifact. Ultimately, the experience of the 9/11 Memorial Museum would be multi-dimensional: a place of learning, remembrance, and inspiration set within a space of palpable authenticity. These multiple functions defined the work of creating this Museum.

PRELIMINARY PLANNING

The effort to conceive and develop the Museum's programmatic content was led by a core planning team operating under the auspices of the National September 11 Memorial & Museum Foundation (known in 2006 as the World Trade Center Memorial Foundation) with the guidance of the Foundation's leadership, including a Board of Directors chaired by Michael R. Bloomberg and President and CEO Joe Daniels. Initially composed of the Museum Director, the Chief Curator, a creative director for museum planning, a museum educator, a public historian with an expertise in memory studies, and an exhibition developer,[1] the core content planning team worked closely with the Foundation's design and construction staff and two architectural teams already on board (Snøhetta for the aboveground entry pavilion and Davis Brody Bond [DBB] for the Museum's belowground spaces). The early planning work benefited from a set of recommendations for an interpretive facility, originally proposed in Studio Daniel Libeskind's 2003 master site plan, *Memory Foundations*, and referred to by the Lower Manhattan Development Corporation (LMDC) as a Memorial Center. Convened by Anita Contini of the LMDC in April 2004, a Memorial Center Advisory Committee consisting of a wide range of 9/11 stakeholders articulated the broad purposes of such a facility, suggesting the scope of subject matter to be addressed through exhibitions. This two-page list of recommended contents and focal points served as a foundational blueprint for the work now to be undertaken by the Museum's core planning team.

From the start of planning in spring 2006, the team consciously embraced a spirit of collaboration. We understood the imperatives of listening to various constituencies and hearing multiple points of view. The process of decision making would involve consensus, often hard won after passionate debate. We also recognized the primacy of storytelling. Unlike more traditional museum practice, where exhibitions are conventionally built to showcase and contextualize key objects and collection resources, this would be a museum in which the selection and sequencing of artifacts and images, the determination of spatial program allocation, and the incorporation of media would all be placed in the service of the story being told.

All museums that document events defined by unimaginable personal loss and collective trauma will inevitably face challenges during the planning phase. The 9/11 Memorial Museum was no exception. But the work to create this particular museum also took place within the context of intense public scrutiny, divergent expectations of what would be appropriate to present at such an emotionally charged site, and the daunting responsibility to construct an exhibition narrative that would effectively codify a history not yet written. A fundamental challenge was how to balance the imperatives and sensibilities of commemoration with education, historical documentation, and the presentation of information that could be both graphic and provocative. Adding to these complications were our temporal proximity to the event itself; key constituencies' continuing personal and communal grief; and the extremely public, and at times politicized, planning process for a museum commemorating an event at once highly local, distinctly national, and essentially global.

Negotiating all of these pressures and considerations required a process that would be both transparent and inclusive.

MUSEUM PLANNING CONVERSATION SERIES

Museums are morphing. Once they were chroniclers or collectors,
gathering objects and facts and putting them on display.
Now many have become crucibles: places where a cultural identity
is hammered out, refined and reshaped.

—Edward Rothstein, *New York Times*, July 20, 2006

As a first step, it seemed essential to create a forum in which representatives of many diverse constituent groups—those who understandably felt an "ownership" of the Museum's content—could come together to be better informed about working assumptions for the museum planning process and contribute to a shared vision and vocabulary for this undertaking. We began with an exercise of collective imagination: envisioning with others what this Memorial Museum should and could become.

In the summer of 2006, the Museum Planning Conversation Series was convened, involving a broadly representative group of project stakeholders: family members of victims, survivors, appointed liaisons from the New York City Police Department (NYPD), the New York City Fire Department (FDNY), and the Port Authority Police Department (PAPD), local residents, downtown businesses, interfaith clergy, architects and landmark preservationists, colleagues in the museum and cultural communities, government personnel, exhibition designers, and other interested parties. Over the course of five presentations that first summer, a distinguished roster of expert advisers engaged participants (averaging well over 90 in attendance) in considering the Memorial Museum's core exhibitions and content programming in light of the following considerations:

- the potential and character of 21st-century museums;

- the particular requirements and sensitivities of memorial museums that must balance the concerns of privacy with the imperative to educate;

- the challenge of understanding the Museum's role and responsibility to present visually difficult imagery without re-traumatizing the public and in an age-appropriate way to younger visitors;

- the recognition that the story told in the Museum would inevitably contribute to the writing of history, and that the emerging story already echoed key themes of the American historical narrative; and,

- the role museums play as instruments of civic renewal.

The discussions and insights shared during this first season of the Conversation Series would continue to influence the evolution of the Museum's content design over the subsequent eight years. Among the guiding principles articulated that summer were those of museum theorist and performance studies professor Dr. Barbara Kirshenblatt-Gimblett, who advised that visitors can experience an emotional and intellectual alchemy in museums that encourages self-reflection, which in turn can lead to moral understanding. She stated that visitors should "find themselves" in the Museum, even if the story is not their personal story; and that site specificity was a critical factor: this Memorial Museum had to be fully "in conversation" with its location at Ground Zero. A key observation that strongly influenced the exhibition design was that memorial museums are performance spaces, not unlike theaters. Where, in a theater, the audience is static and actors move onstage, in a museum, visitors move through exhibitions, enacting the performance of memory and engagement.

Dr. Edward T. Linenthal, battlefield historian and author of books about the creation of the United States Holocaust Memorial Museum and the Oklahoma City National Memorial & Museum, cautioned that compromises would be necessary as the planning team tried to balance unavoidable tensions between commemoration and historical documentation. He affirmed that "controversy doesn't mean that something's wrong; it means that people are passionately engaged."

Dr. Grady Bray, a disaster psychologist and authority on emergency response who had worked with FDNY families after 9/11, wisely instructed the planning team to make curatorial and design selections bearing in mind that anyone who witnessed the events of 9/11—even at the remove of watching televised reports, seen by billions that day—would have experienced a degree of psychological trauma. He urged the team to prepare for intense emotional responses, and to anticipate that *what* would be displayed and *how* it would be displayed had the potential to impact people traumatically, however unintentionally.

Civil War historian Dr. David Blight and American Social History Project cofounder Dr. Stephen Brier guided the Conversation Series participants through a discussion of how public understandings of recent events coalesce into "collective memory," and how the social power of public memory intersects with the evolution of a "national narrative" in American history. With an event that, at the time of this conversation, was a mere five years past, these historians acknowledged that the narrative of the Museum's exhibitions would contribute to the codification of the history, shaping not just how the events would be remembered, but also how they would eventually be understood.

Finally, Dr. Harold Skramstad, president emeritus of the Henry Ford Museum and Greenfield Village, and a museum theorist whose writings had focused on museums as instruments of civic renewal, closed the opening season of the Museum Planning Conversation Series with a charge to focus on the centrality of the visitor experience and to create exhibitions that could realize the educational potential of 21st-century museums as laboratories of participatory learning. In Dr. Skramstad's words, a museum "should not tell visitors what to think, but rather, what to think about."

PLANNING AND DESIGN

In planning the museum, we wanted not only to give visitors the facts but to impress upon them that history is not simply a fixed story of the past but a continuum—and that asking questions and being observant are critical in our ever more interconnected world.

—Michael Shulan, Creative Director, Museum Planning

Those first sessions of the Conversation Series effectively launched the process of envisioning the 9/11 Memorial Museum. Bearing in mind the advice and input of the participants, the creative team began to imagine the visitor experience in a foundational document known as the Journey Narrative. The team worked closely with project architects, planning consultants, key advisers, and especially the Program Committee—the Board-designated group composed of victims' family members and professionals from cultural organizations and museums[2]—to ratify a museum mission statement, clarify project objectives, and identify core programmatic components.

Following a six-month international search, the Foundation engaged the services of a lead exhibition design team, Thinc Design in collaboration with media designers Local Projects, in May 2007. With the lead exhibition designers on board and a clearly articulated mission for the Museum, the schematic design process began in earnest that summer. Among the first steps undertaken by the Thinc and Local Projects team was a pre-design exercise to identify the diverse audiences that the Museum would serve.

To be experienced by a broad range of people as truly authentic, the 9/11 Museum must support the paradoxically contemporaneous functions of bringing closure and acknowledging 9/11's continuing impact. At the same time, it must provide a coherent journey through this complex emotional terrain.

—Tom Hennes, Principal, Thinc Design; Lead Exhibition Designer

The visitor segmentation analysis identified eight fundamental activities that an effective design would need to help visitors to do: remember; understand the space and be oriented to it; learn ways of using the Museum; encounter the story of 9/11; feel the experience is authentic; recognize or discover oneself in the story; experience uplift and pride; and move toward an embrace of complexity.

Before exhibition design could fully begin, it was essential to allocate programmatic content within the existing spaces of the physical plant of the Museum. This exercise of program allocation was not a simple one. The space of the Museum was exceedingly complex: ceiling heights ranged from nine to 60 feet; there were cavernous halls, and federal preservation law required that in-situ archaeological remnants 70 feet belowground be made accessible, thus necessitating the placement of core elements at the foundation level of the site. This particular constraint inspired DBB to insert a winding ramp that in turn called for some level of introductory information while not interfering with the architectural objective of offering progressive views into the spaces below.

Adding to these complexities were considerations of propriety. The open spaces of the Museum—what came to be referred to as the Interstitial Spaces, the areas outside the tower footprints—needed to be age-appropriate, meaning that the most emotionally difficult and explicitly violent content would have to be sequestered in enclosed spaces that visitors would choose to enter rather than simply encounter. Additionally, we had to accommodate monumentally scaled artifacts, accepting the practical necessity of placing them where they could fit and still be meaningful, rather than where they might otherwise support a specific point in the exhibition narrative.

Another exercise that helped to clarify intention for the exhibition design was Thinc Design's Visitor Experience Map, an early attempt to visualize a visitor's pathway through the spaces of the Museum, capturing the affective or emotional objective for each location and stage of the visitor's journey.

While the early assumptions about program components, their placement, and even the names of the spaces would evolve and change over time, the core assumptions about the visitor experience remained remarkably unchanged as the Museum took shape.

Even at this early stage, members of the planning team understood that the exhibition program for this museum would be defined by a commitment to create environments that spur sensory and emotional cognition even before a visitor might fully comprehend narrative content. Artifacts, images, sound, digital visualizations, and text would combine to cue visitors to an unfolding story line. Visitors would move along a pathway that opened to views of in-situ remnants of the original World Trade Center site; encounters with monumental artifacts would convey an unfamiliar (and unexpected) enormity of scale; and the sequence of the core historical exhibition would allow information about what happened on 9/11—not only in New York City, but in Arlington, Virginia, and near Shanksville, Pennsylvania—to unfold as it was revealed and perceived during the course of that day. Segments within that exhibition would be keyed to distinct time periods, marking not only the developments as they occurred but a real and significant alteration of emotion, awareness, and understanding experienced by witnesses both near and far.

Multiple considerations influenced the determination of where to place program content: among them, visitor capacity and circulation patterns; operational efficiencies; temperature and relative humidity requirements for

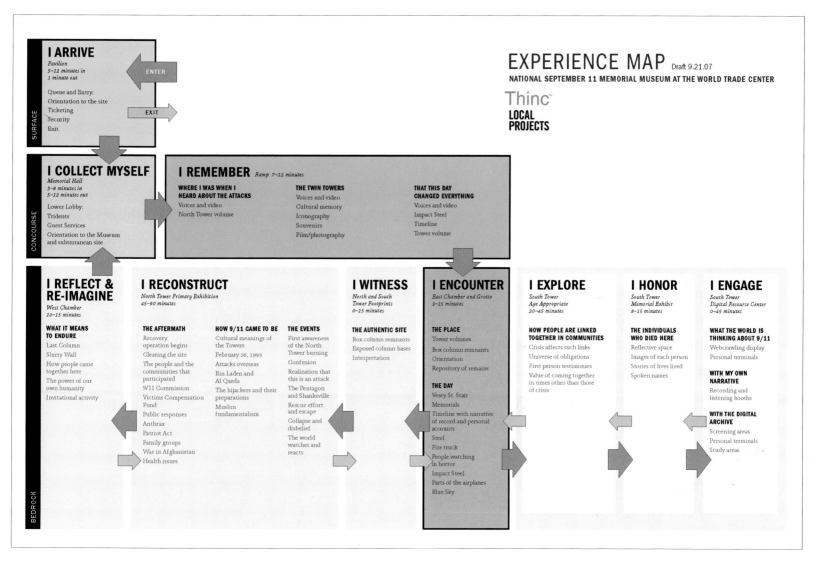

VISITOR EXPERIENCE MAP CREATED BY LEAD EXHIBITION DESIGNERS THINC DESIGN WITH LOCAL PROJECTS

artifacts; the scale, visibility, and emotional impact of certain key artifacts; and whether, given the realities of the physical plant and finite funding, a program component could be prioritized as essential, contributing, or supporting a set of agreed-upon programmatic objectives.

LOCATING THE MEMORIAL EXHIBITION

One essential component—a presentation that would individually honor all 2,983 victims of the terrorist attacks of September 11, 2001 and February 26, 1993, referred to from the start of planning simply as the "memorial exhibition"—was never in question. Its location, however, was.

As early as 2007, planners determined that the two core exhibitions of the Museum—one focusing on commemoration and the other on historical documentation—would each occupy space directly on the foundational footprints of the Twin Towers. This placement tied the core exhibitions to the archaeological authenticity of the site and signaled the fundamental significance of these exhibitions as privileged spaces, while at the same time providing a sense of parity for the two exhibitions regardless of their relative sizes. The historical exhibition, which would require significant square footage to address a multiplicity of topics and accommodate some of the larger artifacts and first response vehicles, would be located within the North Tower footprint, whose dimensions very nearly matched the full acre size of the floor span of the original One World Trade Center building. The memorial exhibition—requiring less physical space for the presentation of portraits, digital databases, and intimate personal effects items—would be placed within the South Tower footprint, of which only half the original floor span was accessible within the space of the Museum. This was due to the fact that the PATH train tracks, as they had for decades, crossed directly over the other half of the foundation of what had been Two World Trade Center.

The first design studies for the memorial exhibition drew inspiration from Michael Arad's design for the Memorial, in which two pools occupy the vacant spaces left by the now absent Twin Towers. These two acre-sized pools with 30-foot waterfalls cascading down all four sides would be distinguished by a center void into which the water falls a second time, perpetually disappearing out of view. Working closely with the Museum's creative director, the Thinc design team argued forcefully for placing the memorial exhibition at what would be the center of the South Tower's foundational footprint, exactly below the center void in the south Memorial pool seven stories above. The poetry of this concept lay in the idea that where the Memorial reflected absence, the Museum's memorial exhibition would focus on the "presence" of those who were killed through its presentation of a portrait-lined "wall of faces," the alphabetical sequencing of their names, touchscreen tables that would invite visitors to learn more about each individual, and recorded remembrances spoken by those who knew and loved them.

By January 2008, when draft schematic design studies for the memorial exhibition were brought to the Program Committee for consideration, the response was robust and surprising. While there was strong, majority support for the proposed location below the Memorial void, a forceful argument against it was put forward by the co-chair of the Program Committee, Howard W. Lutnick. As Chairman and CEO of Cantor Fitzgerald, which occupied floors 101 through 105 of the North Tower in 2001, Lutnick had lost 658 employees and friends, including his own brother, **Gary Frederick Lutnick**, on 9/11. While acknowledging the symbolic intention of the design proposal, Howard focused on what was in his mind the overriding need for the memorial exhibition to be the most visually prominent feature of all the various program elements in the South Tower, and for this exhibition, in particular, to

THE MEMORIAL EXHIBITION, LOCATED WITHIN THE SOUTH TOWER FOOTPRINT

be immediately accessible to visitors when they arrived at bedrock. His perspective, passionately and persuasively advanced, influenced the ultimate design. Today, the memorial exhibition, *In Memoriam*, sits at the northwest corner of the South Tower footprint, the first of the core exhibitions that visitors encounter at bedrock.

As the Museum design process progressed through schematic design toward full design development, the Program Committee would be consulted regularly, as would the participants in the Conversation Series, which was reconvened on a periodic basis to ensure a level of transparency and to solicit reactions and guidance from those closely invested in the Museum's successful realization. Over the next six years, these groups—welcoming new members along the way—would gather to review design studies and consider some of the most challenging aspects of the project.

THE OCME REPOSITORY

Chief among those challenges was an obligation dating back to 2002, when a Families Advisory Council convened by the LMDC recommended that the unidentified remains of many who had been killed at the World Trade Center on 9/11 be housed within the Memorial Complex being planned for the site. By 2003, the Coalition of 9/11 Families, a consortium of 9/11 family groups that had formed support and advocacy organizations in the aftermath of the attacks, secured the agreement of New York Governor George Pataki for this position. The commitment was to provide a private space within the Memorial Complex for the New York City Office of Chief Medical Examiner (OCME) to maintain a repository containing both unidentified and unclaimed remains.

The OCME faced an unusual situation. Due to the horrific circumstances of the tower collapses, many of the nearly 22,000 human remains eventually recovered at the site were either minuscule in size or significantly degraded to a degree that existing forensic technologies were not applicable. Six years after the attacks, when the Museum design process was just beginning, the physical remains of more than 1,100 victims—41 percent of all 9/11 victims at the World Trade Center—had not been identified. This meant that their families had received no physical remains of loved ones. By the anniversary in 2015, the OCME had made 20 new identifications, dropping the figure to 40 percent. The OCME committed to continuing its work to identify these remains as technologies evolved, and to do so in perpetuity.

Without remains, families had no places of rest for their deceased. Many 9/11 families advocated for an area within the Memorial Complex to serve this purpose. The repository would be neither a mausoleum nor a working laboratory; it would be a dignified place of repose, from which OCME staff members would periodically remove remains in order to conduct increasingly precise analysis in the hopes of making positive identifications.

Identifying a placement for the OCME's repository was formally written into the program requirements for the Lower Manhattan Development Corporation's Memorial design competition. In response, the Coalition of 9/11 Families asserted the need for the repository to be placed "in the area encased by the 'slurry wall,'" the retaining wall built when the original World Trade Center was constructed that had—some felt miraculously—withstood the building collapses on 9/11. Following the selection of the Michael Arad–Peter Walker design, *Reflecting Absence*, in January 2004, the placement of the repository at bedrock became fixed, though its actual location would shift as the Memorial design evolved in the spring of 2006 through a process undertaken to consolidate the Memorial, Museum, and a planned Visitor Orientation and Education Center and reduce escalating project costs.

The location and configuration of space for a museum at the site evolved in conjunction with this process. While the fundamental concept of the Memorial—two one-acre pools set within the voids where the Twin Towers once stood, each with waterfalls surrounded by the names of the dead—remained unchanged, the Memorial design shifted from its original plan of having multiple levels and of going down 70 feet to bedrock to being two pools accessed at street level. With this change, previously separate elements of the master plan for the World Trade Center redevelopment site—the Memorial Center and a Visitor Orientation and Education Center—were combined into the single entity of the Memorial Museum, which would now be entered through an aboveground pavilion building with exhibition areas occupying the underground space below the Memorial pools.

By May 2006, responses to the Memorial design revisions from 9/11 families included a request to place the OCME repository between the Twin Tower footprints at bedrock, so as not to privilege one footprint over the other. Concurrent with the launch of the Museum planning process, these two requirements—to place the repository of unidentified victim remains at bedrock within an area encased by the slurry wall and to situate it between the two footprints, rather than on either one of them—left only one possible location for the OCME space. Though not operated by the Museum, and neither visible nor accessible to visitors, it would be adjacent to the Museum's public spaces, situated behind a wall on the eastern perimeter of the exhibition level at bedrock. Moreover, as the Museum's own configuration began to take shape, and as the architects from Davis Brody Bond refined their concept for a slightly graded descent into the space of the Museum along a ramp or "ribbon" that would connect the plaza level to bedrock, the wall behind which the repository would be placed dominated and defined the contours of the very first space visitors would come to, when they arrived at bedrock. In the words of one adviser, this location was at the symbolically "charged center of the site."

The presence of the OCME repository of remains thus became a given of the Museum planning effort, and it would remain among the most sensitive areas to be addressed. Recognizing the challenge of integrating respectful public awareness of the OCME repository with the broader experience of visiting the 9/11 Memorial Museum, planners sought advice from interfaith advisers and also brought this issue to the Museum Planning Conversation Series in its second season.

THE EAST PERIMETER WALL

The question of how to treat a massive, raw concrete wall, measuring 140 linear feet and standing 34 feet high, that separates the public space and primary visitor pathway of the Museum from the private OCME repository became a focus of design deliberation involving, at various times, the architects, exhibition designers, Museum planning team, and the Program Committee of the Board. Not only would it be critical to find an appropriately respectful way to signal to visitors what was behind the wall, there was the fundamental challenge that the space demarcated by this wall (eventually named Memorial Hall) would be a prominent and central area of the Museum serving as a kind of lower lobby and orientation area. As visitors follow the ramped pathway of the introductory exhibits and then descend along a stairway to their arrival at bedrock, they would see this monumental wall even before they arrived physically in the hall. All visitors would have to pass through this area at least once in their journey to the core exhibitions (situated within the actual footprints of the towers at bedrock); many visitors would pass through the hall multiple times during a museum visit.

Numerous design proposals were put forward and rejected. But there was one idea that all parties agreed upon, from the very start of planning: that it would be disingenuous and disrespectful if we did not clearly indicate the presence of the OCME repository behind this wall. Straightforward and matter-of-fact language for a plaque to be placed on the wall in two locations was developed in the earliest stages of design development: *Reposed behind this wall are the remains of many who perished at the World Trade Center site on September 11, 2001. The Repository is maintained by the Office of Chief Medical Examiner of the City of New York.*

While the plaques would ensure visitor awareness of the repository in a literal sense, they did not address the programmatic need to facilitate the visitor's encounter with such an emotionally charged space. As early as 2006, team members had identified a quote from Virgil's *Aeneid* that seemed to capture the essence of the Museum's

PLAQUE ON THE MUSEUM'S EAST PERIMETER WALL

commemorative mission: "No day shall erase you from the memory of time." Planners felt that integrating this quote into the design of the wall would frame the overall memorial context of the Museum experience and at the same time provide a poetic reference to those killed.

Tom Hennes, principal of Thinc Design, advanced the idea that we might engage an artisan blacksmith to forge the letters of the Virgil quote out of recovered World Trade Center steel, and thereby transform wounded remnants from the site into elements of hope and beauty. New Mexico artist Tom Joyce understood the directive to capture the concept of the transformative potential of remembrance by harnessing the transformational process that occurs when iron is touched by fire. His process of forging and folding the metal actually changed the surface of the steel, so that it took on both a bluish cast and an almost iridescent quality. The resulting work of art is a stunning reminder that Virgil's words are not just a statement; in this context, they are a promise.

While the selection of this quote elicited critical reactions from some classicists who objected to its use because of the much-contested passage in *The Aeneid* in which this particular line appears, other scholars vigorously supported its use in this location, citing a time-honored tradition of appropriating classical quotations regardless of the original context.

Even as the design work for the Virgil quote was underway, feedback from 9/11 family members and other participants in the Conversation Series suggested that the large, raw concrete surface of this wall needed to be treated in a more reverential and respectful manner so that, acknowledging the OCME repository behind it, the wall would be distinguished from the rest of the Museum at bedrock where raw concrete was valued for its simplicity and authenticity. Planners investigated various strategies including facing the wall with stone or archival World Trade Center travertine, providing distinctive lighting to wash the wall, and creating an opportunity for visitors to engage in a memorial gesture at this location; none of the strategies were satisfactory, and in the words of one adviser, the wall remained "30 degrees below zero emotionally."

By early 2011, at the suggestion of Program Committee member Kate D. Levin, the design focus for the wall shifted to the idea of a site-specific art installation. Museum planners convened a small group of advisers with expertise in public art installations to help guide them.[3] The group identified seven artists; of them, six were invited to visit the Museum construction site to offer potential solutions to the challenge of the wall, understanding that whatever would be placed there needed to work with the Virgil quote. Three of the artists submitted proposals; each of them was deeply thoughtful, inventive, and had the potential to inspire. One submission—Spencer Finch's *Trying to Remember the Color of the Sky on That September Morning*, which focused on collective memory of the color and clarity of the blue sky on 9/11—was originally conceived as light projections. While there were many questions yet to be answered, it was felt that in the simplicity of Finch's proposal was a "flash of something poetic." The design would be tested in mock-ups and revisions, eventually morphing into Finch's vision of the entire wall covered with 2,983 individually painted, 10.5" x 10.5" watercolors, the same number as the number of victims from the attacks on September 11, 2001, and in the bombing of the World Trade Center in February 1993, being commemorated at the Memorial and Museum.

Finch proposed to paint each of these paper tiles in a different shade of blue—creating a panoramic mosaic, each blue square unique and individual, yet together creating a unified field of color. In his artist statement, Finch explained: "The creation of each work is a specific act of memory, what I remember might not be what you remember, what I see as blue may not be what you see as blue, but collectively, we share a common point of reference. Each of the people killed on 9/11 and in 1993 was a unique person, yet part of a collective as a result of the circumstances of their deaths. These squares subtly recall the missing posters and tributes affixed to fences and walls and public surfaces, and it is my hope that the very ephemerality of the paper and the watercolor will suggest the process of remembering, a kind of living memorial."

The concept for the wall was now complete. Though neither visible nor accessible to visitors, the repository could now be respectfully acknowledged and experienced in a deeply personal way without morbidity, through the expressive lens of art.

WORKS BY ARTISTS TOM JOYCE AND SPENCER FINCH IN MEMORIAL HALL

DISPLAYING SENSITIVE SUBJECT MATTER

The question of how to approach the presence of human remains went beyond the OCME repository. The content planning team and its advisers also had to consider the implications of presenting artifacts in a museum that, given the specific, historical circumstances of 9/11, would be particularly charged and potentially controversial because of the presumption or possibility that they might contain microscopic traces of human remains, whether in dust or in other forms.

Numerous planning discussions, variously with Conversation Series attendees, Program Committee members, interfaith advisers, museum ethicists, a "kitchen cabinet" of expert advisers, and focus group participants, took into consideration questions of propriety; the obligation to document this historical atrocity with factuality and authenticity; the need for appropriate and meaningful context; and most of all, sensitivity to the sensibilities of victims' family members, survivors, and the visiting public, combined with an awareness of when the boundary might be crossed between reverence and exploitation.

Over time, the planning team evolved a kind of working ethics of presentation. Charged elements would be presented matter-of-factly, but with careful attention to the way exhibition design might mediate the experience for visitors. For example, the curators advised that recovered property—the personal effects of victims found in the rubble of Ground Zero, the debris field at Flight 93's crash site near Shanksville, or at the Pentagon and returned to family members who then made this material available through donation or loan to the Museum—should be treated differently from other artifacts. The design evolved to accommodate this requirement so that recovered property—a wedding ring, the contents of a wallet, an identification card—would be nestled in soft fabric and cradled or embraced by the mount, rather than being installed in a more utilitarian fashion.

Among the most sensitive issues confronted during the planning of the Museum was the question of how to reference the fact that, almost immediately following the crash of hijacked Flight 11 into the North Tower, men and women faced such intolerable conditions that some fell or jumped to the ground below. We can only assume that many of those people had been placed in the unimaginable position of having to make a "choiceless choice": whether to stay inside a building transformed in an instant into an inferno and be burned alive, or to escape the choking smoke and unbearably hot flames by leaping out of the buildings, some from a height of more than 90 stories.

Fairly early on, it became clear that one could not tell the full story of what happened on 9/11 without acknowledging those who faced this agonizing decision. So it was not a matter of whether or not this topic would be addressed in the Museum; the question was how to do this in a manner that would not feel voyeuristic or be in any way disrespectful of the very individuals we were charged to commemorate.

Here again, a number of design studies were put forward and rejected. Framed still photographs on a gallery wall seemed (however unintentionally) to aestheticize the subject matter in a manner that was deeply uncomfortable. Using documentary film footage was considered for a time and then determined to be potentially exploitative (of both the subject matter and the viewer) and, in some profound sense, unfair to the individuals who fell to their deaths—and who, as the video looped, would fall again and again and again. Then there was the question of how many images to use. Would one image suffice to reference this occurrence, and, in effect, stand in for all? Or would only a single image mislead Museum visitors to think that this was an idiosyncratic occurrence? Given that estimates of the number of people who died as a result of falling from the Twin Towers range from 50 to more than 200, we concluded that it would be necessary to document the multiplicity by presenting more than one documentary image. But how many would be appropriate?

The questions that swirled around this very sensitive topic eventually coalesced into a set of criteria for the design. The exhibition strategy needed to be straightforward and factual, without aestheticizing; only still images could be used, but there had to be more than one; there could be no clearly identifiable individuals in any of the photographs; it was important to integrate the reality that the unthinkable fact of numerous individuals falling to their deaths out of skyscrapers was witnessed widely that morning, and it would be essential to prepare our visitors for this extremely disturbing content in such a way that they would be able to make an informed decision about whether they wished to see it. This last requirement was directly influenced by guidance provided in the Conversation Series sessions as early as 2008, when multiple educators and cognitive psychologists cautioned the planning team about the need, when chronicling traumatic experiences, to avoid shocking visitors and, instead, prepare them in advance about exceptionally distressing content, thereby empowering them to make their own choices about what they are or are not willing to see.

This is an unapologetically historical exhibition, and the integrity of its content cannot be compromised. But good design must also anticipate the profound emotions visitors will likely experience.

—David Layman, Principal, Layman Design; Historical Exhibition Designer

A solution was put forward by David Layman, principal of Layman Design, the firm brought on board in 2010 to advance and finalize design development of the historical exhibition. Bearing in mind all of the requirements, Layman proposed to project multiple still images (eventually, a total of five) onto a concrete panel above eye level, requiring that one look up to see them. An image would appear, hold for a few seconds, and then fade out, with the timing of sequencing being neither fast nor slow, but appropriately elegiac. These images would be authentic but never simply documentary. The respectful pace of their sequenced, ephemeral

EXTERIOR OF "FALLING FROM THE TOWERS" ALCOVE IN THE HISTORICAL EXHIBITION

presentation would add a sacred quality to the experience. This would not be voyeuristic; it was meant as an invitation to pay one's respects. The design called for the projections to be located behind a stele-like, freestanding wall that could serve both to shield unintentional views of this sensitive subject matter by those passing by and to require visitors to elect consciously to enter the space behind the wall. Furthermore, the entire display would be isolated off the main visitor pathway in its own discrete space or alcove area, and a cautionary sign, unique to this installation, would signal that the content contained within this area of the exhibition might be particularly disturbing.

As it developed, the design ensured that visitors, before ever entering the space, would be cued to the subject matter through a structured sequence of content elements. First, a photograph of witnesses, eyes wide with horror, hands over their mouths, would reference what was seen by so many that morning. An introductory text panel (a strategy rarely used in this section of the historical exhibition, which tends to be more experiential) would state the facts. As visitors move off the main path into the alcove, they would see on the outside of the freestanding wall a photograph establishing the impossible conditions faced by people leaning out of windows, trapped on the upper floors of one of the burning towers. And, finally, before going behind that freestanding wall, visitors could read a selection of quotes from eyewitnesses. Testifying to a range of reactions—the impulse not to look; the obligation not to turn away; a profound recognition of the human cost that morning—these quotes might, it was hoped, give visitors permission to accept the legitimacy of their own range of emotional responses to the projected images behind the wall.

TELLING THE STORY

This concept held as the overall design for the historical exhibition evolved and solidified. Early in the conceptual planning for the first part of the historical exhibition—the section chronicling the events of the day on September 11, 2001—it was determined that the story would be told in three distinct but complementary ways. First, there would be a central path of witness, evoking through displays of artifacts, photographs, and video and sound recordings the progressive, escalating disbelief and terror of that morning and the shock and uncertainty of that afternoon and evening. It would mirror those emotions as they were experienced globally by the two billion people estimated to have witnessed the events, either as they unfolded in real time on televised news reports or during the endlessly repeating broadcasts that followed.

Concurrently, a timeline would wrap the perimeter wall, providing information that those who watched the attacks, collapses, and immediate aftermath were, for the most part, unaware of on that day: specifically, what was happening in the skies above (as more airplanes were hijacked) and on the ground below, in terms of how government leaders and agencies at the local, state, and federal levels were responding. The timeline would track the path of witness, so that specific timestamps would correlate to the moment in the narrative of the day where a visitor would be standing in the main path. In synoptic fashion, the timeline would present, above and below those timestamps, what was happening elsewhere that morning so that visitors might gain a clearer sense of the simultaneity of these various developments.

Finally, the story would be told "from the inside" in intimate audio alcoves where visitors could listen to first-person accounts of escape and evacuation from the towers in New York as well as at the Pentagon, along with archived radio transmissions from first responders. With great deliberation, and with a self-imposed requirement to secure permissions from next of kin, we also elected to include real-time messages and calls to 9-1-1 from those trapped within the buildings and—in the Flight 93 alcove—voice-mail messages left for loved ones by passengers and crew aboard the hijacked flight. What our media producers, Jake Barton and his gifted team at Local Projects, ultimately delivered were programs that fashioned a coherent narrative arc out of a compilation of recorded testimonies and archival audio, creating an extraordinarily vivid sense of immediacy for listeners and establishing an entirely new way for oral histories to be presented in museums.

Our use of the archival clips demanded exceptionally careful consideration of visitors' emotional thresholds. When is listening to a recording of someone's final words in the public space of a museum appropriate? When does historical documentation violate individual privacy and dignity? These questions were at the heart of every decision made.

Opinions varied widely among members of the core planning team, with some advocating an obligation to present audio content just as evidence might be presented in a court of law, as the unvarnished truth. Others argued that just because we had certain recordings did not mean we were obligated to use them; that certain circumstances demanded discretion out of respect for those who died and consideration for their families. Most often, consensus could be reached. When there were, however, certain issues of a particularly sensitive or potentially controversial nature, the team sought resolution through guidance from key advisers, most often the Program Committee or the "kitchen cabinet,"[4] a small group convened beginning in March 2009 to serve as a kind of independent brain trust. Including historians, museum professionals, a theorist of memory and memorialization, a cultural critic, a public policy expert, and representatives from the Program Committee, the Cabinet met periodically over a period of four years to provide objective responses to curatorial and design decisions as a means of ensuring that the exhibition program of the Museum was meeting best-practice standards from a variety of perspectives: the presentation of historical narratives, storytelling within museum settings, visitor learning in museums, the transformative power of immersive environments and experiential design, and the integration of memorial considerations and sensitivities with the presentation of historical fact.

INCLUDING THE PERPETRATORS AND THEIR SUPPORTERS

Among the most critical topics considered by the "kitchen cabinet," Program Committee, and participants in the Conversation Series was the issue of how the Memorial Museum would approach the complex subject of the perpetrators. In deciding early on in the planning process to segregate the historical and memorial exhibitions, Museum planners had already acknowledged the tension between commemoration and historical documentation. But, in committing to a historical exhibition, the team had already pledged to tell the story of the attacks—not just the experience of the day and the impact on victims, their families, colleagues, and communities, but also the broader historical context for the attacks, including those who carried them out and the ongoing global repercussions.

As the content and design for the exhibition progressed, there would be many flash points along this road. How should we explain the roots of al-Qaeda and Islamist terrorism? Where would we begin that story? With the Crusades? The end of the Ottoman Empire? Or might there be a starting point more specifically connected to the events of 2001 and 1993 that we were specifically chronicling? Should we include images of the terrorists? If we did choose to portray the hijackers, how would we do so? What images would we use? What size should they be? And where should they be placed physically, and in what context? The answers to all of these questions evolved over several years, aided by meetings and consultations with a number of academic advisers specializing in Middle Eastern history and counterterrorism.

Two issues that became the subject of particular focus for the Program Committee were the use of hijacker voices and the inclusion of references to the relatively isolated anti-American celebrations that took place abroad in the wake of the 2001 attacks.

Throughout the first part of the historical exhibition, which chronicles the events of the day on September 11, 2001, the dominant perspective of the storytelling is that of witness or, in the context of the audio alcoves, those who experienced the attacks directly: first responders, survivors, those aboard the flights (passengers and flight crew), and the people inside the buildings (World Trade Center and Pentagon survivors; some individuals trapped in the towers). Since this part of the exhibition was intended to mirror the experiences of that day when not much was certain about who was behind the attacks, there is little mention of who had perpetrated them. That topic was left to be explored in the second part of the exhibition.

However, in 2011, as the audio alcove was being developed for the Flight 93 story, it became clear that the transcripts and actual voice-mail recordings of passengers and crew told only part of that story. The plane's cockpit voice recorder had captured the conversations and intercom broadcasts of the hijackers, providing critical information about what had actually happened aboard that flight on 9/11. We knew we had to include this content;[5] the question was whether to present the content in transcription or to use the actual recording—and in doing so, have our visitors hear the voice of the hijacker pilot. The question extended to other moments in the second part of the historical exhibition, where visitors would hear the voice of Osama bin Laden in a news clip featured in a documentary media installation and the voice of one of the Flight 11 hijackers heard via an audio wand alongside a transcription on an adjacent timeline.

The debate centered on the inherent tension between honoring the obligation to present authentic, historical documentation and the equal imperative to honor and memorialize the victims, requiring solutions that are sensitive, respectful, and responsible. A majority of Program Committee members advised prioritizing the authenticity and veracity of historic documentation in the exhibition and strongly favored use of the audio recordings. It was noted that this content had already been made public in feature films about Flight 93, and one family member on the committee noted that because most of the public did not know what actually happened on the planes, it would honor the memory of the passengers and crew to include these recordings. Another family member observed that the Memorial would have to have a strong rationale for why it did not include significant and available archival material.

Still, the guidance provided early on by Conversation Series adviser and trauma psychologist Grady Bray about the power of aural content continued to have influence. Dr. Bray had emphatically cautioned extreme care when using oral recordings in memorial museum settings, stating that the timbre of a human voice had the potential to intensify the emotional impact. And so the decision of whether to include the voice of a perpetrator was considered so sensitive that staff elected to invite the parents of one of the passengers aboard hijacked Flight 93 to join in the discussion.

The parents of **Todd M. Beamer**, Peggy and David (who is a member of the 9/11 Memorial Board but was not a member of the Program Committee), graciously agreed to view two versions of the Flight 93 alcove program in development. In one version, the voice of a perpetrator could be heard in two separate instances. The first time, the speaker—presumed to be hijacker pilot Ziad Jarrah—is attempting to tell passengers:[6] *Ladies and gentlemen, here is the captain. Please sit down; keep remaining sitting. We have a bomb on board. So, sit.* Some minutes later, a voice confirmed to be Jarrah's is heard saying: *Uh, this is the captain. Would like you all to remain seated. There is a bomb on board and are going back to the airport and to have our demands. So, please remain quiet.* The alternate version shared with the Beamers simply provided the transcript of these two communications.

It was clearly an emotionally fraught experience for both of them. Nevertheless, with dignity and quiet courage, both asserted that there was no question for them. In their minds, it was critical to present history as it happened, and hard as it was to hear the voice of the hijacker pilot, the use of the actual recording was essential. A decision was made to move forward accordingly. The final alcove program includes these two audio clips. Transcripts of other hijacker voices are presented in the program without accompanying audio since those recordings remain under seal.[7]

Another issue addressed by the Program Committee concerned the portrayal of international vigils and gatherings in the immediate aftermath of the 9/11 attacks. A multimedia display was being developed with the goal of documenting how the world came together in the wake of the attacks, specifically demonstrated by the widespread expressions of sympathy and support as people spontaneously assembled in places like New York City's Union Square and various locations around the world. Early prototypes of this installation typically brought viewers to

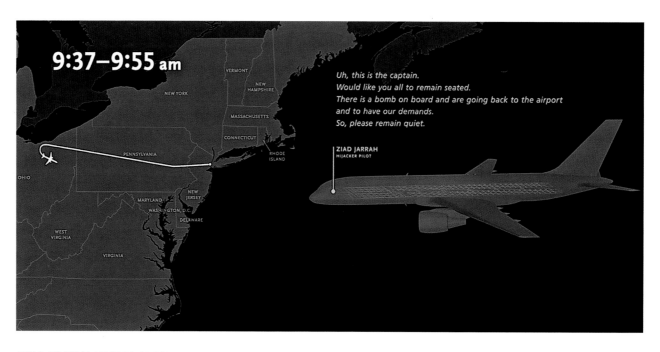

9:37–9:55 am

Uh, this is the captain.
Would like you all to remain seated.
There is a bomb on board and are going back to the airport
and to have our demands.
So, please remain quiet.

ZIAD JARRAH
HIJACKER PILOT

STILL FROM FLIGHT 93 ALCOVE IN THE HISTORICAL EXHIBITION

tears, as image after image of people from around the globe offered a powerful reminder of our shared grief and sense of common humanity at that moment in time.

In the wake of the attacks, however, there were also isolated, spontaneous public celebrations abroad. The question for the exhibition team was how best to acknowledge that these protests and demonstrations—which expressed opposition to American foreign policy and support for Osama bin Laden and violent Islamism—took place, without suggesting equivalence with the significantly more numerous expressions of condolence and solidarity.

Early design studies explored integrating the relatively few examples of post-9/11, anti-American celebrations into the same media program that presented the vigils. This was deemed not to be a successful strategy—since, proportionately, the negative responses were so limited in number; not only did they get lost in the sequence of images but presenting them in this fashion risked criticism that we were obscuring the fact that they had taken place at all. A proposal to place three still documentary images on the railing surrounding the vigils' media program was brought to the Program Committee in April 2012. While accepting the necessity of this approach, some committee members took issue with the draft interpretive text, expressing concern that the text seemed to characterize entire nations as being antagonistic to the United States, rather than focusing on radical Islamist extremism as an international ideology defined not by places but by ideas and their adherents. Others on the committee asserted that there was ample evidence from polls conducted in 2001 and 2002 that majority populations of certain countries were indeed anti-American. A decision was made to revise the interpretive text to eliminate ambiguities and imprecise language. Ultimately, the final text provided straightforward acknowledgment of celebrations by proponents of radical Islamism and groups unhappy with American foreign policy, without characterizing these expressions as national activities of particular countries. The specific locations where these demonstrations took place would, however, still be referenced in the individual photo captions.

Over the course of creating the Museum, the exhibition team—together with its advisers—negotiated all manner of concerns and considerations, whether it be the nuances of language in an interpretive text or visitors' and stakeholders' sensitivities and sensibilities with respect to object, image, and audio selections. Throughout, the dedication to telling the story as it happened never wavered.

THE REALIZED MUSEUM

Four key principles ultimately informed the 9/11 Museum's fundamental character. The first of these is **authenticity**. At sites of memory, authenticity is *the* critical element for achieving moral authority. Our location at Ground Zero in the presence of archaeological remnants of the original site reinforced this value. Equally important, establishing the authenticity of our narrative was imperative.

As an educational institution, our commitment was to the narration of fact-based history. This Museum strives to establish a level of literacy about the historical context for the events of September 11, the nature of the world in which we live, the reality of terrorism, and the often incompatible political forces that remain in tension with one another. This tragedy was *not* the result of a natural disaster; 9/11 was planned and carried out by human beings. In the end, we did not shy away from including the recorded voices of the perpetrators, nor did we fail to include the historical context in which al-Qaeda arose, the primary participants in its evolution, and the names and faces of those who plotted and carried out the attacks. In the effort to address who did this and why, we consulted scholars, historians, and experts in various fields to locate the artifacts, images, and content that could most effectively and accurately tell this story.

But this Museum isn't only about documenting history. It is about understanding our humanity. And so the second principle is **engagement**. A museum dedicated to commemoration and education cannot merely testify to what happened. It must also provide inspiration and the opportunity for response.

> *Inviting those who survived the event to share their experience with visitors catalyzed the Museum's commitment to broadening the use of oral history to include the visitor's own voice. Whether telling one's own 9/11 story, recording a remembrance for someone who was killed, or adding an opinion about some of the more challenging questions raised by 9/11, visitors are invited to contribute their own stories to the Museum.*
>
> —Jake Barton, Principal, Local Projects; Media Designer

Throughout the Museum, there are many moments when visitors are invited to engage, whether by exploring touchscreen interfaces that provide enrichment through access to additional content; by recording memories and personal reflections that can be selected for inclusion in the Museum's exhibitions; or by sharing comments and observations with other visitors via an electronic message board and archive.

In so many ways, the 9/11 Museum is as much about the human potential for courage and compassion as it is about the terrible events perpetrated on that unforgettable day. We tell stories of people who acted with extraordinary bravery and kindness: helping strangers evacuate; refusing to leave colleagues behind, even if doing so meant certain death; running into danger, selflessly, so others could live; volunteering at Ground Zero, doing whatever one could. These expressions of empathy and acts of public service significantly contributed to the cleanup and recovery efforts. In celebrating that spirit of generosity—born of shared grief and a fundamental recognition of shared humanity—the Museum offers a model for how to live in an interconnected world.

Connection is the third principle. A memorial museum should facilitate a sense of connection with those who suffered an atrocity or a social injustice, whether as victims, survivors, or witnesses. It is essential that visitors see themselves in the story being told.

At the 9/11 Memorial Museum, the heart of our story is about the people most directly affected by this event. From the start of planning, we recognized that a core responsibility of the Museum was to undercut the very presumption of terrorism, that victims of such acts—in this case, mostly civilians who neither signed up for active combat nor were aware that terrible morning of the grave threat facing them—become nameless abstractions.

The Museum staff worked with families, friends, and colleagues of the victims as well as partners like Voices of September 11th, StoryCorps, and the 9/11 Tribute Center to secure as much material as possible about every individual killed, so that our visitors could be introduced to these people by those who knew them. In the 9/11 Memorial Museum, we want to remember people for *how they lived*, not just for how they died. And, in this sacred space, the number 2,983 is never an abstraction.

The message we strove to convey was this: the people killed on 9/11 could have been any one of us, arriving at work or boarding a plane one morning. They were ages two and a half to 85 years old, from more than 90 nations, representing a wide diversity of economic sectors, ethnicities, and faith traditions. In deliberately focusing—throughout the Memorial Museum—on the individuality of these people, we aspired to fulfill the mandate of remembrance at contemporary memorials which, in the words of historian Ed Linenthal, is all too often "an act of protest against the anonymity of mass death in our time."

The fourth and final principle is **storytelling**. The 9/11 Memorial Museum's dynamic blend of architecture, archaeology, history, and commemoration creates an indelible encounter with the story of the attacks and their aftermath. The experience reminds visitors that history is not an abstraction but rather a compilation of lived narratives that weave into collective memory. As a storytelling museum, our focus has been not so much on historians' interpretations of history but on the human experience of this historical event.

At the heart of this Museum is a fundamental conviction: that bearing witness to the unimaginable is the only way to imagine a way beyond it.

The National September 11 Memorial Museum is a place for understanding ourselves and the world in which we live. It is place for all of us, set within the foundations of the World Trade Center—at the epicenter of Ground Zero—to begin to imagine together the kind of world we want to build for the generations that will follow us.

MUSEUM MISSION STATEMENT

The National September 11 Memorial Museum, located at the World Trade Center site, bears solemn witness to the terrorist attacks of September 11, 2001 and February 26, 1993. The Museum honors the 2,983 victims of these attacks and all those who risked their lives to save others. It further recognizes the thousands who survived and all who demonstrated extraordinary compassion in the aftermath. Demonstrating the consequences of terrorism on individual lives and its impact on communities at the local, national, and international levels, the Museum attests to the triumph of human dignity over human depravity and affirms an unwavering commitment to the fundamental value of human life.

THE MUSEUM PAVILION SEEN FROM ACROSS THE MEMORIAL'S NORTH POOL

THE PAVILION

The 9/11 Memorial Museum experience begins at a landing inside the glass atrium of the entry pavilion. Here, we can look out to the Memorial, the north and south reflecting pools on either side signifying that memory and history, absence and presence, are intertwined and complementary. Immediately in front of us, standing like sentries, are the tridents, two steel columns more than 80 feet high that formed part of the exterior facade of the North Tower, the original 1 World Trade Center (WTC). Called "trees" by WTC architect Minoru Yamasaki, 84 trident columns formed the perimeter structure of each of the Twin Towers and branched at the top of the fifth story. Where individual columns forked into three branches, they met each other, forming Gothic arches and creating a distinctive, repetitive pattern at the base of the towers.

Because of their size, these two tridents had to be set in place first, and the Museum pavilion was built around them. Visible from outside the pavilion, these structural "trees" complement the swamp white oak trees of the Memorial. They suggest the power and presence of the authentic artifacts presented inside the Museum and signal that, here, we can learn history in the very location where the events took place. Evoking the verticality of the two towers that once stood at this site, the tridents form a spine connecting the aboveground and belowground spaces of the Museum. From within the Museum atrium, visitors can look beyond the tridents to see the new 1,776-foot-high One World Trade Center building, a juxtaposition suggesting continuity between past and present and the promise of renewal through reconstruction.

At this location, we can proceed upstairs to the Atrium Terrace and auditorium or downstairs to Concourse Lobby, where our journey to the Museum's foundation level, known as bedrock, will begin.

INTERNATIONAL FLAGS (PREVIOUS PAGE)

Across from the tridents, a display of international flags establishes the global impact of the 9/11 attacks, in which individuals from more than 90 nations were killed. These flags also recall those of the United Nations member states that once hung from the mezzanine level of the original Twin Tower lobbies, animating architect Minoru Yamasaki's vision of world peace achieved through the exchange of products and ideas.

WORLD TRADE CENTER TRIDENTS

Recovered from the World Trade Center site after September 11, 2001
Collection 9/11 Memorial Museum, Courtesy of the Port Authority of
New York and New Jersey

The Twin Towers were built using modular construction methods. Steel pieces were prefabricated at foundries across the United States and stamped with codes indicating their ultimate placement in the towers' structure. The codes on these two steel columns indicate their original location on the east facade of 1 World Trade Center (North Tower). Anchored into bedrock 70 feet below street level, these columns once rose five stories aboveground before branching into the three prongs that give them the name *tridents*.

Beyond the compelling need to make this a monument to world peace, the World Trade Center should, because of its importance, become a living representation of man's belief in humanity, his need for individual dignity, his beliefs in the cooperation of men, and through this cooperation his ability to find greatness.

—Minoru Yamasaki,
World Trade Center architect, 1964

CONCOURSE LOBBY

Concourse Lobby is located 30 feet belowground and between the two Memorial pools at the same level as the waterfalls' first descent, before they fall a second time and disappear into center voids. Here, in Concourse Lobby, we can glimpse through niches in the walls the vast space we are about to enter, while orienting ourselves spatially between two underground structures visible to either side. These structural volumes are both functional and symbolic. Containers for the Memorial pools, they penetrate this belowground space, as if the towers that once stood here had been inverted. Situated directly above the actual footprints of the Twin Towers and covered with aluminum panels, the volumes evoke the towers' presence without being literal.

As visitors pass through Concourse Lobby to begin their Museum journey and again on their way out, we are reminded of the World Trade Center's Austin J. Tobin Plaza, which was itself a bustling square and gathering place for workers, lower Manhattan residents, and the general public. At the center of the plaza between the Twin Towers stood *The Sphere*, a sculpture by Fritz Koenig. Inside the Museum's Concourse Lobby, a model of *The Sphere* serves a similar function, beckoning visitors to gather and pause to reflect on where they are and what was once here.

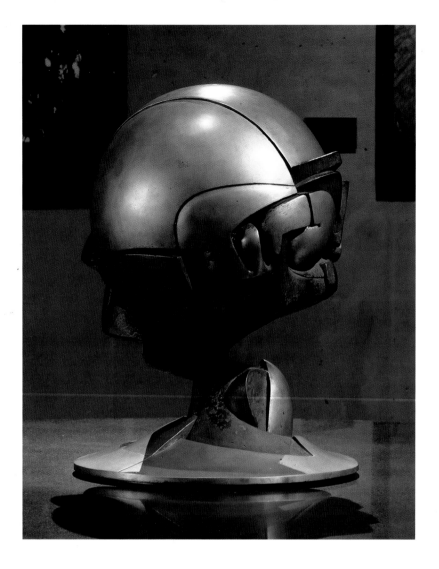

MODEL OF *THE SPHERE* (*GROSSE KUGELKARYATIDE*)

Fritz Koenig (German, b. 1924)
Bronze, on granite
Collection 9/11 Memorial Museum, Gift of Fritz Koenig

This is a 1:12 scale model of Fritz Koenig's *The Sphere*, a monumental sculpture commissioned for the World Trade Center Plaza by architect Minoru Yamasaki and the Port of New York Authority (later renamed the Port Authority of New York and New Jersey). Installed in 1971, the sculpture sat atop a fountain that flowed across a circular expanse of polished stone and was designed to rotate slowly. Regarded as a symbol of world peace, *The Sphere* sustained significant damage in the terrorist attacks on 9/11 and emerged as a lasting symbol of resilience. In March 2002, it was installed in Battery Park as a temporary memorial to the victims of 9/11.

WORLD TRADE CENTER PLAZA, CIRCA 2000

Photograph by Andre R. Aragon / © Bernstein Associates Photographers

LOWER MANHATTAN, ABOUT 8:30 A.M., SEPTEMBER 11, 2001

Photograph by David Monderer

Photographer David Monderer took this photograph of the lower Manhattan skyline, as seen across the East River from Brooklyn, approximately 15 minutes before hijacked Flight 11 crashed into the North Tower on September 11, 2001.

ABOUT **8:30**AM
SEPTEMBER 11, 2001

LOWER MANHATTAN,
VIEW FROM BROOKLYN

SEPTEMBER 11, 2001

On September 11, 2001, nineteen terrorists who were members of al-Qaeda, an Islamist extremist network, hijacked four California-bound commercial airplanes shortly after their departures from airports in Boston, Massachusetts; Newark, New Jersey; and Washington, D.C. In a coordinated attack that transformed the planes into weapons, the hijackers intentionally flew two of the planes into the Twin Towers of the World Trade Center, and another into the Pentagon in Arlington, Virginia. Learning about the other hijackings through telephone calls, passengers and crew members on the fourth plane launched a counterattack. When the passengers attempted to breach the cockpit, the hijacker pilot, who had changed course toward the nation's capital, crashed the plane into a field in Somerset County, Pennsylvania, near the town of Shanksville.

Nearly 3,000 people were killed on that day, the single largest loss of life resulting from a foreign attack on American soil, and the greatest single loss of rescue personnel in American history. Approximately two billion people, almost one third of the world's population, are estimated to have witnessed these horrific events directly or via television, radio, and Internet broadcasts that day.

THE RAMP

The Museum is not simply located *at* the site of the attacks; its main exhibition level is seven stories belowground in a space defined by in-situ historical remnants. Rather than arrive via elevator or escalator at the original foundation level of the World Trade Center, we instead follow a processional descent along a gently sloped ramp. The Ramp recalls construction ramps used at this site, one to build the World Trade Center complex in the 1960s and another installed during the post-9/11 recovery period to haul debris out of the site and to provide access to victims' family members and visiting dignitaries who came to pay their respects at Ground Zero. The Museum's ramped descent also invites an attitude of reverence and, along the way, offers progressive views into a space whose enormous scale cannot be anticipated.

As we begin our descent at the head of the Ramp, a large, picture-perfect photograph of lower Manhattan comes into view. The Twin Towers glisten against a vivid blue sky, conjuring the world before 9/11. Taken at approximately 8:30 a.m. on September 11, 2001, roughly 15 minutes before the first hijacked plane crashed into the North Tower, this image marks the threshold between the world before and the day we can never forget.

Beyond the photo is a global map that appears to fracture into six vertical panels as we move toward it and enter a sound environment, hearing the voices of people from around the world remembering where they were when they first learned about the attacks in New York. It is estimated that nearly two billion people witnessed the attacks of 9/11, via television, radio, and the Internet, either as the events unfolded in real time or in repeated broadcasts that afternoon and evening. The introductory exhibition, *We Remember*, testifies to this global community of witness and, by extension, recognizes that many visitors bring with them their own memories of that day.

Moving beyond this experience of shared, global witness, we pass images showing actual witnesses near two of the three attack sites—New York City and Arlington, Virginia—taken on the morning of 9/11. Proceeding toward an overlook offering a view into the enormous space below, we ourselves become witnesses *here*, at the World Trade Center site.

As the Ramp winds around the volume that sits directly above the North Tower footprint, artifacts and images recall the buildings that were here and are no longer here. Projected missing posters come into view, and the focus shifts to the heart of the matter: people who were here and are no longer here. A second overlook reveals Memorial Hall, the space at bedrock located between the two tower footprints.

WE REMEMBER

Hundreds of voices in many languages spoken by people from around the world comprise this sound environment demonstrating the extent and global reach of shared witness to the events of 9/11. The recordings are drawn from the Museum's archives, to which visitors can add their own 9/11 stories later in the Museum experience.

WITNESS

Photographs (left to right, from top row) by Doug Hamilton; Amy Sancetta, AP Photo; Doug Hamilton; Aristide Economopoulos, The Star-Ledger; Gabrielle Stubbert, Here is New York Collection, New-York Historical Society, Gift of Here is New York; Gus Powell; Frankie Shaw, Here is New York Collection, New-York Historical Society, Gift of Here is New York; Ellen K. Jaffe, Here is New York Collection, New-York Historical Society, Gift of Here is New York; Patrick Witty, Here is New York Collection, New-York Historical Society, Gift of Here is New York

Thousands of people directly witnessed the attacks on the World Trade Center and the Pentagon. Whether running from danger or at a distance, many on the streets felt compelled to stop, unable to avert their eyes from the unfolding scenes of horror. In this installation, as one image fades to the next, the eyes of those watching remain in the same location on the screens, reinforcing the idea of shared, collective witness to the events.

APPROACH TO WEST OVERLOOK (PREVIOUS PAGE)

WEST OVERLOOK

The West Overlook gives us our first view into Foundation Hall, a cathedral-like space with soaring ceiling heights, located at the foundation level of the Museum. Dominating the view is a portion of the original slurry wall, the retaining wall built to keep Hudson River water out of the excavation site when the original World Trade Center was built—a wall that withstood the devastation of 9/11. At the center of the hall stands the Last Column, a core column from the South Tower and the final piece of Twin Tower steel to be brought out of the site in May 2002, at the end of the recovery period. This 36-foot-tall column is covered top to bottom with inscriptions, signatures, prayer cards, and memorabilia affixed by first responders, recovery workers, and others. Visitors will reencounter the wall and the column later in their visit, bringing a deeper understanding to subsequent viewings.

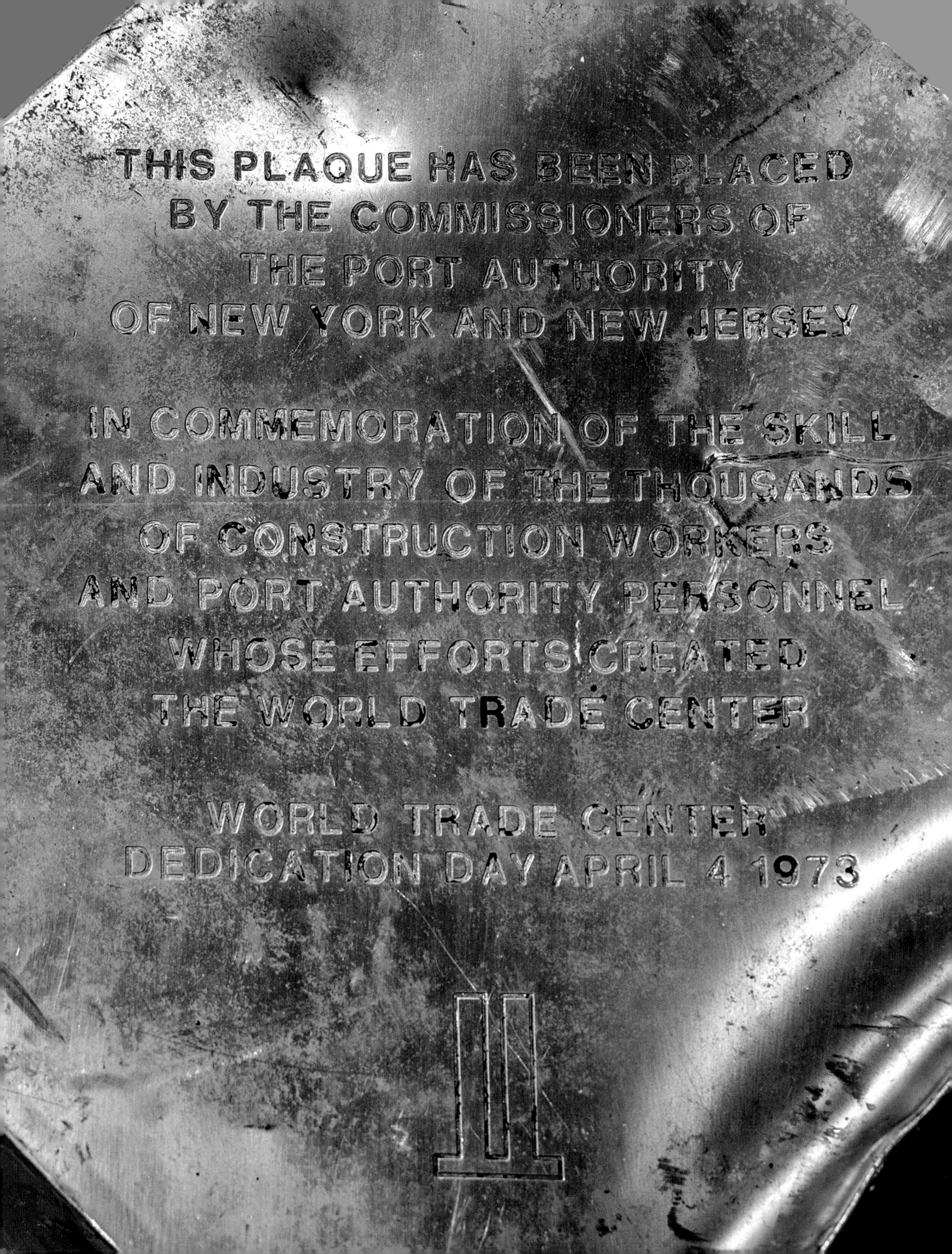

THIS PLAQUE HAS BEEN PLACED
BY THE COMMISSIONERS OF
THE PORT AUTHORITY
OF NEW YORK AND NEW JERSEY

IN COMMEMORATION OF THE SKILL
AND INDUSTRY OF THE THOUSANDS
OF CONSTRUCTION WORKERS
AND PORT AUTHORITY PERSONNEL
WHOSE EFFORTS CREATED
THE WORLD TRADE CENTER

WORLD TRADE CENTER
DEDICATION DAY APRIL 4 1973

DEDICATION PEDESTAL

Recovered from the World Trade Center site after September 11, 2001
Collection 9/11 Memorial Museum, Courtesy of the Port Authority of New York and New Jersey

Construction of the World Trade Center began in August 1966, under the auspices of the Port of New York Authority (now known as the Port Authority of New York and New Jersey). Attesting to the life cycle of the towers, this stainless steel pedestal is inscribed with the date April 4, 1973, when the world's tallest buildings were dedicated in a ribbon-cutting ceremony; it also bears evidence of damage inflicted on September 11, 2001.

SECTION OF STEEL FACADE, NORTH TOWER, FLOORS 96-99

Recovered from the World Trade Center site after September 11, 2001
Collection 9/11 Memorial Museum, Courtesy of the Port Authority
of New York and New Jersey

Visible only partially from the Ramp, a remnant panel of contorted steel columns is suspended off the adjacent facade. At this point in the visitor journey, the steel conveys only the idea of wounded metal, of buildings that sustained injury as a result of tremendous force. When viewed again from below, its full meaning will be revealed.

LOWER MANHATTAN, VIEWS FROM JERSEY CITY,
NEW JERSEY, SEPTEMBER 1995 AND SEPTEMBER 11, 2001

Photographs by Masatomo Kuriya / Yancey Richardson Gallery, New York

MISSING POSTERS

Collection 9/11 Memorial Museum, Gift of 9/11 family members and Sisters of Charity of New York, St. Vincent's Hospital

In the days immediately following 9/11, relatives and friends of those who had not returned home from the World Trade Center posted missing person flyers at hospitals, family assistance centers, and public places throughout the city. As hope for survivors faded, the missing posters themselves became memorials. Here, along the Ramp, images of missing posters fade in and out on multiple surfaces, bringing to mind the posters that papered the surfaces of the city, from building walls to construction fences to bus shelters, giving a human face to unimaginable loss.

APPROACH TO EAST OVERLOOK

A wall of vivid blue beckons visitors to approach the East Overlook where, standing between the North and South Tower volumes, they take in the actual distance that separated the Twin Towers. Memorial Hall opens below.

MEMORIAL HALL FROM EAST OVERLOOK (NEXT PAGE)

NO DAY SHALL ERASE YOU FROM THE MEMORY OF TIME, 2014 (NEXT PAGE)

Tom Joyce (American, b. 1956)
Steel

TRYING TO REMEMBER THE COLOR OF THE SKY ON THAT SEPTEMBER MORNING, 2014 (NEXT PAGE)

Spencer Finch (American, b. 1962)
Watercolor on paper

VESEY STREET STAIR REMNANT: THE SURVIVORS' STAIRS
Recovered from the World Trade Center site after September 11, 2001
Collection 9/11 Memorial Museum, Courtesy of the Port Authority of New York and New Jersey

EVACUEES DESCENDING VESEY STREET STAIRS ON 9/11
Photograph by Shannon Stapleton, Reuters

VESEY STREET STAIR REMNANT, NOVEMBER 15, 2001
Photograph by Joel Meyerowitz, Courtesy Howard Greenberg Gallery

The final descent to bedrock flanks one of the Museum's largest artifacts: a staircase that once connected the northern edge of the World Trade Center Plaza to the Vesey Street sidewalk below. On September 11, 2001, these stairs and an adjacent escalator provided an unobstructed exit for hundreds seeking to escape. The Vesey Street stairs withstood 9/11. (Most of the damage now visible was inflicted during the cleanup operation at the World Trade Center site.) The stairs were slated for demolition until a federal review process involving preservationists, survivors, and other advocates eventually assured that this symbolic remnant, now known as the Survivors' Stairs, would be saved. It was the first artifact to be placed into the Museum site.

Descending alongside the stairs, we follow the path of survival to arrive in Memorial Hall—suggesting that, in some sense, we are all survivors, living in the post-9/11 world.

ARCHAEOLOGY, ARCHITECTURE, AND CREATING A SPACE FOR MEMORY

BY AMY S. WEISSER

Senior Vice President for Exhibitions

The historic importance of the site and its symbolism made it essential for us to find a balance between the collective and the individual experience. We relied on four principles to guide our work: memory, authenticity, scale, and emotion, hoping to provide the most sensitive, respectful, and informative experience for visitors.

—Steven M. Davis, FAIA, Partner, Davis Brody Bond; Museum Architects

In laying out the programmatic requirements for a museum designated for both memorialization and education and working with the project team of the 9/11 Memorial, architects Davis Brody Bond (DBB) established key design strategies for the belowground Museum spaces. First, the architectural design would highlight the archaeological remnants of the site, which include the site's original retaining wall or slurry wall; the remainders of the structural steel columns that formed the perimeter of the two towers, generally referred to as the box column remnants; and a staircase used on 9/11 for evacuation to Vesey Street from the World Trade Center Plaza, now known as the Survivors' Stairs.

A second strategy was to emphasize the original location of the Twin Towers within the 9/11 Memorial Museum. The Museum's main exhibition level, 70 feet belowground and sometimes referred to as "bedrock," encompasses nearly the entire footprint of the North Tower and half of the South Tower footprint along with the areas between and around these two footprints. The architects evoked the Twin Towers with two distinct volumes.

Third, visitors would arrive at the exhibition level along a gently sloping ramp gradually introducing them to the enormous cavity of the former World Trade Center, the space now occupied by the Museum. The decision to insert a ramped descent, rather than use an elevator as the primary means by which visitors would reach the bedrock level seven stories down, was conditioned by several factors and intentions. As an architectural insertion into the authentic space of the World Trade Center's foundation, the ramp would provide a clear distinction between the built environment of the Museum and the archaeological elements incorporated within it. A gradual descent would enable progressive views into the enormous space occupied by the Museum, helping visitors to comprehend the monumental scale that had always been a characteristic of the World Trade Center site. Furthermore, this descent would reference construction ramps at the site when the World Trade Center was first being built, as well as the ramp installed for the removal of debris from Ground Zero in the aftermath of the attacks. It was that ramp which dignitaries and family members of the victims used to access the site and pay their respects during anniversary commemorations before the Memorial was built. Similarly, it was hoped, the ramp inside the Museum would encourage an attitude of reverence, as visitors made their way down to the lowest level of the site.

After DBB established these guiding architectural strategies, the project's lead exhibition design firm, Thinc Design, together with media design partner Local Projects, worked with Museum staff to build on the architectural intention. Together, we crafted an exhibition master plan that joins authenticity with memory, history, and storytelling. Visitors begin their exhibition experience at the top of the Ramp, moving through a media installation that communicates the breadth and simultaneity of global witness to the attacks of

September 11, 2001. Worldwide awareness transitions to images of people witnessing the events at the actual sites; and then, the vista opens to the vast underground space of the Museum, giving visitors a dramatic view of a remnant of the site, the slurry wall.

Slurry wall construction is a technique for building a concrete wall in an environment close to open water, necessary here due to the proximity of the Hudson River. When the World Trade Center was built, a slurry wall ringed the perimeter of the site, creating an inverted bathtub that kept water out. In the Museum, visitors see a large expanse of rough concrete, punctuated evenly by the caps of tiebacks, or cables that anchor the wall to bedrock.

This historic remnant of the original World Trade Center, 60 feet tall and 62 feet wide, is illuminated like a jewel. It defines the west side of the Museum's largest space, Foundation Hall. On the hall's east side, a line of hollow steel rectangles set within concrete articulate the western edge of the North Tower footprint. Slightly varied, with some elements missing, similar rectangles line all sides of this footprint as well as that of the portion of the South Tower footprint within the Museum. These rectangles are the remnants of the box columns that once formed the perimeter structure of the Twin Towers. The column remnants are also theatrically lit, each with its own downlight. They are distinguished from the built environment of the new Museum; visitors cross on bridges set over the archaeological zone to enter the tower footprints. Subtly, architecture and design ensure that visitors know these column remnants are historical elements.

While architectural and exhibition design ultimately determined how these elements would be presented, the mandate to preserve the remnants resulted from impassioned advocacy by a range of stakeholders and was ultimately secured by a federal statute. Redevelopment of the World Trade Center was first managed by the Lower Manhattan Development Corporation (LMDC) in association with the Port Authority of New York and New Jersey, the owner of the site, with funds allocated by the U.S. Department of Housing and Urban Development. As a recipient of federal funds, LMDC was obligated to meet applicable federal requirements. Among these requirements was an assessment of the historic remnants of the site.

Section 106 of the National Historic Preservation Act of 1966 required that a determination be made regarding the World Trade Center site's eligibility for the National Register of Historic Places. Typically, a property is not considered for the register until 50 years after it achieves significance, and so the Twin Towers themselves never reached eligibility. The site, however, met a different eligibility criterion because of its association with a significant historical event. It was deemed to be "exceptionally significant in the history of the United States as the location of events that immediately and profoundly influenced the lives of millions of American citizens." In February 2004, the site became eligible.

To guide its Section 106 compliance, LMDC signed a programmatic agreement with federal and state preservation groups in April 2004. Working with redevelopment officials in an advisory capacity, consulting parties helped to identify historic assets for preservation and reviewed provisions for meaningful access to these elements. The consulting parties included preservationists, architects, urban planners, government representatives, community advocates, family members of those killed at the World Trade Center, survivors, and local residents.

The programmatic agreement named two specific components of the site that required preservation and provisions for public access as part of the site-wide development. They were portions of the slurry wall and the "truncated box beam column bases." It added five elements for which it also advocated preservation and meaningful access. These included the slurry wall tiebacks; the Vesey Street stair remnant; "slab and column remnants of below-grade parking garage at [the] northwest corner of World Trade Center site with smoke scars or other visible evidence of the September 11 attacks;" a "steel column and crossbeam;" and remnants of the Hudson & Manhattan Tubes, century-old tunnels containing former railroad lines that pierced the eastern slurry wall near the Port Authority's railroad tracks. Ultimately, only the Tubes' remnants would not be inside the 9/11 Memorial Museum. When construction of the Museum began, the slurry wall, its tiebacks, and the box column remnants were left in place within the Museum's contours. The stairs, garage slab, and crossbeam would be transferred in and installed as artifacts.

By 2005, preservation advocates turned their attention to the Vesey Street stairs. This stairway was located at what had been the northern edge of the World Trade Center's Austin J. Tobin Plaza. In keeping with the standards of 1960s urban redevelopment, the World Trade Center was designed as a "superblock," its campus situated on a plaza covering 16 acres with a flat plane. The streets of the surrounding area, however, had varied topography, and on this edge of the site, the Plaza was approximately 20 feet above the sidewalk for Vesey Street.

After 9/11, as workers cleared the site of the 1.8 million tons of debris from the collapsed towers and their surrounding buildings, the Vesey Street stairs were left in place because they sheltered a maintenance access into the subway station below. The programmatic agreement thus recognized this stairway, however minor a component during the time of the World Trade Center, as the last aboveground vestige of the original campus.

The stairs held additional meaning for some who had escaped from the World Trade Center on the terrible morning of 9/11. The South Tower, the second building hit by the hijacked planes, was the first to fall. After its collapse, many escaping the devastated site had to run to the north. Sheltered by 5 World Trade Center, the Vesey Street stairs became a path to safety. Some who escaped down its two flights later looked back at the still-standing stairs as the emblem of their survival.

In accordance with the master site plan for rebuilding the World Trade Center, a new tower—2 World Trade Center—was to be located at the northeast corner of the redeveloped site, where the Vesey Street stair remnant stood. As new construction broke ground, advocates raised concerns about the impact of the new tower's perimeter on public access to what had by now come to be known as the Survivors' Stairs. Following much debate, the Section 106 consulting parties joined the LMDC and the 9/11 Memorial in recommending placement of the stairs inside the planned Museum.

At about 17 feet wide, 64 feet long, 21 feet tall, and weighing 175 tons, the stairway itself was massive. The Museum's architects and exhibition designers explored the few locations available for an artifact of this size. Consideration was given to displaying it in Foundation Hall, but DBB ultimately recommended a solution that not only integrated the stairs into the narrative of the introductory exhibition sequence but that also, in a kinesthetic manner, would intensify the visitor's experiential journey. With extraordinary finesse, given the size and weight of the artifact, the 38-step stairway, separated from its escalator bed, was inserted into the ceremonial staircase that links the final stretch of the Ramp to the Museum's exhibition level at bedrock. Visitors now descend alongside the Survivors' Stairs, set off as a protected but visually accessible archaeological artifact. Moving in the same direction many evacuees took on that fateful day, visitors arrive in the Museum's Memorial Hall in the context of survival.

> *By the time people reach bedrock, we have given them a*
> *chance to react to their own memories.*
>
> —Carl Krebs, FAIA, Partner, Davis Brody Bond; Museum Architects

Consulting parties advocated for another historic component not specifically named in the programmatic agreement: remnants of the concrete slab at the lowest level (B-6) of the Twin Towers. This concrete slab had been heavily damaged during the cleanup of the site; parts of it were dug up entirely, and heavy construction equipment had left what remained in pieces. The request to exhibit a damaged floor slab that occupants or visitors to the complex would never have seen initially seemed challenging. But as Thinc Design mulled over the options, and with the advice of participants in the Museum's Conversation Series, the designers realized that the B-6 slab could elucidate authenticity of "place" in the memorial exhibition.

Fulfilling the Museum's mission to honor the lives of those killed in the events of September 11, 2001 and February 26, 1993, the memorial exhibition, *In Memoriam*, iterates its relationship to the site by taking its form—a square within a square—from the Memorial pools above. In its initial design, the gallery provided no visual access to archaeological reminders of the Museum's historic location. Then, Thinc proposed that the exhibition's inner chamber, where visitors learn about the lives of individual victims, might sit directly above an exposed portion of the remaining B-6 slab. A glass floor would simultaneously protect and draw attention to the actual remnant of the building's lowest level. Visitors literally walk over the remnant in this space, and as they do, they hear the voices of loved ones recalling particular and treasured qualities of those who were killed. Again, lighting, here carefully concealed under the glass, was crucial in turning a prosaic remnant into a poetic reminder of the specificity of this place.

The historical exhibition, *September 11, 2001*, designed by Layman Design and set in the North Tower footprint, reveals a different kind of exhibition space. As the Museum's main storytelling exhibition, it provides a distinct environment in which to focus visitors' attention on the stories of the day of 9/11, the lead-up to that day, and what came after. Authenticity is mainly conveyed through the presentation of historic photographs, documentary film, archival recordings of victims and first responders, and the testimony of survivors, as well as objects ranging from multi-ton fragments of recovered building structure to intimate, personal effects items that survivors carried in their pockets.

Two of the large-scale artifacts mandated for preservation and public access in the programmatic agreement found their place in the historical exhibition. A nine-foot-tall portion of the wall from the B-2 parking garage level, where the car bomb detonated during the February 26, 1993 attack on the World Trade Center, bears soot streaks from the fires caused by the 9/11 attacks. It became the focal point of a gallery devoted to the history of that first terrorist strike at the site. The "steel column and crossbeam" referenced in the programmatic agreement, better known as the Ground Zero Cross, now stands at the center of the gallery chronicling the recovery at Ground Zero. Other large pieces, not explicitly called out in the agreement, are displayed throughout the Museum, both in the historical exhibition and open spaces. These include steel panels from the North Tower's facade that were directly impacted by hijacked Flight 11, damaged FDNY vehicles, components of the North Tower's antenna and one of the towers' elevators, and limestone from the Pentagon. Each is a remainder and reminder of the day.

At one place in the historical exhibition, as in the memorial exhibition, the remains of the original B-6 slab are revealed. After visitors have traveled through the information-rich and emotional retelling of the events of the day on 9/11, they enter a brightly lit gallery dominated by the only known extant architectural model of the complex. Even at 1:200 scale, the model, created by Minoru Yamasaki Associates, is nearly eight feet tall. It has been placed above an exposed portion of concrete slab from the lowest level of the site. The visible remnant reminds visitors of where they are standing, in the same place where the towers once stood.

Exiting the historical exhibition, visitors enter Foundation Hall, where they take in the majestic view of the slurry wall, the towering Last Column—the final piece of Twin Tower steel to be removed from Ground Zero at the end of the recovery—and the volume of the former North Tower.

From there, visitors can explore an excavation of the box column remnants at the northern edge of the North Tower footprint. A similar excavation of column remnants can be found at the south end of the South Tower footprint. Within the context of the Section 106 process, DBB suggested that these relatively narrow areas at the edge of the Museum's space provided an opportunity to further explicate the footings of the towers, uncovering the substantial steel plates on which the columns were mounted.

At the North Tower Excavation, the column remnants are in dialogue with images by photographer Stephane Sednaoui of the rescue efforts undertaken during the first nights after the attacks, showing human effort in the midst of the mangled steel of the destroyed World Trade Center. Together, the column remnants and photographs remind us that, at this site, people worked against time in the determined hope of saving lives. Here, people said no to evil, no to those with the intent to hurt. Here, they affirmed that they would do whatever was in their power to help and heal.

Throughout the Museum, architecture and exhibitions sit within the twin contexts of memory and authenticity, attesting to both the tragedy and the good that happened here. Through a seamless integration of design and content, the space inspires awe and a recognition of the power of place.

MEMORIAL HALL

At the foundation of the World Trade Center site—the main exhibition and education level of the Museum—we encounter in-situ archaeological remnants of the buildings, repatriated artifacts scarred by the attacks, and images of those who were killed. These installations attest to the scale of the building complex, the magnitude of the disaster, and the incalculable cost in human lives. Artifacts are arranged in open areas that surround the separately enclosed historical and memorial exhibitions, housed within the footprints of the Twin Towers.

The first space we reach is Memorial Hall, situated between the two footprints. Here, in the Museum's lower lobby, an immense wall displays a pair of site-specific art installations. This same wall separates the public space of the Museum from a private repository of unidentified and unclaimed remains of victims of 9/11, inaccessible to visitors and Museum staff. Two identical markers at either end of the wall explain: "Reposed behind this wall are the remains of many who perished at the World Trade Center site on September 11, 2001. The repository is maintained by the Office of Chief Medical Examiner of the City of New York." The brutal circumstances attending the collapse of two 110-story skyscrapers rendered thousands of human remains recovered at Ground Zero unidentifiable. Using increasingly precise scientific analysis at laboratories off-site, the New York City Office of Chief Medical Examiner is dedicated to continuing the work to make positive identifications and return the remains of loved ones to their families.

A quotation from Book IX of *The Aeneid* by the Roman poet Virgil suggests the transformative potential of memory. The letters have been forged from pieces of recovered World Trade Center steel by New Mexico artist Tom Joyce. Trained as a blacksmith, Joyce harnessed the process that occurs when iron is touched by fire. He took wounded, remnant steel and shaped it into letters of hope and beauty. The result reminds us that Virgil's words are more than a statement; they are a promise.

A surrounding work is composed of 2,983 individual watercolor paintings, each reflecting artist Spencer Finch's attempt to remember the color of the sky on the morning of September 11, 2001. Commemorating the people killed in the attacks of September 11, 2001 and February 26, 1993, every square is a unique shade of blue, combining to create a panoramic mosaic of color. Finch's work centers on the idea of memory. What one person perceives as blue might not be the same as what another person sees; yet our memories, like our perception of color, share a common reference.

In Memorial Hall, the artwork helps us to acknowledge and pay our respects to those whom we cannot see behind the wall.

IN MEMORIAM
Memorial Exhibition

My dear sister, Mary Jane Booth . . . my uncle, Glenn Jonathan Winuk . . . my husband and eternal soulmate, David Garcia . . .

The soft sound of names being read by family and friends leads into *In Memoriam*, commemorating those killed in the attacks of September 11, 2001 and February 26, 1993. Located on the footprint of the South Tower, this exhibition gallery—a square within a square—echoes the geometry of the Memorial pools above. The outer square is lined with portrait photographs placed floor to ceiling on all four walls, surrounding visitors with the faces and names of all who were killed in the attacks. Immediately conveying the enormity of loss, the "wall of faces" renders the number 2,983 an abstraction no longer. These four walls are made up of people, a true cross-section of humanity, aged two and a half to 85, from more than 90 nations, spanning the spectrum of ethnicities, economic classes, and faith traditions. Using touchscreen tables, visitors can learn more about victims by calling up individual profiles. Nearby artifact cases feature displays of recovered property and small objects reflecting the interests and activities of these people before their lives were cut short. In this place, we remember people for how they lived their lives rather than how they died.

The gallery's inner chamber provides a more intimate space for remembrance, its glass floor revealing a remnant of the original South Tower floor slab from the lowest level of the World Trade Center to remind us of where we stand. Profiles of every victim, each running about a minute in length, are projected onto the walls of this room. Where family members, friends, former colleagues, and others recorded remembrances of their loved ones, brief audio clips have been included so that visitors can be introduced to victims by those who knew them best. The stories are familiar, loving, at times humorous; they are the stories we all tell when we remember those we have cherished. The memorial exhibition serves as a reminder that, given the arbitrary and indiscriminate nature of mass murder, any one of us might have been a victim, and all of us are diminished when others suffer the loss of a loved one through a senseless act of terrorism.

Throughout this book, names in blue signify individuals killed as a result of the terrorist attacks of September 11, 2001 and February 26, 1993.

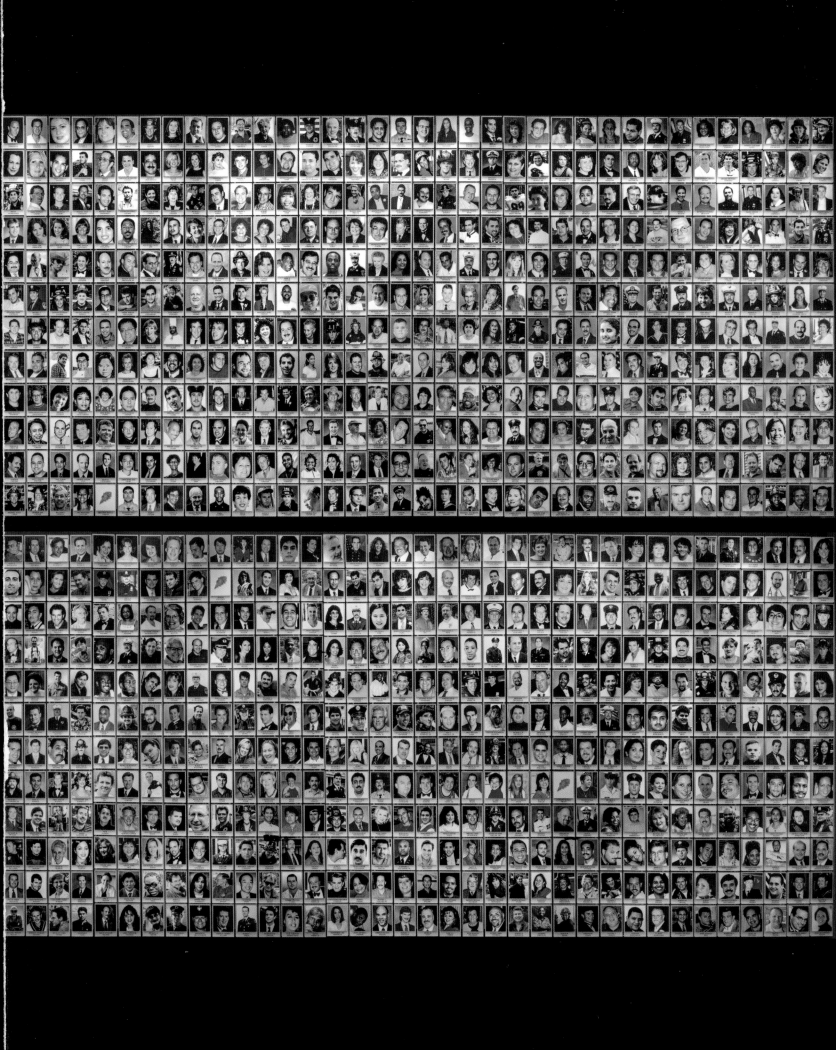

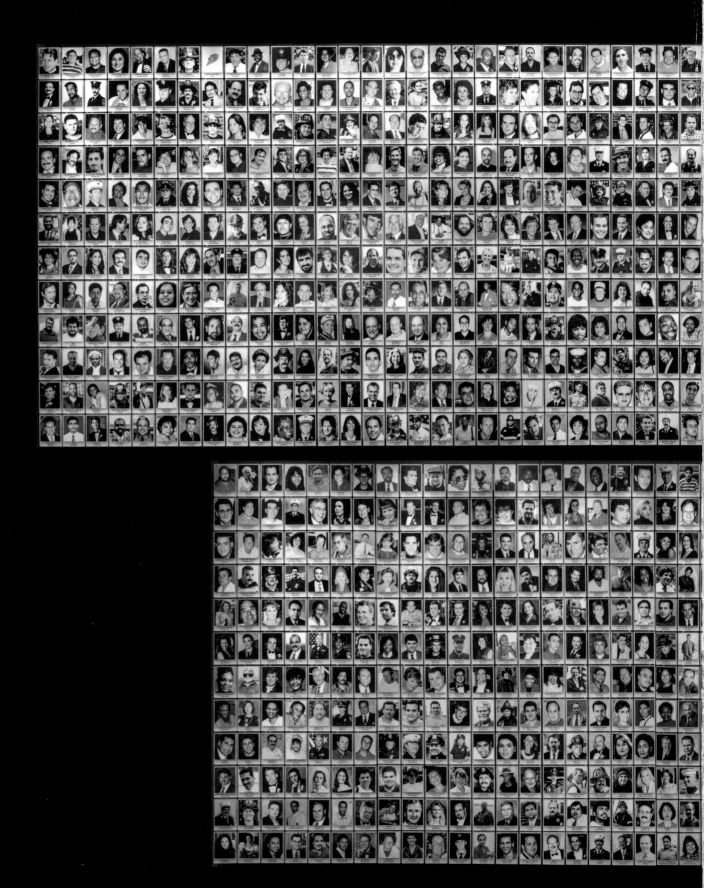

An image of a leaf from a swamp white oak—the type of tree planted on the 9/11 Memorial—appears in place of a portrait when no photograph is available.

SELECTED REMEMBRANCES FROM THE MEMORIAL EXHIBITION

TOURI HAMZAVI BOLOURCHI as remembered by her husband, Akbar Bolourchi
Touri liked the traditions of life very much. She respected proper etiquette. She knew how to be a great host. She would impress people in parties and gatherings. She was very well spoken and always had a smile.

VINCENT G. DANZ as remembered by his wife, Angela Danz
You would never have known he was a police officer if you had met him. He was extremely kindhearted, and there wasn't a tough bone in his body.

DARLENE E. FLAGG as remembered by her son, Marcus W. Flagg
She could do everything, from working in the fields on the farm to hosting a black-tie dinner, perfectly. She was very easygoing, she kept everything together, very, very smart—she was a Mensa—and she could do incredible things.

LEROY W. HOMER, JR., as remembered by his wife, Melodie Homer
LeRoy's just very romantic. You know when you watch romantic comedies and they seem so contrived? He would make me breakfast in bed for no reason. He would go on a trip and write me a postcard, and I'd get it like a week and a half later. I mean, he was just a gentleman.

UHURU G. HOUSTON as remembered by his coworker, Sue Keane
He had the greatest smile in the world, the brightest smile.

KAZUSHIGE ITO as remembered by his father, Tsugio Ito
As a man and as his father, I can say that he was sociable, and he was a man of action. He was persuasive and also had a sense of humor.

SARA ELIZABETH LOW as remembered by her sister, Alyson Low
We had so much left to do, not just as sisters but as friends.

DENNIS MOJICA as remembered by his coworker and friend, Timothy L. Brown
He really, really loved the Fire Department. And he loved, especially, the guys that worked for him.

PATRICK JUDE MURPHY as remembered by his mother, Joan Miller
When he was older and I started to travel, there was nothing that I could talk to him about that he hadn't been, or seen, or read about.

SEAMUS L. ONEAL as remembered by his partner, Thomas Miller
Seamus was unlike anyone I have ever known. He loved life with a fervor and spent every moment experiencing life as fully as possible.

RICHARD ALLEN PEARLMAN as remembered by his mother, Dorie Pearlman
Richard was a unique eighteen-year-old. He was as tender and gentle as a teddy bear and at times as rough and tough as a grizzly bear.

MONICA RODRIGUEZ SMITH as remembered by her husband, Ed Smith
Monica was a vivacious, outgoing person who was full of energy—she was the life of the party. . . . She was seven months pregnant with our first child, a son we planned to name Eddie. . . . She was my best friend and my inspiration.

RING AND WALLET BELONGING TO **ROBERT JOSEPH GSCHAAR** (INSURANCE UNDERWRITER, AON CORPORATION, SOUTH TOWER, 92ND FLOOR)

Collection 9/11 Memorial Museum, Gift of Myrta Gschaar in honor of my beloved husband Robert J. Gschaar

When **Robert Gschaar** proposed to his future wife, Myrta, he presented her with a $2 bill. Both had been previously married and pledged to keep a $2 bill in their respective wallets as a symbol of their second chance at happiness. On September 11, Robert phoned his wife to report that there had been an accident at the World Trade Center and that he would call her when he reached the street outside. More than a year later, Robert's wallet and wedding ring were recovered at Ground Zero. Still tucked inside his wallet was the cherished $2 bill.

EARMUFFS AND WASHINGTON, D.C., PUBLIC LIBRARY CARD BELONGING TO **ASIA S. COTTOM** (PASSENGER, FLIGHT 77)

Collection 9/11 Memorial Museum, Gift of the Asia Sivon Cottom Memorial Scholarship Fund

STUFFED ANIMAL BELONGING TO **CHRISTINE LEE HANSON** (PASSENGER, FLIGHT 175)

Collection 9/11 Memorial Museum, Gift of the Hanson family, Lee, Eunice, and Kathy

Eight children were killed aboard the hijacked planes on September 11, 2001. **Asia Cottom**, a sixth grader, was flying to California with a teacher to attend an educational program at a marine sanctuary. The Peter Rabbit toy belonged to the youngest victim, **Christine Hanson**, age two and a half, who was heading to Disneyland with her parents.

TOUCHSCREEN TABLE IN THE MEMORIAL EXHIBITION (PREVIOUS PAGE)

TRIBUTE WALK

Defined by a soaring concrete wall more than 50 feet high and 200 feet long, running alongside the South Tower footprint, Tribute Walk is a dramatic venue for large-scale works of tribute art displayed on a rotating basis.

In the aftermath of 9/11, professional and amateur artists alike attempted to capture the significance of the attacks, honor those lost, and comfort those left behind. A diverse array of artworks are exhibited, ranging from quilts to children's paintings and including unique items such as a decorated tribute motorcycle and engraved Waterford crystal triangles that formed part of the New Year's Eve Ball dropped at Times Square on December 31, 2001.

SOUTH TOWER EXCAVATION

TRIBUTE WALK

FDNY DREAM BIKE

Collection 9/11 Memorial Museum, Gift of Ladder Company 9 and Engine Company 33, and Michael and Nuri Wernick

In summer 2001, Firefighter **Gerard Baptiste**, FDNY Ladder Company 9, purchased a battered 1979 Honda motorcycle, model CB750. Baptiste believed that he could restore it to good working order. His fellow firefighters joked that it would take time and money just to start the engine.

Following Baptiste's death in the North Tower on 9/11, his colleagues decided to restore the bike in his memory. Surviving members of Ladder Company 9, with support from Honda and motorcycle enthusiasts nationwide, transformed the motorcycle into a "bike of healing" known as the Dream Bike. Ten roses painted on the cover of its gas tank symbolize the members of Ladder Company 9 and Engine Company 33 who were killed on 9/11.

ENGRAVED WATERFORD CRYSTAL TRIANGLES FROM THE TIMES SQUARE NEW YEAR'S EVE BALL

Collection 9/11 Memorial Museum, Gift of Waterford Crystal Times Square New Year's Eve Ball

At 11:59 p.m. on December 31, 2001, atop 1 Times Square, outgoing New York City Mayor Rudolph Giuliani ushered in the New Year by pressing a button that released an illuminated crystal ball memorializing the victims of 9/11 and honoring first responders. Six feet in diameter and weighing 1,070 pounds, the Times Square Ball was composed of 504 Waterford crystal triangles. Inscriptions on the crystals acknowledged losses from the terrorist attacks at the World Trade Center, the Pentagon, and aboard all four hijacked flights, as well as from the first responder agencies, and the home countries of the victims.

9/11 MEMORIAL URN

Tom Lane (American, b. 1949)
Porcelain
Collection 9/11 Memorial Museum

Cast in porcelain, ceramicist Tom Lane's classically shaped urn honors the lives of those lost on 9/11. This is an urn in concept only, as the vessel is empty. Fired into its faceted surface are the names of all 2,977 victims of 9/11. The words of the speech delivered by U.S. President George W. Bush on the night of the attacks wind around its tapered lid.

EDUCATION CENTER

The vestibule of the Education Center—located within the South Tower footprint adjacent to Tribute Walk—provides a complementary display space for works of tribute art. Throughout the year, programs for students, teachers, and intergenerational audiences, as well as civic education training programs for military, intelligence, and law enforcement officials, are offered in the Center's classrooms.

THE SHIELD, 2002

Red Grooms (American, b. 1937)
Enamel on epoxy
Collection 9/11 Memorial Museum, Gift of Dr. Albert and Margarita Waxman
© 2016 Red Grooms / Artist Rights Society (ARS), New York

Deeply affected by the September 11 terrorist attacks, lower Manhattan resident and artist Red Grooms felt inspired to create *The Shield*, a composition that combines painting and sculpture in tribute to the recovery workers at Ground Zero. The shape of *The Shield* is reminiscent of a police officer's badge. The work includes a reference to photographer Thomas E. Franklin's iconic image of three firefighters raising an American flag at Ground Zero and others wearing hard hats set against the ruins of the Twin Towers. At the shield's base, Grooms depicts military and law enforcement personnel who were stationed around the World Trade Center site in the immediate aftermath of 9/11.

PAINTING TO COMMEMORATE A GIFT OF COWS BY THE MAASAI TO THE UNITED STATES

Collection 9/11 Memorial Museum, Gift of Wilson Kimeli Naiyomah and the Maasai people of Kenya

Living in a remote region of eastern Africa, many of the Maasai people of Kenya did not learn about the magnitude of the 9/11 attacks for months. Wilson Kimeli Naiyomah, a Maasai student attending a university in California, witnessed the attacks on the World Trade Center during a visit to New York City and told his community what had happened when he returned home to visit in spring 2002. In response, the community offered 14 cows—a gift of compassion and generosity—to the United States. For the Maasai, cows are a sacred symbol of life. The U.S. ambassador accepted the gift on behalf of the nation. It was determined, however, that the herd should remain in Kenya to be cared for properly. Naiyomah asked an American friend, James Cloutier, to create two identical paintings to commemorate the gift—one for Kenya and one for the United States.

LADY LIBERTY

Collection 9/11 Memorial Museum, Gift in memory of the courageous firefighters from Engine 54/Ladder 4/Battalion 9 killed at the World Trade Center on September 11, 2001
Object photograph by Bruce M. White

Soon after 9/11, a Statue of Liberty replica appeared on the sidewalk in front of a midtown Manhattan firehouse. Home to FDNY Engine Company 54, Ladder Company 4, and Battalion 9, the firehouse lost 15 firefighters at the World Trade Center on 9/11. People walking past the building began to affix small American flags, condolence messages, prayer cards and rosary beads, patches bearing military and uniformed service insignia, money, and other tribute items on the statue, which soon became known as Lady Liberty.

SOUTH TOWER EXCAVATION

Archaeology, history, and memory intersect at the South Tower Excavation. Here, the actual footings of structural columns that once formed the south facade of the South Tower are revealed, providing a dramatic backdrop for the story of the Twin Towers' construction.

The Twin Towers received mixed architectural reviews when they first dominated the New York City skyline as the tallest buildings on earth. The engineering innovations that made their height possible were, however, universally acclaimed. From exterior walls that supported roughly half of the building's weight, freeing up space on the floors, to the self-elevating "kangaroo cranes"—the first used in America—that jumped from floor to floor as the structures rose, to a damping system that allowed the towers to sway as much as 12 inches on windy days, the Twin Towers lifted high-rise construction to new heights. Planning and completing the complex took 13 years, including seven years of construction. When the Twin Towers were dedicated in 1973, they were the tallest buildings in the world, reaching more than a quarter mile into the sky.

The excavated column footings, along with other elements of the Museum, are in situ, having been preserved as historic assets in their original locations. However, it is an artifact not in situ but returned to the site—a contorted piece of North Tower steel—that draws visitors to the South Tower Excavation.

BOX COLUMN REMNANTS, SOUTH TOWER, WORLD TRADE CENTER (PREVIOUS PAGE)

Seventy-three box columns—so called because of their rectangular shape and hollow center—formed the one-acre perimeter of the World Trade Center's South Tower at bedrock. The tower soared 1,362 feet aboveground, supported by these steel columns anchored 70 feet belowground. During cleanup operations following 9/11, recovery workers sheared what remained of the North and South Towers' exterior structural columns, leaving the stumps, which were set within a concrete base secured to a bedrock layer of Manhattan schist.

Many 9/11 victims' family members joined with landmark preservationists to advocate for both towers' column remnants to be designated as permanent historic assets of the World Trade Center site. Today, they are visible in the Museum, where they articulate the perimeters of the two towers' footprints.

SECTION OF STEEL FACADE, NORTH TOWER, FLOORS 93-96

*Recovered from the World Trade Center site after September 11, 2001
Collection 9/11 Memorial Museum, Courtesy of the Port Authority of
New York and New Jersey*

On 9/11, hijacked Flight 11 tore into the north facade of the North Tower, creating a gash from the 93rd through the 99th floors and tearing apart steel columns weighing many tons. The underbelly of the aircraft mangled the top of this facade segment with force sufficient to twist and shred the steel. It forms a pair with the section of steel facade visible from the Ramp.

Situated at the far end of Tribute Walk, this piece of facade steel is a reminder of the violent demise of the towers. A curve in the steel bends down toward the excavated footings of the South Tower, inviting contemplation of both the beginning and the end of the Twin Towers.

IRONWORKER THERMOSES

Collection 9/11 Memorial Museum, Gift of Brian Delisle and Gift of
Peter J. Stacey

Many of the ironworkers who helped build the World Trade Center belonged to the Kahnawake and Akwesasne Mohawk Nations, located in upper New York State and Canada. Their work placing structural steel for the Twin Towers put them several floors above the elevators that transported the construction workers. As the towers neared their final heights, the half-mile round trip to ground level and back at lunchtime became increasingly time-consuming. Workers employed by Karl Koch Erecting Company were given thermoses in which they could bring a hot beverage or meal for their lunch breaks, eliminating the need to climb up and down stairways and make the long elevator trip.

STREET SIGN, PRE-1968

Courtesy of Charles Maikish

Construction of the World Trade Center in the late 1960s created an urban superblock over what had previously been a maze of commercial and residential streets. Among the neighborhoods eliminated was the stretch of Greenwich Street between Dey Street, to the north, and Liberty Street, to the south, nicknamed Radio Row. A commercial district known for its numerous mom-and-pop electronics shops, Radio Row was home to more than 350 small businesses in 1966, when construction of the World Trade Center began.

MANHATTAN SCHIST FROM THE WORLD TRADE CENTER SITE

Recovered from the World Trade Center site after September 11, 2001
Collection 9/11 Memorial Museum, Courtesy of the Port Authority of New York
and New Jersey

A durable metamorphic rock, schist is the major geological formation running below the streets of lower Manhattan. Manhattan schist is sturdy enough to support the massive weight of skyscrapers. In New York City, tall towers were built where schist appears close to the surface. Major outcroppings exist in lower Manhattan and in midtown.

SOUTH TOWER GALLERY

Linking the South Tower Excavation and Tribute Walk, the South Tower Gallery is a space for special exhibitions of photography and other two-dimensional works. An adjacent theater plays *Rebirth at Ground Zero*, a 270-degree panoramic and immersive media installation created exclusively for the Museum. Through time-lapse footage and testimonies gathered in the 10 years after 9/11, *Rebirth at Ground Zero* chronicles the human spirit coping with disaster and affirms the possibility of renewal.

REBIRTH AT GROUND ZERO

Six months after 9/11, Project Rebirth, a nonprofit organization founded by filmmaker Jim Whitaker, placed time-lapse cameras in strategic locations at and around Ground Zero. This 11-minute immersive film experience was created from the resulting footage. While cameras followed the physical transformation and renewal at the World Trade Center site, the project also charted the emotional journeys of individuals who were profoundly affected by 9/11.

CENTER PASSAGE

Center Passage runs east-west between the North and South Tower footprints, linking Memorial Hall and Foundation Hall. Sheltered below the Ramp, the corridor evokes the Roman Forum—a field of debris where each fragment testifies to something once vital, immense, and impressive. The artifacts on display are physical remains of the day, pulled from the wreckage at Ground Zero. Singular and enigmatic in appearance, not immediately recognizable, they are presented to visitors with minimal context: a section of the communications antenna from the North Tower; a motor that powered one of the Twin Towers' 198 elevators; the crushed truck of FDNY Ladder Company 3; steel twisted by the impact of hijacked Flight 11. Each bears silent witness to the magnitude of what was here and the enormity of the devastation. And each, in its own way, is a kind of memorial, standing in for those no longer with us: broadcast engineers trapped above the impact zone; the estimated 200 people who perished in the worst passenger elevator disaster in history; first responders who ran into danger to save others; passengers and crew aboard the hijacked planes; and all who died inside the buildings into which those aircraft crashed.

SEGMENT OF RADIO AND TELEVISION ANTENNA, NORTH TOWER

Recovered from the World Trade Center site after September 11, 2001
Collection 9/11 Memorial Museum, Courtesy of the Port Authority of New York and New Jersey

A transmission tower approximately 360 feet tall stood atop the North Tower, distinguishing the building from its twin. This antenna began broadcasting television signals in 1980. Transmissions for most stations failed shortly after hijacked Flight 11 pierced the North Tower on 9/11. All transmissions ceased by 10:28 a.m., when the tower collapsed. This 19.8-foot-long fragment was approximately one-twentieth of the whole antenna.

ELEVATOR MOTOR

Recovered from the World Trade Center site after September 11, 2001
Collection 9/11 Memorial Museum, Courtesy of the Port Authority of New York
and New Jersey

The Twin Towers were the first skyscrapers to employ a system of local and express elevators, an innovation that reduced elevator travel time and made the buildings attractive to occupants of the upper floors. In addition to elevators servicing basement levels, each tower's 99 elevators included freight, local, and high-speed express cars. Two express cars traveled directly to the Windows on the World restaurant in the North Tower, and two went to the South Tower Observation Deck. This elevator motor, the largest model in the world when installed, powered one of the express or service cars, which moved at a speed of 1,600 feet per minute.

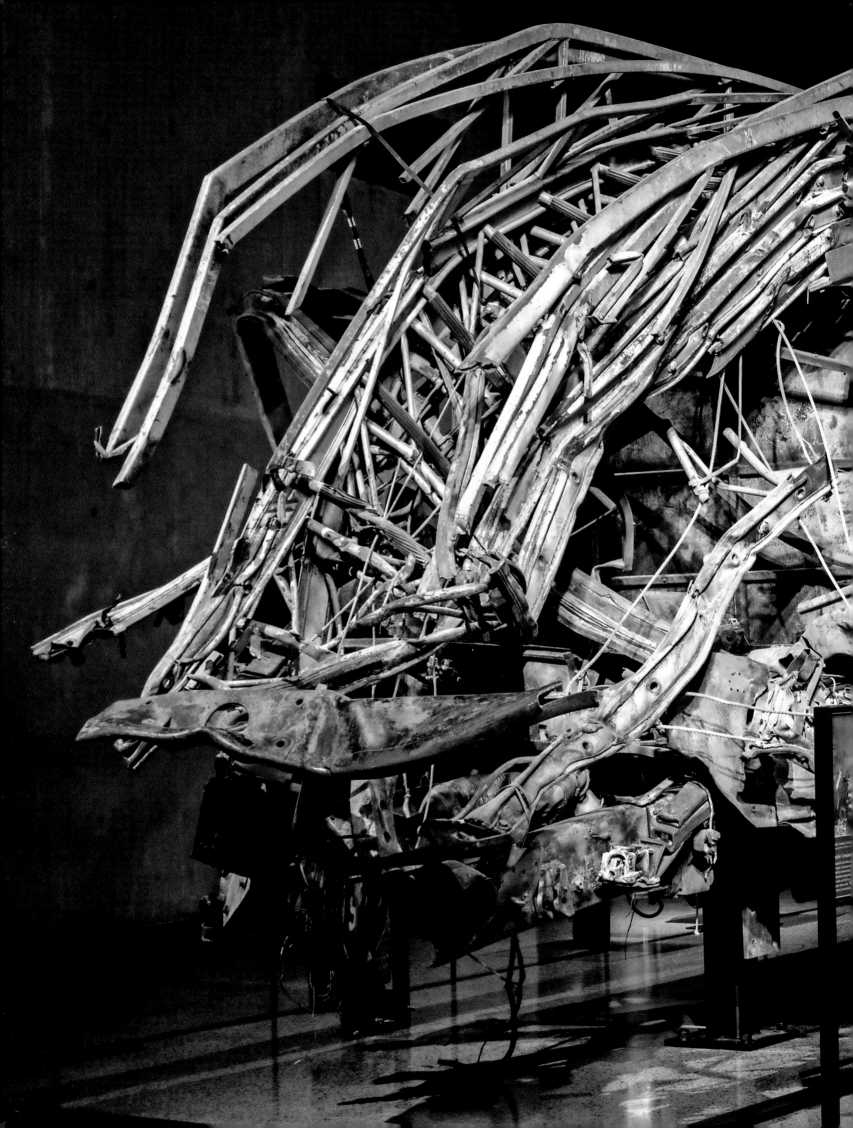

LADDER COMPANY 3 TRUCK, NEW YORK CITY FIRE DEPARTMENT (PREVIOUS PAGE)

Recovered from the World Trade Center site after September 11, 2001
Collection 9/11 Memorial Museum, Courtesy of the Port Authority of New York
and New Jersey, Presented with permission of the New York City Fire Department

FDNY Ladder Company 3 is located in the East Village neighborhood of Manhattan. On September 11, 2001, led by its highly decorated captain, **Patrick "Paddy" John Brown**, the company asked a dispatcher to deploy its members to the World Trade Center disaster. Those who had just started their shift parked the ladder truck on West Street near Vesey Street. Others who had just gone off duty after completing overnight shifts also responded. Eleven members in all entered the North Tower. Some are known to have reached the 35th floor by 9:21 a.m. In his last recorded transmission, Captain Brown said, "Three Truck, and we are still heading up." All 11 responding members were inside the building and killed when it collapsed at 10:28 a.m. The collapse sheared off the front cab of this truck.

SECTION OF STEEL FACADE, WORLD TRADE CENTER, NORTH TOWER, FLOORS 96-99 (AS SEEN FROM CENTER PASSAGE LOOKING UP)

Recovered from the World Trade Center site after September 11, 2001
Collection 9/11 Memorial Museum, Courtesy of the Port Authority of New York
and New Jersey

This piece of steel, once part of the north facade of the North Tower, was located at the point of impact where hijacked Flight 11 pierced the building at the 93rd through the 99th floors. Museum visitors first encounter this piece during their descent on the Ramp. Here in Center Passage, they see it from its underside, where the force of the crashing airplane bent the multi-ton steel columns inward.

Forming a pair with the section of steel facade displayed near the South Tower Excavation, this piece is suspended above the entry to the historical exhibition. In this location, it signals the moment of impact, 8:46 a.m.—the time at which the world first became aware of the events unfolding in lower Manhattan that morning as well as the starting point for the story told inside the historical exhibition, *September 11, 2001.*

SEPTEMBER 11, 2001

SEPTEMBER 11, 2001
Historical Exhibition

The historical exhibition, *September 11, 2001*, is located within the original footprint of the North Tower. It tells the story of 9/11 using artifacts, images, first-person testimony, and archival audio and video recordings. 9/11 is shorthand for four coordinated terrorist attacks that occurred on the morning of September 11, 2001. The attacks killed 2,977 people.

The exhibition is divided into three parts. The first part covers the events of the day as they unfolded. The second section provides the historical context leading up to the attacks, including the 1993 World Trade Center bombing and other antecedents to 9/11. The third and final area addresses the world after 9/11, covering the immediate aftermath of the attacks through the end of the recovery at the three attack sites, and exploring the ongoing ramifications of 9/11.

Throughout this book, names in blue signify individuals killed as a result of the terrorist attacks of September 11, 2001 and February 26, 1993.

EVENTS OF THE DAY

Crossing a bridge over the exposed box column remnants that once formed the exterior structural support of the North Tower, we enter into the first part of the historical exhibition, which focuses on the events of the day. Beginning with the impact of the first hijacked airliner—the point at which most of the world became aware of the unfolding events on that Tuesday morning in 2001—and continuing to the end of the day on 9/11, the first part of the exhibition presents the escalation of events as witnessed that day, whether in New York City or in the areas near the Pentagon and western Pennsylvania, or by watching the repeated television broadcasts worldwide.

As we encounter these unfolding events along a main path of witness, a sequential account of other events—many of them not necessarily seen or known on the day of 9/11—is presented on a timeline that wraps the outer walls of the exhibition. Timestamps appear along a central, horizontal band on this timeline, becoming visible when we stand directly in front of them and then disappearing when we move beyond the spot (a signal that, as in life, the moment has passed). These timestamps provide specific temporal coordinates for the events being documented along the main path. They also provide the point of intersection for other developments occurring simultaneously in multiple locations elsewhere, even as the world maintained its focus on the events transpiring in lower Manhattan.

The timeline itself has two registers, one above and one below the horizontal band of timestamps. The upper register chronicles what was happening in the air that morning, tracking the activities and responses of civilian aviation professionals, military personnel, and passengers and crew aboard the hijacked planes. The lower register tracks what was happening on the ground, as federal, state, and municipal officials implemented emergency response plans, adapting established procedures as the disaster continued to unfold throughout the day. Where the main path presents us with the perspective of public witness on 9/11, this synoptic timeline conveys a fuller picture of all that was happening that fateful morning, much of which would not be pieced together until later.

The experiences of those closest to the events—rescuers, survivors, and victims—are presented in intimate spaces where we listen to first-person accounts of escape and evacuation and the activity of first responders from within the towers. Among the more sensitive recordings in these alcoves are real-time messages and calls to emergency services from those trapped within the buildings. A separate listening alcove covers stories of escape and rescue at the Pentagon, and another covers the story of Flight 93. Here, phone calls and messages from those on the flight and excerpts from the cockpit voice recorder attest to the valiant efforts of passengers and crew who struggled to wrest control of the plane from the hijackers.

We continue along the path, witness to the collapses of both towers at the World Trade Center that in turn created apocalyptic dust plumes blanketing lower Manhattan and visible from space. Our journey continues through the rest of the day as shock and disbelief gave way to the urgency of rescue and response. With news coverage around the world focused exclusively on the attacks, Americans, and indeed, people everywhere faced a new and uncertain reality, sensing that there would now forever be a "before 9/11" and an "after 9/11."

EXCERPTS FROM *2001*

Tuesday, September 11, 2001, 8:46 a.m., New York City; Time-lapse compilation of video footage, extracted at four-second intervals
© 2001 Wolfgang Staehle (German, b. 1950)

The approach of hijacked Flight 11 (seen in the top right of the middle image) and its shattering impact into the north face of the North Tower were unwittingly captured by two webcams set up by an artist just days before in Brooklyn. Fixed on lower Manhattan, the cameras' shutters had been calibrated to trip at precise intervals, continuously snapping skyline views that were transmitted live to an art gallery in Manhattan's Chelsea neighborhood. Titled *2001*, the installation, which ran in real time from September 6 to October 3, was conceived to convey the unchanging and predictable normalcy of life at the start of the 21st century.

8:46 AM

**NORTH TOWER (1 WTC)
WORLD TRADE CENTER**

NORMALCY INTERRUPTED

In New York City, the major news story before the attacks was the primary election for mayor and other local offices taking place on September 11, 2001. Many parents and child-care providers around the city were escorting children to school. As on any business day, tens of thousands of commuters were arriving in lower Manhattan by car, ferry, subway, bus, bicycle, and train. That normalcy was interrupted at 8:46 a.m. by a plane crash at the World Trade Center. Reports soon dominated morning radio and television programs around the country and later cut into regular programming around the world. American Airlines Flight 11, hijacked by five terrorists and carrying 76 passengers and 11 crew members on board, had been flown into the North Tower. The tremendous force of the collision sent broken glass, pieces of metal, burning paper, and other office supplies to the streets below. Inside the building, on floors rapidly growing hot and filling with smoke, people broke windows in an effort to breathe fresh air. The smoke from the upper floors could be seen for many blocks north of the World Trade Center and was visible at least 45 miles away.

NORTH TOWER BURNING
Photograph by Stephane Sednaoui

IN THE AIR
On September 11, 2001, civilian aviation professionals, military personnel, and passengers respond to the crisis.

ON THE GROUND
Federal, state, and municipal officials implement emergency response plans, adapting established procedures as the disaster unfolds throughout the day.

8:46 AM

NORTH TOWER ATTACK
Five hijackers crash American Airlines Flight 11 into 1 World Trade Center (North Tower). The 76 passengers and 11 crew members on board perish, and hundreds are killed instantly inside the building. The crash severs all three emergency stairwells and traps hundreds of people above the 91st floor.

RESPONDERS MOBILIZE
New York City emergency dispatchers send paramedics and responders from the New York City Fire Department (FDNY) and the New York City Police Department (NYPD) to the North Tower.

NORTH TOWER EVACUATION
The Port Authority Police Department (PAPD), responsible for the safety and security of the World Trade Center in addition to regional bridges, tunnels, airports, and the port of New York and New Jersey, initiates the evacuation of the North Tower. Additional PAPD units from other posts dispatch to the World Trade Center to aid in evacuation and rescue.

8:48 AM

OEM ACTIVATES CRISIS CENTER

The New York City Mayor's Office of Emergency Management (OEM) contacts federal, state, and municipal emergency response agencies. OEM requests that city agencies send representatives to OEM's Emergency Operations Center located in 7 World Trade Center, a 47-story office building across the street from the North Tower.

8:50 AM

U.S. PRESIDENT ALERTED

At an elementary school in Sarasota, Florida, U.S. President George W. Bush learns that a plane has hit the North Tower. Bush and his advisers assume that the crash is a tragic accident.

CIA RESPONDS

Around this time, Director of Central Intelligence George Tenet calls for a meeting of his top counterterrorism advisers at the Central Intelligence Agency (CIA) in Langley, Virginia. Tenet's deputies suspect that the plane crash is a terrorist attack.

8:51 AM

AIR FORCE AWARENESS

The Northeast Air Defense Sector (NEADS), a division of the U.S. Air Force responsible for monitoring and defending the airspace above the northeastern United States, is alerted to a plane crash at the World Trade Center. NEADS had been informed approximately 13 minutes earlier of a possible hijacking.

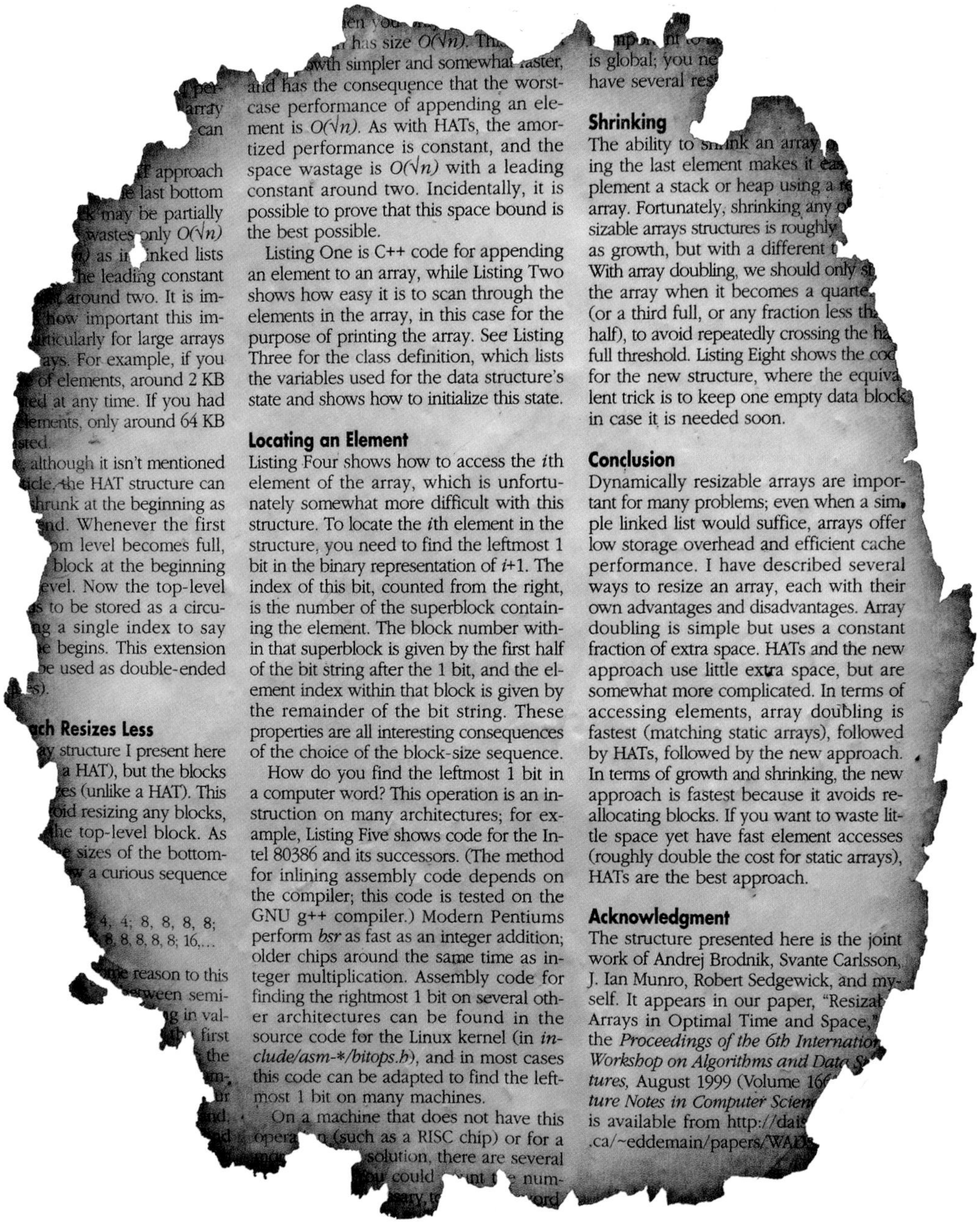

...per ...array ...can

...f approach ...e last bottom ...k may be partially ...wastes only $O(\sqrt{n})$ ...) as i...nked lists ...he leading constant ...around two. It is im... ...how important this im... ...ticularly for large arrays ...ays. For example, if you ...of elements, around 2 KB ...ed at any time. If you had ...ements, only around 64 KB ...sted.

...although it isn't mentioned ...icle, the HAT structure can ...hrunk at the beginning as ...nd. Whenever the first ...om level becomes full, ...block at the beginning ...evel. Now the top-level ...s to be stored as a circu... ...g a single index to say ...e begins. This extension ...be used as double-ended ...es).

...ch Resizes Less

...y structure I present here ...a HAT), but the blocks ...es (unlike a HAT). This ...oid resizing any blocks, ...he top-level block. As ...sizes of the bottom... ...y a curious sequence

...4, 4, 8, 8, 8, 8; ...8, 8, 8, 8, 16,...

...e reason to this ...tween semi... ...g in val... ...first ...the ...

...en you... ...has size $O(\sqrt{n})$. Th... ...wth simpler and somewhat faster, and has the consequence that the worst-case performance of appending an element is $O(\sqrt{n})$. As with HATs, the amortized performance is constant, and the space wastage is $O(\sqrt{n})$ with a leading constant around two. Incidentally, it is possible to prove that this space bound is the best possible.

Listing One is C++ code for appending an element to an array, while Listing Two shows how easy it is to scan through the elements in the array, in this case for the purpose of printing the array. See Listing Three for the class definition, which lists the variables used for the data structure's state and shows how to initialize this state.

Locating an Element

Listing Four shows how to access the *i*th element of the array, which is unfortunately somewhat more difficult with this structure. To locate the *i*th element in the structure, you need to find the leftmost 1 bit in the binary representation of *i*+1. The index of this bit, counted from the right, is the number of the superblock containing the element. The block number within that superblock is given by the first half of the bit string after the 1 bit, and the element index within that block is given by the remainder of the bit string. These properties are all interesting consequences of the choice of the block-size sequence.

How do you find the leftmost 1 bit in a computer word? This operation is an instruction on many architectures; for example, Listing Five shows code for the Intel 80386 and its successors. (The method for inlining assembly code depends on the compiler; this code is tested on the GNU g++ compiler.) Modern Pentiums perform *bsr* as fast as an integer addition; older chips around the same time as integer multiplication. Assembly code for finding the rightmost 1 bit on several other architectures can be found in the source code for the Linux kernel (in *include/asm-*/bitops.h*), and in most cases this code can be adapted to find the leftmost 1 bit on many machines.

On a machine that does not have this opera... (such as a RISC chip) or for a ... solution, there are several ...ou could ...nt ... num... ...ary, ...ord

...impo... ...is global; you ne... have several res...

Shrinking

The ability to sh...nk an array... ing the last element makes it ea... plement a stack or heap using a ... array. Fortunately, shrinking any ... sizable arrays structures is roughly ... as growth, but with a different ... With array doubling, we should only sh... the array when it becomes a quarte... (or a third full, or any fraction less th... half), to avoid repeatedly crossing the ha... full threshold. Listing Eight shows the cod... for the new structure, where the equiva... lent trick is to keep one empty data block in case it is needed soon.

Conclusion

Dynamically resizable arrays are important for many problems; even when a simple linked list would suffice, arrays offer low storage overhead and efficient cache performance. I have described several ways to resize an array, each with their own advantages and disadvantages. Array doubling is simple but uses a constant fraction of extra space. HATs and the new approach use little extra space, but are somewhat more complicated. In terms of accessing elements, array doubling is fastest (matching static arrays), followed by HATs, followed by the new approach. In terms of growth and shrinking, the new approach is fastest because it avoids reallocating blocks. If you want to waste little space yet have fast element accesses (roughly double the cost for static arrays), HATs are the best approach.

Acknowledgment

The structure presented here is the joint work of Andrej Brodnik, Svante Carlsson, J. Ian Munro, Robert Sedgewick, and myself. It appears in our paper, "Resizab... Arrays in Optimal Time and Space," ... the *Proceedings of the 6th Internatio... Workshop on Algorithms and Data S... tures*, August 1999 (Volume 16... *...ture Notes in Computer Scien...* is available from http://dai... .ca/~eddemain/papers/WAD...

PROGRAM FOR WATERS 2001 FINANCIAL TECHNOLOGY CONGRESS

Collection 9/11 Memorial Museum, Gift of Jared Kotz, Courtesy of Incisive Media

The World Trade Center was home to a variety of enterprises, including multinational corporations, and a site for business meetings. By 8:46 a.m., roughly 80 people had gathered at Windows on the World on the 106th floor of the North Tower to participate in a financial technology conference presented by Risk Waters Group. Seventy-two restaurant staff had arrived earlier in advance of the morning's breakfast service and conference preparation.

PAPER

Collection 9/11 Memorial Museum, Gift of Alex Zablocki, in memory of all those lost on 9/11

When hijacked Flight 11 pierced the North Tower, pieces of paper, some of them on fire, blew out of shattered windows. Some drifted onto lower Manhattan rooftops, balconies, and streets. Others were carried by wind for miles.

NBC *TODAY SHOW*, SEPTEMBER 11, 2001, 8:51 A.M.

Courtesy of NBCUniversal Archives

8:52 AM

PATH TRAIN SERVICE SUSPENDED
The Port Authority Trans-Hudson Corporation (PATH) suspends all service into and out of the World Trade Center. PATH employees direct one train to turn around without unloading passengers and another to reboard all passengers who had just disembarked. An empty train passes through the station to pick up remaining passengers and PATH employees.

8:53 AM

AIR TRAFFIC CONTROL SUSPECTS SECOND HIJACKING
After noticing a change in altitude and unusual transmissions from Flight 175, an air traffic controller radios the cockpit. Unable to contact the flight crew, the controller reports that the flight might have been hijacked. Flight 175 had taken off from Boston's Logan International Airport for Los Angeles, California, at 8:14 a.m. Fifty-one passengers, nine crew members, and five hijackers are on board.

MILITARY JETS TAKE OFF
Following orders issued earlier by NEADS at 8:37 a.m. in response to the hijacking of Flight 11, two fighter jets depart Otis Air National Guard Base in Cape Cod, Massachusetts, under orders to head toward New York City.

8:54 AM

FLIGHT 77 HIJACKED
Five hijackers gain control of American Airlines Flight 77 about half an hour after the plane has taken off from Washington, D.C., for Los Angeles. Fifty-three passengers and six crew members are on board. The hijackers reverse course, aiming for the nation's capital.

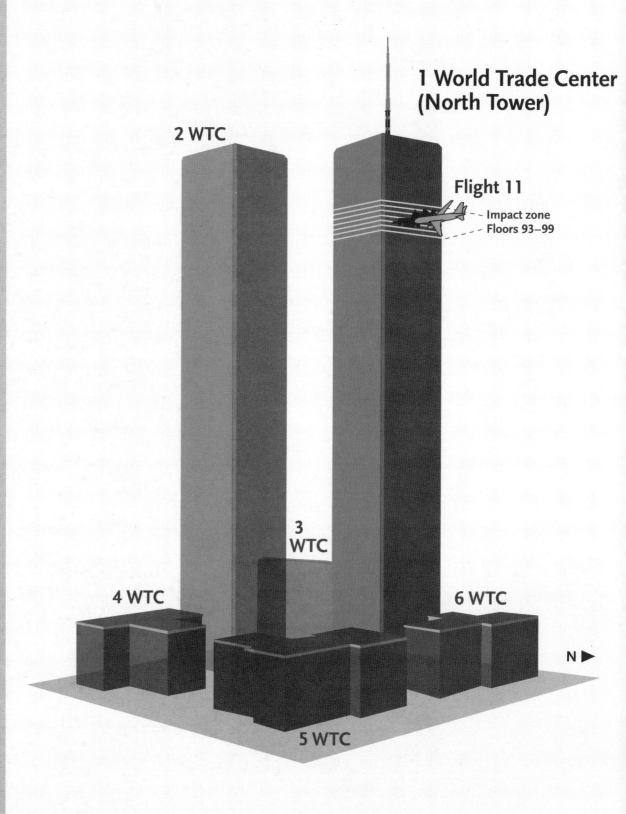

1 World Trade Center (North Tower)

2 WTC

Flight 11

Impact zone
Floors 93–99

3 WTC

4 WTC

6 WTC

5 WTC

N ▶

NORTH TOWER IMPACT ZONE

Collection 9/11 Memorial Museum, Roberto Rabanne Archive, Photograph by Roberto Rabanne

The hijacker piloting Flight 11 intentionally crashed the airplane into the north face of the North Tower, tearing a gash from the 93rd to the 99th floors. From a rooftop several blocks away, photographer Roberto Rabanne captured images of people at windows and near the edges of the impact zone. One was later identified as **Edna Cintron**, the woman wearing white pants and a blue blouse visible near the center of this photograph.

EMERGENCY RESPONSE

The crash of hijacked Flight 11 into the North Tower triggered the largest rescue operation in the history of New York City. Numerous civilians telephoned the 9-1-1 emergency system. Within minutes of the plane crash, New York City emergency dispatchers sent police officers, paramedics, and firefighters to the North Tower. The New York City Mayor's Office of Emergency Management (OEM) contacted federal and state emergency response agencies and coordinated efforts with responders from the New York City Fire Department (FDNY) and New York City Police Department (NYPD). The Port Authority Police Department (PAPD), Office of Chief Medical Examiner (OCME), and area hospitals also responded rapidly to the scene.

"EMERGENCY RESPONSE" INSTALLATION IN THE HISTORICAL EXHIBITION

HELMET WORN BY BATTALION CHIEF JOSEPH PFEIFER ON 9/11

Collection 9/11 Memorial Museum, Gift of the Pfeifer family in memory of FDNY's 343 heroes

At 8:46 a.m., a group of firefighters from FDNY Engine Company 7 and Ladder Company 1 were on a routine assignment with the chief of Battalion 1, Joseph Pfeifer, investigating a reported gas leak several blocks north of the World Trade Center. Hearing a rumble, they looked up to see a large, low-flying plane. In horror, they watched as it crashed into the North Tower. Battalion Chief Pfeifer immediately signaled a "second alarm," communicating the severity of the situation. Within two minutes, Pfeifer then ordered the transmission of a "third alarm," which called for the deployment of 23 engine and ladder companies, 12 chiefs, and 10 specialized units to the World Trade Center.

FIRST RESPONDERS CONVERGE AT THE WORLD TRADE CENTER

Video by Jules Naudet and Gédéon Naudet, © Goldfish Pictures, Inc.

FDNY firefighters with Battalion Chief Joseph Pfeifer were the first members of the FDNY to arrive at the disaster scene. Entering the North Tower lobby, Pfeifer set up the Incident Command Post and consulted with the PAPD and the Port Authority's fire safety staff, already on site, as other firefighters converged at the World Trade Center. Pfeifer's actions and those of other emergency responders and witnesses to the events were filmed by brothers Gédéon and Jules Naudet who were making a documentary film during the summer of 2001 in collaboration with FDNY Firefighter James Hanlon about FDNY Ladder Company 1.

EMERGENCY RESPONSE AGENCY PATCHES

Collection 9/11 Memorial Museum, Gifts of Henry Jackson, NYC Office of Chief Medical Examiner, Mickey Kross, Larry Fields in memory of all Port Authority Police who perished on 9/11, and Larry Mannion

8:55 AM

SOUTH TOWER DECLARED SECURE

Around 8:55 a.m., a Port Authority fire safety employee announces over the South Tower's public address system, "Your attention, please, ladies and gentlemen. Building Two is secure. There is no need to evacuate Building Two. If you are in the midst of evacuation, you may use the reentry doors and the elevators to return to your office. Repeat, Building Two is secure."

8:56 AM

FLIGHT 77 MISSING

Air traffic controllers alert the Federal Aviation Administration (FAA) after Flight 77 disappears from their radar screens. Attempts to contact the pilots fail.

8:58 AM

NYPD AND FDNY MOBILIZATIONS ESCALATE

The NYPD issues a Level 4 mobilization, the department's highest alert, dispatching more than 900 officers to the World Trade Center. Moments later, FDNY dispatch relays a fifth alarm, the Fire Department's highest response level. This raises the number of mobilized personnel to approximately 250 firefighters, including teams trained to respond to high-rise fires and hazardous materials specialists. Additional units are mobilized to staging areas nearby.

8:59 AM

PAPD ORDERS EVACUATION OF TWIN TOWERS
The PAPD issues an order to commence the evacuation of the North and South Towers. One minute later, the order is expanded to include all civilians in the World Trade Center complex.

9:00 AM

AIRLINE ALERTS FBI
Around this time, an American Airlines corporate security director calls the Federal Bureau of Investigation (FBI) to report distress calls received earlier from Flight 11 flight attendants Betty Ann Ong and Madeline Amy Sweeney in which they relayed the hijackers' seat numbers and reported that the cockpit was unreachable.

ON BOARD FLIGHT 175
Earlier, at 8:52 a.m., a flight attendant, likely Robert John Fangman, reached a United Airlines operator in San Francisco, California, and reported a hijacking. By 9:00 a.m., passengers Garnet Ace Bailey, Peter Burton Hanson, and Brian David Sweeney call family members.

VICE PRESIDENT ALERTED
At the White House, U.S. Vice President Dick Cheney learns of the crash at the World Trade Center and begins monitoring the events.

REACTIONS AROUND THE WORLD TRADE CENTER COMPLEX

Reactions to the plane crash varied across the World Trade Center complex. Inside the North Tower, many people began to evacuate as soon as they felt the building shake. Some paused to document the conditions visible from their office windows: smoke billowing above and metal, glass, paper, and other debris strewn over every surface below. Others made telephone calls reassuring loved ones of their safety or describing their peril. Some occupants of the South Tower, either seeing the crash or hearing what sounded like an explosion, chose to leave at once; others sheltered in place, soon to hear a public address system announcement informing them that their building remained secure. Partial views of the crash, limited information, and confusion influenced decisions to stay or evacuate in the adjacent Marriott hotel located at 3 World Trade Center, the neighboring office buildings of 4, 5, 6, and 7 World Trade Center, the concourse-level shopping mall, and belowground local train stations. Local residents in nearby apartment buildings faced similar choices, as many viewed the burning tower outside their windows and witnessed the increasing arrivals of rescue personnel.

A plane crashed into World Trade Center One.
We're fine.
We're in World Trade Center Two.
—Bradley James Fetchet, calling his mother from the 89th floor of the South Tower

TWO-WAY RADIO
Collection 9/11 Memorial Museum, Gift of Ada Dolch

The High School for Leadership and Public Service just south of the World Trade Center was a designated polling station for the city's primary election. After the first plane crashed, Principal Ada Dolch used her two-way radio to communicate with teachers on the school's upper floors, where students could see flames engulfing the North Tower. When the second plane hit, Dolch initiated a school-wide evacuation. She was forced to jettison existing emergency plans that called for mustering closer to the World Trade Center and instead guided approximately 600 students and staff southward to safety in Battery Park. Fulfilling her professional responsibility to students, staff, and voters, Dolch could not yet address a private worry: the welfare of her sister, Wendy Alice Rosario Wakeford, who worked on the 105th floor of the North Tower.

PHONE CALLS FROM SEAN PAUL ROONEY **TO HIS WIFE, BEVERLY ECKERT**

Collection 9/11 Memorial Museum, Gift of Beverly Eckert

*Hey, Beverly, this is Sean. In case you
get this message, there's been an explosion in World Trade One,
it's the other building. It looks like a plane struck it.
It's on fire at about the 90th floor. And it's, it's, it's horrible. Bye.*

—Sean Rooney, calling from the 98th floor of the South Tower, 8:59 a.m.

*Yeah, honey, this is Sean again. Looks
like we'll be in this tower for a while. It's, it's secure here.
I'll talk to you later. Bye.*

—Sean Rooney, calling from the 98th floor of the South Tower, 9:02 a.m

PUBLIC ADDRESS ANNOUNCEMENT HEARD IN THE BACKGROUND OF ROONEY'S PHONE CALL

*May I have your attention, please. Repeating this message.
The situation occurred in Building One. If the conditions warrant on
your floor, you may wish to start an orderly evacuation.*

—Port Authority announcement, 9:02 a.m.

MAP OF THE WORLD TRADE CENTER COMPLEX AND SURROUNDING NEIGHBORHOOD

9:00 AM

**WASHINGTON RESPONDS
TO CRISIS**

National Security Council
counterterrorism coordinator
Richard A. Clarke calls for an
emergency teleconference in the
White House Situation Room.
Clarke believes that the crash
is an act of terrorism and asks
his team to prepare for the
possibility of additional attacks.

Aware that an airplane had hit
the World Trade Center, U.S.
Secretary of Defense Donald
Rumsfeld convenes his scheduled
daily intelligence briefing by the
CIA at the Pentagon.

9:02 AM

**REALIZATION OF
MULTIPLE HIJACKINGS**

Personnel at Boston Air Traffic
Control Center review radio
transmissions made earlier
that morning from the cockpit
of Flight 11. While listening to a
transmission recording made
before the crash into the North
Tower, they hear a male voice
reference multiple aircraft: "We
have some planes. Just stay
quiet and you'll be okay. We are
returning to the airport."

**EVACUATION ORDER
BROADCAST IN
THE SOUTH TOWER**

A second announcement is
broadcast by a Port Authority fire
safety employee over the South
Tower's public address system:
"May I have your attention,
please. Repeating this message.
The situation occurred in Building
One. If the conditions warrant on
your floor, you may wish to start
an orderly evacuation."

9:03 AM

**SOUTH TOWER (2 WTC)
WORLD TRADE CENTER**

*From the right of the
screen comes another plane, and
it was no Cessna.... It didn't
take me too long to figure
out that we were under attack.*

—Michael Garcia, Officer, Pentagon Defense Protective
Service, watching television in suburban Virginia

IMPACT OF FLIGHT 175

As onlookers across the city and in front of their televisions across the country gazed at the gaping hole in the North Tower, a second hijacked plane entered New York City airspace. Commandeered by five terrorists, United Airlines Flight 175 crashed into the South Tower at 9:03 a.m., carrying 51 passengers and nine crew members. As events at the World Trade Center escalated and the realization set in that the country was under attack, thousands of people photographed and filmed the scene, making 9/11 the most widely documented breaking news event of its time.

HIJACKED FLIGHT 175 STRIKING THE SOUTH TOWER
Photographs by Sean Adair, Reuters

VIEW OF THE TWIN TOWERS, LOOKING SOUTH
Photograph by Jennifer Clifford Danner

MILITARY ASSISTANCE
The FAA requests flyover assistance from jets under the command of the U.S. Air Force's Northeast Air Defense Sector (NEADS).

SOUTH TOWER ATTACK
Five hijackers crash United Airlines Flight 175 into the South Tower of the World Trade Center, killing an unknown number of people inside the building. The 51 passengers and nine crew members on board perish. The impact renders two of the three emergency stairwells impassable and severs a majority of the elevator cables in this area, trapping many above the impact zone and inside elevator cars.

NYPD REQUESTS CLOSING OF NEW YORK AIRSPACE
In addition to requesting the shutdown of airspace over New York City, the NYPD calls for a second Level 4 mobilization, bringing its total deployment to nearly 2,000 officers.

INCREASING RESPONSE
The FDNY issues a fifth alarm for the South Tower, deploying several hundred additional firefighters to the disaster. Additional companies and off-duty personnel from across the metropolitan area travel to the scene.

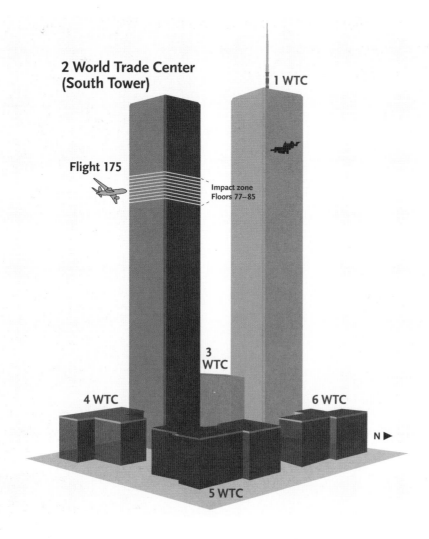

2 World Trade Center
(South Tower)

1 WTC

Flight 175

Impact zone
Floors 77–85

3 WTC

4 WTC

6 WTC

N ▶

5 WTC

"ON THE STREET" INSTALLATION IN THE HISTORICAL EXHIBITION

**FUSELAGE FRAGMENT
WITH PASSENGER WINDOW
(OPPOSITE PAGE)**

*Collection 9/11 Memorial Museum,
Gift of the Port Authority Police Department
9/11 Traveling Memorial*

Pieces of the two hijacked aircraft landed on rooftops and streets surrounding the World Trade Center. Pedestrians encountered unfamiliar metal objects on the ground, but not everyone immediately recognized these items as parts of the aircraft that had just struck the Twin Towers.

There were people running, there were some people standing with their mouths open looking at the buildings, people sitting on the sidewalk crying. . . . Mayhem.

—Hazem Gamal, outside a subway station in lower Manhattan

ON THE STREET

After two hijacked aircraft crashed into the Twin Towers, the mass exodus from inside the buildings intensified. Coworkers and strangers helped one another during their evacuations. Some stayed together even after they exited the Twin Towers, offering mutual comfort and support. Once outside, they were confronted with material that had plunged to the streets. Some used briefcases, serving trays, and other available objects to protect their heads from falling debris. Building and airplane fragments had injured and killed pedestrians and damaged surrounding buildings. Paramedics and emergency medical technicians set up triage stations and treated injured survivors on the streets surrounding the World Trade Center. Many suffering from burns or wounded by shards of metal, glass, and other hazardous debris were transported to hospitals. Other evacuees suffering from shock and seemingly minor injuries walked to infirmaries for treatment or sought medical attention after going home.

9:05 AM

INFORMING THE U.S. PRESIDENT
White House Chief of Staff Andrew Card reports to U.S. President George W. Bush that "a second plane hit the second tower. America is under attack."

NEW YORK CITY MAYOR GIULIANI ARRIVES AT THE NYPD COMMAND POST
Mayor Rudolph Giuliani rushes to the NYPD command post near the World Trade Center.

9:12 AM

ON BOARD FLIGHT 77
Flight attendant Renée A. May calls her mother, Nancy May, and tells her that hijackers have seized control of the plane, forcing passengers and crew members to the rear. When they are disconnected, Nancy May calls American Airlines.

NATIONAL GUARD MOBILIZED
Within minutes of the second attack, New York State Governor George Pataki activates the New York National Guard to respond to the disaster.

9:19 AM

U.S. DEPARTMENT OF JUSTICE RECEIVES A CALL
Around this time, Flight 77 passenger Barbara K. Olson calls her husband, Theodore Olson, the U.S. Solicitor General, who is at his desk in the Department of Justice. She tells him that hijackers have taken over the flight using knives and box cutters. Theodore Olson alerts other federal officials.

9:21 AM

**ALL BRIDGES AND TUNNELS
INTO MANHATTAN ARE CLOSED**

9:25 AM

**AIR NATIONAL GUARD FIGHTER
JETS ESTABLISH COMBAT AIR
PATROLS OVER NEW YORK CITY**

9:28 AM

FLIGHT 93 HIJACKED
Hijackers break into the cockpit
of United Airlines Flight 93. The
struggle is broadcast over the
radio to air traffic control and
other aircraft nearby. Flight 93
had taken off from Newark
International Airport at 8:42 a.m.
with 33 passengers, seven
crew members, and four hijackers
on board.

9:29 AM

**FDNY ISSUES OFF-DUTY
RECALL ORDER**
The FDNY orders all uniformed
personnel to report for
duty. Some firefighters report
to their assigned firehouses.
Others go directly to the World
Trade Center.

*You could see that they knew . . . it was dangerous.
Those people were concentrated, focused on doing their job. . . .
They were going up to their death. And I was walking down to live.*

—Bruno Dellinger, evacuee from the 47th floor of the North Tower, recalling firefighters in the stairwell

INSIDE THE WORLD TRADE CENTER

Many people on the upper floors within the impact zones were killed when the planes struck the buildings. Hundreds were killed inside elevators, and others were severely injured when jet fuel flowing down elevator shafts caused fireballs to erupt as elevator doors opened. As fires raged high in the towers, sirens blared steadily and conditions in the emergency stairwells grew progressively warmer. Still, evacuation from both towers proceeded in an orderly fashion. People generally stayed to the right, leaving a clear path for rescue personnel heading upstairs and making room for injured survivors coming down. Some office workers also walked up to higher floors to search for people trapped and in need of assistance.

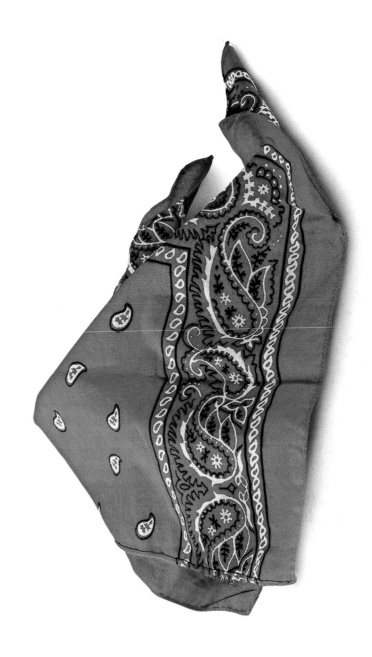

The police were telling us to run. They were saying, "Get out of the building! Run!" We were going up the escalator in Borders and there was a fireman who couldn't have been more than nineteen years old, with a hose on his shoulder. And I remember looking at him and saying to him, "There's nothing you can do, don't go in there." And he just said, "Lady, it's my job, I have to do it."

—Jeannine Ali, Morgan Stanley

Yeah, hi. I'm on the 106th floor of the World Trade Center, and we just heard an explosion on, like, the 105th floor. We have smoke and it's pretty bad. Yeah, we can't get down the stairs. There's smoke and we got about a hundred people up here. We can't open the windows unless we break it. Please hurry.

—Christopher Hanley, Risk Waters conference attendee from Radianz, emergency call to 9-1-1

BANDANA

Collection 9/11 Memorial Museum, Gift of Alison and Jefferson Crowther and family
Object photograph by Matt Flynn

Welles Remy Crowther, a 24-year-old equities trader for Sandler O'Neill & Partners, was working on the 104th floor of the South Tower when hijacked Flight 11 struck the other tower. He telephoned a friend and said that he would try to help people in the North Tower. Crowther had just reached the 78th floor of the South Tower when the second hijacked aircraft, Flight 175, tore through the 77th through 85th floors. Wearing a red bandana over his mouth and nose to guard against smoke, Crowther drew on his training as a volunteer firefighter to guide evacuees and help the injured.

Crowther's remains were eventually found in the wreckage of the South Tower. In May 2002, the *New York Times* reported the acts of a courageous civilian wearing a red bandana. When shown Crowther's photograph, survivors confirmed that he was the man in the red bandana. This bandana was one of his many spares.

NOTE WRITTEN BY RANDOLPH SCOTT

Courtesy of the family of Randolph Scott, with thanks to the Federal Reserve Bank of New York for preserving this note

A woman saw this note in the street as she was fleeing the World Trade Center vicinity. Recognizing the significance of the message "84th floor, west office, 12 people trapped," she handed it to a security officer for the Federal Reserve Bank of New York, two blocks east of the complex, hoping that the officer would be able to communicate directly with emergency personnel.

A report by a U.S. Secret Service agent of the possibility of additional hijacked planes prompts OEM to evacuate its headquarters at 7 World Trade Center.

U.S. PRESIDENT ADDRESSES THE NATION FROM SARASOTA, FLORIDA

From the elementary school he is visiting in Sarasota, Florida, President George W. Bush states, "Today we've had a national tragedy. Two airplanes have crashed into the World Trade Center in an apparent terrorist attack on our country."

9:33AM

AIR TRAFFIC CONTROL SPOTS FAST-MOVING PLANE HEADING TOWARD WASHINGTON, D.C.

Suspecting another attack, a supervisor at Ronald Reagan Washington National Airport alerts U.S. Secret Service agents, who initiate the evacuation of the White House.

9:36AM

EVACUATION OF U.S. VICE PRESIDENT CHENEY

U.S. Secret Service agents evacuate Vice President Cheney to the Presidential Emergency Operations Center beneath the White House.

*I kept looking up, saying,
"I want to help you guys, hold on, please hold on."
But I knew there was nothing I could do.*

—David Brink, Officer, NYPD Emergency Service Unit Squad 3

FALLING FROM THE TOWERS

Almost immediately after hijacked Flight 11 punctured the North Tower, men and women faced such intolerable conditions of smoke and heat that some fell or jumped to the ground below. Estimates of the number of people who died as a result of falling from the Twin Towers range from 50 to more than 200.

EYEWITNESSES *Photograph by Don Halasy, Courtesy of the Library of Congress*

TRAPPED

Photograph by Jose Jimenez/Primera Hora, Getty Images

She had a business suit on, her hair was all askew. . . .
This woman stood there for what seemed like minutes,
then she held down her skirt and then stepped off the ledge. . . .
I thought, how human, how modest, to hold down her skirt before she jumped. . . .
I couldn't look anymore.

—James Gilroy, lower Manhattan resident

You felt compelled to watch out of respect to them.
They were ending their life without a choice and to turn
away from them would have been wrong.

—Louisa Griffith-Jones, lower Manhattan resident

While we still looked up, a man jumped from the building.
White shirt, black pants, end-over-end tumbling to the ground. . . .
At that instant, the towering glass and metal mass
of billowing smoke became human.

—Victor Colantonio, eyewitness

CONTINUED EMERGENCY RESPONSE

Approximately 2,000 police officers and nearly 1,000 firefighters deployed in response to the attacks on the World Trade Center. More than 100 city and volunteer ambulances were dispatched to the scene within the first hour. As the situation at the World Trade Center escalated, civilians with training in first aid, crisis counseling, law enforcement, and firefighting made their way to the scene of the disaster. The primary mission of emergency response efforts at the World Trade Center focused on rescue, evacuation, and medical treatment. Many responders put their own lives at risk to help and save others.

NYPD helicopter pilots hovered in the vicinity of the Twin Towers, assessing the possibility of rooftop rescues. The North Tower roof was crowded with electrical equipment, and the helipad on the South Tower roof was obscured by smoke. Extreme temperatures prevented helicopters from getting close enough to the roof of either tower to attempt any rescue. Officers in the helicopters were, however, able to relay information about the fire to police officials on the ground.

SHIELD AND MEDAL RACK WORN BY OFFICER MOIRA ANN SMITH ON 9/11

Presented with permission of the City of New York and the New York City Police Department. All rights reserved.

Officer Moira Smith, a 13-year veteran of the NYPD, was on patrol in the 13th Precinct a few miles north of the World Trade Center, when the North Tower was hit by hijacked Flight 11. She immediately rushed downtown to the disaster site. Many South Tower survivors recall seeing her in the lobby calmly but forcefully directing them out of the building.

JERICHO FIRE DEPARTMENT IDENTIFICATION CARRIED BY GLENN J. WINUK ON 9/11

Collection 9/11 Memorial Museum, Gift of the Winuk family

Glenn Winuk, a lawyer who was also certified as an emergency medical technician and had served as a volunteer firefighter in Jericho, New York, self-dispatched from his office two blocks from the towers with a dust mask, gloves, and medical bag.

BADGE AND NAMEPLATE WORN BY PAPD CAPTAIN KATHY N. MAZZA ON 9/11

Courtesy of the Smithsonian Institution, National Museum of American History, Kenneth E. Behring Center
Object photograph by Jaclyn Nash

Captain Kathy Mazza, one of the highest-ranking female officers in the PAPD, responded to the World Trade Center from the Port Authority Police Academy in Jersey City, New Jersey. In the lobby of the North Tower, she assisted evacuees waiting to exit the building by purportedly using her gun to shoot out a large plate-glass window, enabling many to escape. Captain Mazza then made her way up the stairs in search of others needing aid.

"CONTINUED EMERGENCY RESPONSE" INSTALLATIONS IN THE HISTORICAL EXHIBITION

It was just surreal to see the Pentagon like that....
That big monstrous building was so vulnerable.
I never thought anything could hurt that place.

—Gary Tobias, Captain, Arlington County Fire Department

THE PENTAGON, ARLINGTON, VIRGINIA

Courtesy of the U.S. Department of Justice

AT THE PENTAGON

News of a third plane crash interrupted national coverage of the disaster in New York City. At 9:37 a.m., five hijackers crashed American Airlines Flight 77 into the western facade of the Pentagon, the military headquarters of the United States. The aircraft directly hit the Navy Command Center and the adjoining naval operations intelligence office, where civilian and military personnel had congregated in front of office televisions to watch the news from New York. The plane's descent was witnessed by many people on the ground and documented by four security cameras. It was traveling at 530 miles per hour when it reached the Pentagon, so fast that it crossed the Pentagon's lawn in under a second. The plane was flying less than 20 feet above the ground in the moment before impact.

Fragments of the aircraft broke off upon impact, landing on the lawn. Continuing momentum drove the fuselage inside the building and formed a path of destruction roughly 270 feet long through interior offices. All 53 passengers and six crew members on board perished, and the attack killed 125 people on the ground. Within minutes, emergency response agencies from the National Capital Region formed a unified command. The Arlington County Fire Department assumed control of the scene and directed the fight against ensuing fires and the rescue of people trapped inside. Local emergency medical workers arrived on scene, and triage stations were set up on the lawn and in the Pentagon's center courtyard to assist the injured among the approximately 20,000 military and civilian personnel who worked there. A segment of the Pentagon's outer ring collapsed around 10:15 a.m., 38 minutes after the impact of Flight 77. This unthinkable assault on the country's center of military power heightened anxiety about the possibility of additional attacks across the nation.

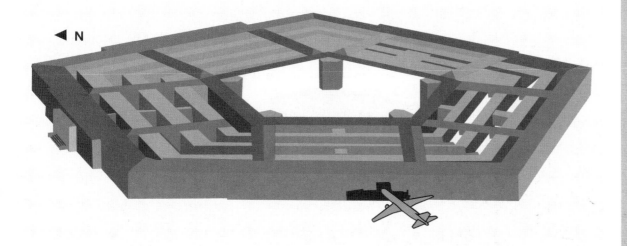

◀ N

9:37 AM

ATTACK AT THE PENTAGON
Five hijackers crash American Airlines Flight 77 into the Pentagon. The 53 passengers and six crew members on board perish. The crash and ensuing fire kill 125 military and civilian personnel on the ground.

9:42 AM

FEDERAL AVIATION ADMINISTRATION GROUNDS ALL FLIGHTS
The FAA orders all civilian planes in U.S. airspace to land and prohibits departures.

9:45 AM

WASHINGTON, D.C., EVACUATIONS
Evacuations begin at the White House and U.S. Capitol, where the House of Representatives and Senate are in session.

of al-Qaeda terrorist Osama bin Laden. The caller reports that he "heard good news" and suggests that a fourth attack was imminent. By the time the call is translated and relayed to the U.S. Department of Defense, the attacks had already been carried out.

9:54 AM

AIR FORCE ONE DEPARTS SARASOTA, FLORIDA
President Bush departs on Air Force One without a clear destination as his advisers seek to keep him out of harm's way.

9:58 AM

9-1-1 CALL FROM FLIGHT 93
Flight 93 passenger Edward P. Felt uses his cell phone to call 9-1-1 from a restroom in the rear of the plane. He reaches an emergency telephone operator in Westmoreland County, Pennsylvania, and reports a "hijacking in progress."

PENTAGON INSTALLATION IN THE HISTORICAL EXHIBITION, INCLUDING PLANE PARTS, DAMAGED OFFICE SUPPLIES, AND LIMESTONE FROM THE BUILDING FACADE

As we walked out, we could see, as I turned around, it was like a volcano—the fire and the flames—and the smoke was just tremendous and to know that we were walking out of a building where all these people had been killed was horrifying.

—Megan Grafton, Pentagon Spokeswoman

COLLAPSE OF THE PENTAGON OUTER RING *Photograph by Corporal Jason Ingersoll, USMC, U.S. Department of Defense*

CHILDREN'S CLOTHING RECOVERED INSIDE THE PENTAGON

Courtesy of the United States Army Historical Collection, U.S. Army Center of Military History

The crash of hijacked Flight 77 killed six crew members and 53 passengers, including five children. **Dana Falkenberg**, age 3, and **Zoe Falkenberg**, age 8, were on the first leg of a family trip to Australia, accompanied by their parents, **Charles S. Falkenberg** and **Leslie A. Whittington**. Sixth graders **Bernard C. Brown II**, **Asia S. Cottom**, and **Rodney Dickens** were traveling to a science conference in California with teachers **Sara M. Clark**, **James D. Debeuneure**, and **Hilda E. Taylor** and National Geographic Society employees **J. Joseph Ferguson** and **Ann C. Judge**.

U.S. SECRETARY OF DEFENSE DONALD RUMSFELD (CENTER) AIDS RESCUE
Still from video courtesy of WUSA9, Washington, D.C.

9:59 AM

**SOUTH TOWER (2 WTC)
WORLD TRADE CENTER**

*It went from that bright crisp
morning to just total blackness,
and then it felt like an earthquake.*

—Michelle Wiley, lower Manhattan resident

SOUTH TOWER COLLAPSING
Photograph by Thomas Nilsson

COLLAPSE OF THE SOUTH TOWER

After burning for 56 minutes, the South Tower collapsed in 10 seconds. Shock waves from the collapse were so strong, seismic recording devices at Columbia University's observation station 21 miles north of the World Trade Center logged a spike of earthquake-level activity measuring 2.1 on the Richter scale. Clouds of smoke and debris rolled through surrounding streets, causing enormous damage to the area and sending thousands running for their lives.

In addition to the 60 passengers and crew aboard Flight 175, more than 800 civilians and first responders inside the building and in the surrounding area were killed as a result of the attack on the South Tower.

JOSEPH MASSIAN (CENTER RIGHT) AND OTHERS RUNNING FROM THE COLLAPSE OF THE SOUTH TOWER
Photograph by Suzanne Plunkett, AP Photo

9:59 AM

SPOTTING FLIGHT 93
A pilot in Latrobe, Pennsylvania, reports seeing a commercial airliner in distress, rolling from side to side.

COLLAPSE OF THE SOUTH TOWER
After burning for 56 minutes, the South Tower collapses in 10 seconds. More than 800 civilians and first responders inside the building and in the surrounding area are killed as a result of the attack on the South Tower.

CONTINUITY-OF-GOVERNMENT PROCEDURES
Continuity-of-government procedures, established to protect high-level government officials during national emergencies, are implemented for the first known time in American history. Key officials evacuate to secure locations around the United States.

10:00 AM

FDNY AND NYPD ISSUE EVACUATION ORDERS
The FDNY and NYPD order the evacuation of rescue units from the North Tower. The NYPD order is heard on police radios. Technical issues impede the FDNY transmission, however, and it is not heard by all personnel.

There was this ripping sound of metal being torn. There was a jet of debris, very fast and several stories high. It just enveloped me, it was almost solid. I prayed to God, and then I thought to myself, this is how the world ends. There was just such a scene of devastation. Smoke everywhere and debris everywhere, and crushed fire engines and emergency vehicles.

—Allan Tannenbaum, photojournalist

RUNNING FROM THE DUST CLOUD DOWN BROADWAY
Photograph by Kelly Grace Price

SHOES WORN ON 9/11
Collection 9/11 Memorial Museum, Gifts of Michele C. Martocci and Linda Raisch-Lopez; and courtesy of Allison Hawke and Colum McCann

Office workers descended hundreds of steps and then walked several miles in dress shoes as they evacuated from the Twin Towers. After evacuating her 62nd-floor office in the South Tower, Morgan Stanley vice president Michele Martocci began walking to a friend's home in Brooklyn, still wearing her high heels. Fiduciary Trust employee Linda Raisch-Lopez began her evacuation on the 97th floor of the South Tower after seeing flames erupt from the North Tower. It was not until she was in line to board a ferry home to New Jersey that Raisch-Lopez noticed that blood from her cut and blistered feet had stained her high heels. In the North Tower Roger Hawke made an almost 90-minute walk down from his 54th-floor office at Sidley Austin Brown & Wood and exited down the Vesey Street stairs—now known as the Survivors' Stairs—moments before his building collapsed. He continued on foot to his daughter's home five miles uptown. Wanting to protect his granddaughter from visible traces of the tragedy, he left his dust-coated shoes at the door. She still asked why he smelled like smoke.

"ONE TOWER STANDING"
Photograph by Robert Adam Mayer

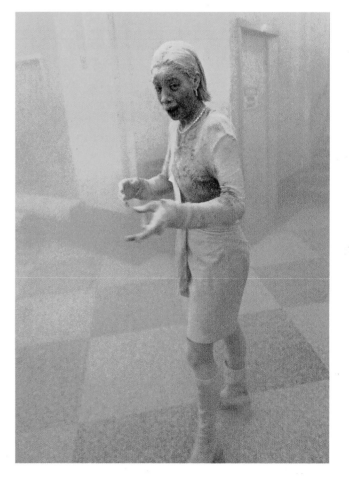

MARCY BORDERS EMERGING FROM THE DUST CLOUD AFTER EVACUATING FROM THE NORTH TOWER
Photograph by Stan Honda, Getty Images

*Don't panic, but a fourth plane is missing
and may be heading our way.*

—Katherine Green, Vice President of News, WTTG-TV, Washington, D.C., to newsroom staff

SOMERSET COUNTY, PENNSYLVANIA, MOMENTS AFTER THE CRASH OF HIJACKED FLIGHT 93

Photograph by Valencia McClatchey

CRASH OF FLIGHT 93

While international coverage focused on the devastating collapse of the South Tower, news was slow to spread of another downed plane, this time in rural Pennsylvania. Four hijackers aboard United Airlines Flight 93 crashed the aircraft in a field near the town of Shanksville in Somerset County. Seven crew members and 33 passengers were on board. The plane burrowed into the soft earth of a reclaimed coal mine, and airplane fragments were scattered over a debris field that stretched for miles. Local volunteer fire departments, emergency medical units, and Pennsylvania State Police troopers converged on the scene within minutes. By the afternoon, agents from the FBI's Pittsburgh field office had arrived to search for evidence and remains. The salvaged flight data recorder showed that the hijackers had set a course for Ronald Reagan Washington National Airport. This information led investigators to conclude that the hijackers' intended target was a landmark in Washington, D.C., probably the U.S. Capitol Building, where Congress was in session. Through a total of 37 phone calls known to have been placed by at least 13 people while aboard the flight, passengers and crew received and shared information about the hijackings with those on the ground. Aware that two hijacked aircraft had struck the Twin Towers, those aboard Flight 93 planned to avoid another deadly attack. The recovered cockpit voice recorder confirmed that they had launched a counterassault against the terrorists in the final minutes before the plane crashed, preventing the hijackers from reaching their target.

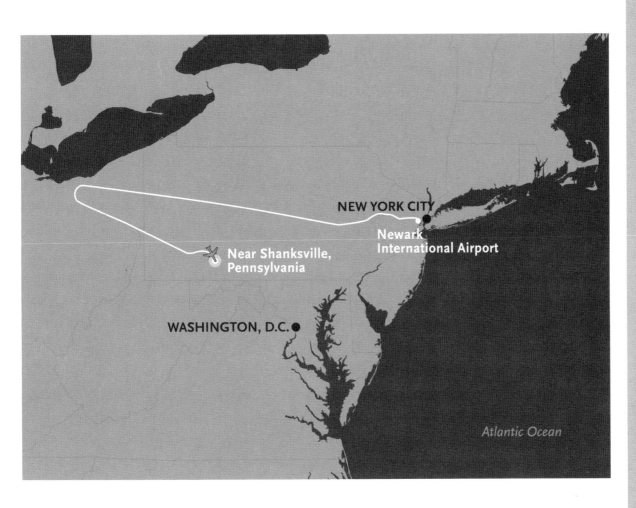

10:03 AM

CRASH OF FLIGHT 93
Four hijackers crash Flight 93 near the town of Shanksville in Somerset County, Pennsylvania, after passengers and crew storm the cockpit. The 33 passengers and seven crew members on board perish. The crash site is approximately 20 minutes' flying time from Washington, D.C.

10:08 AM

NYPD HELICOPTER PILOT CIRCLING THE NORTH TOWER WARNS THE BUILDING MAY FALL

SECURING THE WHITE HOUSE
U.S. Secret Service agents secure the area around the White House and establish armed patrols. Around this time, in the Situation Room, counterterrorism officials call for increased security at borders and harbors.

Hi, baby.

I'm—baby, you have to listen to me carefully.

I'm on a plane that's been hijacked.

I'm on the plane, I'm calling from the plane.

I want to tell you I love you, please tell my children that

I love them very much. And I'm so sorry, babe,

I don't know what to say.

They're three guys, they've hijacked the plane,

I'm trying to be calm.

We're turned around, and I've heard that there's

planes that's been flown into the World Trade Center.

I hope to be able to see your face again, baby.

I love you. Good-bye.

—CeeCee Lyles, flight attendant, phone message
left for her husband, Lorne Lyles

WATCH BELONGING TO
TODD M. BEAMER

Courtesy of the Beamer family

Flight 93's takeoff from Newark International Airport was delayed approximately 25 minutes due to heavy air traffic. By the time Flight 93 was airborne, Flight 11 had been hijacked, and Flights 175 and 77 were minutes away from being taken over. The four hijackers on board Flight 93 attacked at 9:28 a.m., taking a flight attendant hostage and breaching the cockpit. Captain Jason M. Dahl and First Officer LeRoy W. Homer, Jr., resisted the hijackers and activated the radio, alerting air traffic control to the struggle. Passengers and crew members tried to wrest control of the aircraft from the hijackers, who crashed the plane in Somerset County, Pennsylvania. Among the objects recovered at the crash site were business cards and the wristwatch worn by passenger Todd Beamer. The watch's date-keeper still reads 11.

Honey, are you there?

Jack, pick up, sweetie.

Okay, well, I just wanted to tell you I love you.

We're having a little problem on the plane.

I'm totally fine.

I just love you more than anything, just know that.

And, you know, I'm, I'm comfortable,

and I'm okay for now.

It's a little problem. So, I'll—I just love you.

Please tell my family I love them, too.

Bye, honey.

—Lauren Grandcolas, passenger,
phone message left for her husband, Jack Grandcolas

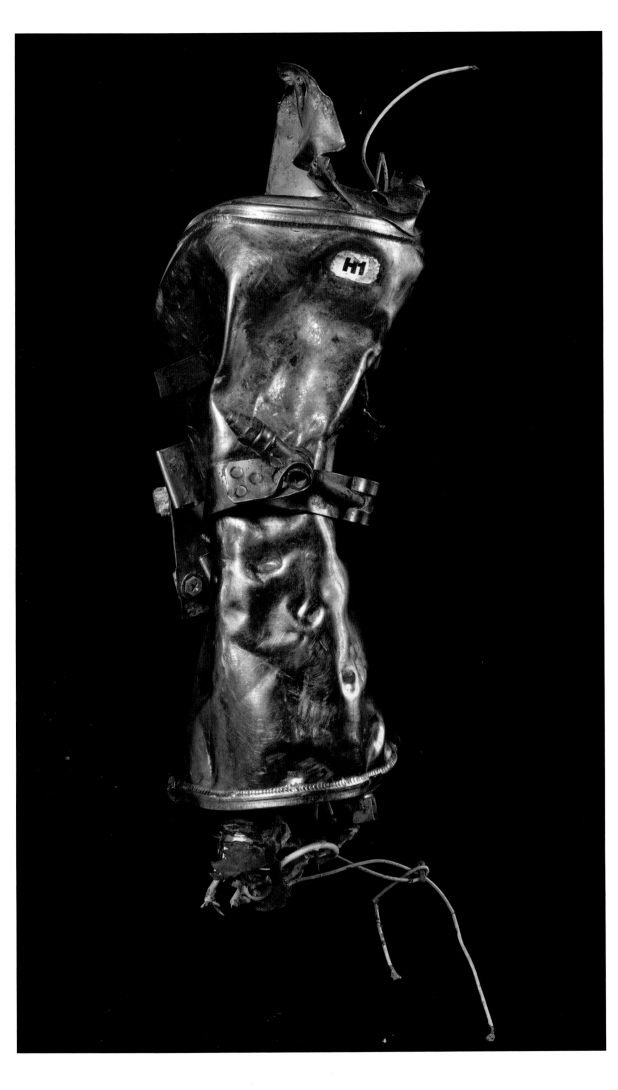

GALLEY WATER HEATER RECOVERED FROM THE FLIGHT 93 CRASH SITE

Courtesy of the Smithsonian Institution,
National Museum of American History,
Kenneth E. Behring Center
Object photograph by Jaclyn Nash

The United Airlines inflight hand-book instructed flight attendants on measures to take in the event of a hijacking on board the aircraft, such as using eye contact to reduce anxiety and distributing food and nonalcoholic beverages. Before 9/11, procedures were based on the assumption that hijackers would negotiate the safe return of passengers and crew to achieve their goals.

Aware that two hijacked aircraft had already struck the World Trade Center, those onboard Flight 93 wanted to avoid another deadly crash. Passengers **Todd M. Beamer, Thomas E. Burnett, Jr.,** and **Jeremy Logan Glick** and flight attendant **Sandy Waugh Bradshaw** each reported that passengers and crew were working together to take back control of the plane. Glick told his wife that they planned to vote on what action to take. Bradshaw reported to her husband that she and some passengers were boiling water in the plane's rear kitchen to throw on the hijackers. In a call connected to an Airfone operator, Beamer explained that the plane was flying erratically and the passengers and crew were planning to fight back. The operator, Lisa Jefferson, recounted the last words she heard as "You ready? Okay. Let's roll!"

The cockpit voice recorder documented the sounds of the passengers' and crew's attempts to enter the cockpit during the six minutes before the plane crashed at 10:03 a.m.

10:15 AM

COLLAPSE OF THE PENTAGON E RING

A damaged section of the Pentagon collapses around this time.

EVACUATIONS ACROSS THE COUNTRY

By this time, officials across the country are in the process of closing buildings, bridges, and other public spaces.

10:18 AM

SHOOT-DOWN ORDER

After conferring with President Bush, Vice President Cheney issues an order to the National Military Command Center authorizing fighter jets to shoot down hijacked aircraft.

10:20 AM

NEW YORK CITY PUBLIC TRANSIT SHUTS DOWN

The Metropolitan Transportation Authority (MTA) suspends public transit in New York City.

The building roared.
Like feeling vibrations of a speedy locomotive in my kitchen. . . .
The lights went out, and water started rushing in. . . .
That's when the panic set in.

—Kayla Bergeron, Port Authority employee, recalling her
evacuation from the North Tower as the South Tower collapsed

CONTINUED ESCAPE FROM THE WORLD TRADE CENTER

As the dust cloud caused by the collapse of the South Tower cleared, one tower remained standing—a single Twin Tower. Inside the North Tower, a full-scale evacuation, intensified by a growing sense of urgency, was under way. Many continued down stairwells unaware of the full extent of the destruction that awaited them outside.

ENTRANCE TO "CONTINUED ESCAPE" ALCOVE IN THE HISTORICAL EXHIBITION

SQUEEGEE HANDLE

Courtesy of the Smithsonian Institution,
National Museum of American History,
Kenneth E. Behring Center
Object photograph by Jaclyn Nash

Window washer Jan Demczur became trapped with five other passengers in an elevator stuck near the 50th floor of the North Tower when hijacked Flight 11 crashed into the building. With his squeegee, the only tool he had, Demczur pried open the elevator doors but encountered drywall. Taking turns, the passengers used the squeegee and its metal handle to cut a hole large enough for them to squeeze through and escape down the stairs.

COLLEAGUES EVACUATE TOGETHER

*Photograph by © **William G. Biggart** NYC*

On the 69th floor of the North Tower, Port Authority comptroller Michael Fabiano was lifted out of his chair when hijacked Flight 11 crashed into the building. Fabiano, the fire warden on the floor, urged his colleagues to evacuate at once. Among the people in the office that morning was John Abruzzo, a quadriplegic who relied on a battery-powered wheelchair for mobility. A group of 10 coworkers transferred Abruzzo to a portable evacuation chair, retrieved a backpack filled with first-aid supplies, and entered the stairwell. As they neared the building's lower floors, taking turns carrying Abruzzo, firefighters encouraged the group to speed their exit by leaving Abruzzo with them. Choosing instead to continue together, the group proceeded to the lobby and exited the tower through a broken window, minutes before the tower collapsed.

All we hear is one boom after another.
All of a sudden the windows blew in and everything
turned black. It was like a tornado went through.
It just sucked the air out of your lungs.
I just now started picking people up and saying,
"Wait here, I'm gonna step out and look up
and when I tell you to go,
you need to go like you've never gone before."
As we're going along, you're like kind of
picking up people that are wandering.
People are disoriented,
because nothing looks the way it did an hour ago.
The whole area was gray.
Even when you looked up, all you saw was gray.

—Officer Sue Keane, PAPD Liaison Officer to the NYPD Court System

You could hear Maydays going over the radio. . . .
It was just so many.
—Thomas Turilli, Firefighter, FDNY Engine Company 47

IMMINENT COLLAPSE

After the South Tower collapsed, NYPD helicopter pilots warned that the North Tower appeared to be on the brink of falling. Because the NYPD and FDNY did not use compatible radios or regularly coordinate command and control functions as part of their standard response procedures, this critical information did not reach FDNY responders in the towers. Furthermore, FDNY radios historically performed poorly inside steel and concrete high-rise buildings. While a repeater system had been installed to bolster the signal within the towers, radio communications between lobby command posts and emergency responders on the floors above were sporadic and unreliable, and not all FDNY personnel received commands to evacuate the North Tower before it collapsed.

FATHER MYCHAL F. JUDGE CARRIED FROM THE WORLD TRADE CENTER

Photograph by Shannon Stapleton, Reuters

After learning that a plane had crashed into the World Trade Center, Father Mychal Judge, chaplain to the FDNY since 1992, replaced his friar's robes with an FDNY uniform and made his way to the World Trade Center. He entered the North Tower to offer spiritual support and the sacrament of anointing the sick, commonly known as last rites. Seeing the carnage, Father Judge stopped to pray. He died after a hail of debris from the collapse of the South Tower penetrated the North Tower lobby. FDNY Firefighter Christian Waugh, NYPD Lieutenant William Cosgrove, FDNY Firefighter Zachary Vause, Goldman Sachs employee John Maguire, and OEM field responder Kevin Allen carried the body of Father Judge from the Plaza, down the Vesey Street stairs. His body was brought shortly thereafter to St. Peter's Church a few blocks away.

IDENTIFICATION CARDS

Collection 9/11 Memorial Museum, Gifts of the Burke family in memory of Captain William F. Burke, Jr., E-21; the Beyea family in memory of Edward; and Jack and Evelyn Zelmanowitz in loving memory of Abe Zelmanowitz

Having reached the 27th floor of the North Tower and aware that the South Tower had collapsed, FDNY Engine Company 21 Captain **William Francis Burke, Jr.**, ordered the men under his command to evacuate, promising to meet them later "at the rig." Burke stayed behind to assist **Edward Frank Beyea** and **Abraham J. Zelmanowitz**, Empire BlueCross BlueShield computer programmers. Zelmanowitz refused to abandon Beyea, his colleague and friend, a wheelchair-bound quadriplegic. The men telephoned family and friends. Beyea assured his mother that he would be okay. Zelmanowitz told his family that they were with a firefighter. Burke called a friend, who begged him to be safe. He is reported to have told her, "This is my job. This is who I am." The three were last seen together before the North Tower collapsed. Burke was the only member of his firehouse to perish on September 11.

FDNY ENGINE COMPANY 21 RIG (OPPOSITE PAGE)

*Recovered from the World Trade Center site after September 11, 2001
Collection 9/11 Memorial Museum, Courtesy of the Port Authority of New York and New Jersey, Presented with permission of the New York City Fire Department*

Engine Company 21, led by Captain **William Francis Burke, Jr.**, reported to the North Tower's command post. The company's rig was parked on Vesey Street under a pedestrian overpass, with the cab exposed. The front of the vehicle was damaged by flaming debris.

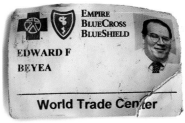

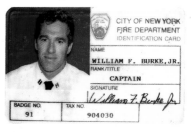

10:28AM

COLLAPSE OF THE NORTH TOWER

The North Tower collapses after burning for 102 minutes. More than 1,600 people are killed as a result of the attack on the North Tower.

10:31AM

NEADS RECEIVES SHOOT-DOWN ORDER

After Vice President Cheney issues the order at 10:18 a.m., the authorization to shoot down hijacked aircraft reaches NEADS. The order is not transmitted to the fighter jet pilots patrolling the skies over Washington, D.C., and New York City. Minutes later, Air National Guard fighter planes take off from Andrews Air Force Base with permission conveyed by the U.S. Secret Service to shoot down airplanes approaching the White House or the Capitol.

EMERGENCY RESPONSE COORDINATION

By this time, the New York State Emergency Management Office in Albany is coordinating the state's response to the attacks.

11:00AM

RESPONSE AT THE PENTAGON

Firefighters attempt to control the blaze as it spreads beyond the impact area. Key personnel continue working in their offices in unaffected sections of the Pentagon. That afternoon, investigators begin to search the grounds for evidence.

10:28AM

**NORTH TOWER (1 WTC)
WORLD TRADE CENTER**

Everything was gone.
—Mickey Kross, Lieutenant, FDNY Engine Company 16

COLLAPSE OF THE NORTH TOWER

At 10:28 a.m., 102 minutes after the first plane crashed into the World Trade Center, the North Tower collapses.

In addition to the 87 passengers and crew aboard Flight 11, more than 1,600 people were killed as a result of the attack on the North Tower.

Nineteen hijackers had coordinated attacks that transformed four commercial airliners into weapons. Fires raged at the Pentagon outside the nation's capital. Plumes of smoke rose over a field in western Pennsylvania. The Twin Towers were gone from the New York City skyline, leaving a massive debris cloud billowing over lower Manhattan that could be seen from outer space. The ash settled and covered everything: streets, parks, playgrounds, fruit and vegetable stands. In the momentary stillness, witnesses remained shocked and stunned. The world was forever changed.

VIEW OF NEW YORK CITY FROM SPACE

Video by Frank Culbertson, Courtesy of National Aeronautics Space Administration

NASA Astronaut Frank Culbertson was the only American not on the planet on September 11, 2001. He was aboard the International Space Station, orbiting the Earth, when he learned about the attacks. As the spacecraft passed over the East Coast, Culbertson grabbed a video camera. Even at a distance of more than 200 miles, he could see smoke billowing ominously over New York City. In a transmission to NASA, he stated, "I just wanted the folks to know that their city still looks very beautiful from space. I know it's very difficult for everybody in America right now, and I know folks are struggling very hard to deal with this and recover from it, but the country still looks good. And for New Yorkers, your city still looks great from up here."

LOWER MANHATTAN AFTER THE COLLAPSE OF THE NORTH TOWER

11:02AM

MAYOR GIULIANI ORDERS
EVACUATION OF LOWER
MANHATTAN

11:17AM

AIRLINES BEGIN TO CONFIRM
CRASH OF FOUR FLIGHTS
In various press releases,
United Airlines announces that
Flight 175 crashed in New York
and that Flight 93 crashed in
Pennsylvania. American Airlines
confirms that Flights 11 and 77 are
missing. Passenger manifests are
provided to the FBI but are not
publicly released.

12:16PM

U.S. AIRSPACE CLOSED
The last flight still in the air
above the continental United
States lands. In two and a half
hours, U.S. airspace has been
cleared of an estimated
4,500 planes.

12:30PM

GROUP OF 14 SURVIVORS
LOCATED IN THE RUINS OF
NORTH TOWER'S STAIRWELL B
A lower section of the North
Tower's stairwell B survives the
building's collapse, protecting
a group of 13 first responders
and one civilian who had been
attempting to evacuate down the
stairs. Within hours of the tower's
collapse, the first responders
emerge from the debris and
direct rescuers to the civilian.

For the rest of the day, we just searched through rubble.

—Adrienne Walsh, Firefighter, FDNY Ladder Company 20

RENEWED ACTIVITY AT THE WORLD TRADE CENTER SITE

The collapse of two 110-story buildings created compressed piles of mangled steel and rubble measuring multiple stories high and seven stories belowground. The steel wreckage was sharp-edged, extremely hot, and coated with layers of dust, posing hazards for rescue workers searching for survivors. On surrounding streets, isolated fires, ignited by flaming debris, flared throughout the day. Some vehicles parked nearby caught fire. Explosions from burning fuel tanks reverberated for blocks. After burning for hours, the 47-story office building 7 World Trade Center collapsed at 5:20 p.m.

Many people with skills and tools that could be used to search for survivors continued to arrive at the World Trade Center site throughout the late morning, afternoon, and evening. Medical personnel came to the site anticipating that lifesaving measures would be needed, and thousands in the metropolitan region began forming lines to donate blood at hospitals and other locations. Clergy members arrived preparing to administer last rites to the dying. However, as hours passed and few survivors were rescued, there was a growing realization that few people would be pulled alive from the debris. In the end, only 18 people were found alive.

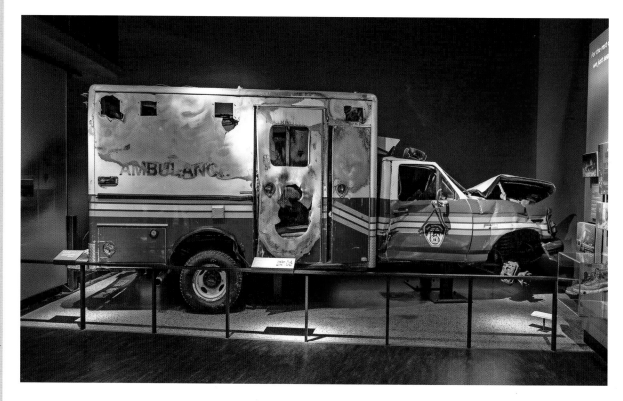

FDNY AMBULANCE, EMS BATTALION 17
Recovered from the World Trade Center site after September 11, 2001, Collection 9/11 Memorial Museum, Courtesy of the Port Authority of New York and New Jersey, Presented with permission of the New York City Fire Department

EVACUATING LOWER MANHATTAN AND CLEARING U.S. AIRSPACE

The U.S. Coast Guard called for all boats, commercial and private, in the vicinity of New York to respond to the emergency. Captains of commuter ferries and water taxis disregarded posted schedules and capacity restrictions to carry as many people to safety as quickly as possible. An estimated 300,000 to 500,000 people were transported to safety in the largest waterborne evacuation in New York City history.

With subway service suspended, tens of thousands of people began their exodus from lower Manhattan by walking north. City highways and bridges to Brooklyn and Queens normally choked with vehicular traffic became pedestrian thoroughfares, closed to all but emergency response vehicles. Retail stores, houses of worship, and other establishments opened their doors to people walking out of lower Manhattan. Evacuees were offered bottled water, dust masks, sneakers, and other necessities.

In an effort to safeguard against any further hijackings, U.S. airspace was closed and cleared of an estimated 4,500 commercial and general aviation planes in flight that morning. Plane passengers became stranded as flights were canceled or diverted. Others attempting to travel nationally by train, bus, or rental car found most options canceled or sold out within hours of the attacks.

WATERBORNE EVACUATION FROM LOWER MANHATTAN
Used with permission of the City of New York and the New York City Police Department. All rights reserved.

U.S. AIRSPACE (RIGHT)
Courtesy of National Aeronautics Space Administration

2:30 PM

FBI AGENTS ARRIVE AT THE FLIGHT 93 CRASH SITE

The FBI joins local law enforcement officers and forensic scientists in the search for criminal evidence and remains.

2:40 PM

U.S. SECRETARY OF DEFENSE PLANS MILITARY RESPONSE

At the Pentagon, Secretary of Defense Donald Rumsfeld speaks with General Richard Myers, vice chairman of the Joint Chiefs of Staff, regarding the likely perpetrators. Early intelligence implicates terrorist Osama bin Laden, already wanted for directing prior attacks on American embassies and U.S. troops stationed abroad.

3:00 PM

FDNY RESCUES SURVIVOR AT WORLD TRADE CENTER SITE

About an hour after the FDNY initiates a roll call to determine the status of its own members, rescuers free Port Authority employee Pasquale Buzzelli from the rubble of the North Tower.

5:20 PM

COLLAPSE OF 7 WORLD TRADE CENTER

After burning for hours, 7 World Trade Center collapses. The 47-story tower had been evacuated earlier. There are no casualties.

6:15 PM

PENNSYLVANIA GOVERNOR TOM RIDGE INSPECTS THE FLIGHT 93 CRASH SITE

FLAG RAISING

Photograph by Thomas E. Franklin/The Record (Bergen County, New Jersey), ©2001 North Jersey Media Group

FDNY Firefighter Dan McWilliams found a flag on a yacht docked near the World Trade Center on the afternoon of September 11. He, along with FDNY Firefighters Billy Eisengrein and George Johnson, raised the flag on a 20-foot pile of debris near West Street. The flag raising lifted the spirits of rescue workers at the site. To many, the widely circulated image of the flag raising at Ground Zero was reminiscent of the World War II photograph of U.S. Marines raising an American flag at Iwo Jima.

FRAGMENT OF THE SEAL OF THE NYC MAYOR'S OFFICE OF EMERGENCY MANAGEMENT, 7 WORLD TRADE CENTER

Used with permission of the City of New York and the New York City Office of Emergency Management, Courtesy of Richard Sheirer

7 World Trade Center was a 47-story office building just north of the Twin Towers. It housed a diversity of private tenants and government agencies, including the U.S. Secret Service and the New York City Mayor's Office of Emergency Management (OEM). Many of the building's occupants evacuated immediately after the North Tower was struck by hijacked Flight 11. OEM temporarily shifted its operations to a command bus located nearby. The collapse of the North Tower caused significant damage to 7 World Trade Center and ignited intense fires. After burning for hours, the building collapsed at 5:20 p.m., destroying OEM's high-tech command center on the 23rd floor.

STORIES OF SURVIVAL

FLASHLIGHT
Collection 9/11 Memorial Museum,
Gift of Brian Clark and Stanley Praimnath

Brian Clark and Stanley Praimnath, working in separate offices high in the South Tower, each heard the impact when hijacked Flight 11 struck the North Tower. On the 84th floor, volunteer fire warden Clark saw fireballs outside his window. Praimnath, on the 81st floor, began evacuating with colleagues. Returning upstairs at the direction of a security guard who assured Praimnath that the danger was confined to the other tower, he was at his desk when hijacked Flight 175 struck his floor, leaving one of its burning wings lodged in a nearby office door. Trapped behind a wall of debris, he banged on the wall and called for help. Clark, heading downstairs, heard Praimnath's distress, assisted him out of the rubble, and used his flashlight to light their way down the stairwell. They exited the South Tower minutes before it collapsed and were separated when the North Tower fell. One year later, Clark gave Praimnath the flashlight that had guided their evacuation as a memento of their survival.

TRIAGE TAG
Collection 9/11 Memorial Museum,
Gift of Allison Gilbert

Allison Gilbert, an investigative producer for WNBC-TV, anticipated that her work on September 11 would focus on the day's planned mayoral primary. Instead, she was directed to cover breaking news of a plane crash at the World Trade Center. Gilbert used her press credentials to access the site, arriving moments before the North Tower collapsed. Covered in dust and debris and having difficulty breathing, Gilbert was assisted by emergency responders and taken to a triage center set up in the Millenium Hilton hotel. Receiving a triage tag that described her condition, she was transported by ambulance to Bellevue Hospital. Before leaving the hospital, she transmitted a live report on what she had seen and experienced at the World Trade Center that morning.

HOTEL LUGGAGE CLAIM TICKET
Courtesy of Joyce Ng

Joyce Ng was in her room on the 13th floor of the New York Marriott World Trade Center hotel when she felt what seemed like an explosion. Looking out of her window, she saw people shielding their heads from falling pieces of metal, glass, and burning paper. Ng grabbed her room key and the wallet containing her luggage claim ticket and left the building. Outside, she saw the North Tower in flames and a low-flying airplane overhead. Thinking a military plane was on a rescue mission, Ng was shocked to see a commercial jetliner strike the South Tower. Ng found shelter at another Marriott hotel near Times Square, which provided rollaway cots to many who were stranded, before she was able to return home to Massachusetts.

6:54 PM

PRESIDENT BUSH RETURNS TO WASHINGTON, D.C.
After Air Force One keeps the President airborne and out of harm's way for most of the day, the President's advisers determine that it is safe for him to return to the White House.

7:15 PM

FEMA ANNOUNCES URBAN SEARCH AND RESCUE TEAMS DEPLOYMENT
The Federal Emergency Management Agency (FEMA) announces that it has deployed Urban Search and Rescue Teams to the World Trade Center and the Pentagon.

7:47 PM

THE WORLD TRADE CENTER SITE BECOMES KNOWN AS GROUND ZERO
While on the air, CBS News reporter Jim Axelrod uses the words "Ground Zero" to describe the World Trade Center site, attributing the reference to rescue workers. National media adopts the terminology.

8:30 PM

PRESIDENT BUSH ADDRESSES THE NATION FROM THE WHITE HOUSE
In a televised statement from the Oval Office, President Bush declares, "The search is under way for those who are behind these evil acts. I've directed the full resources of our intelligence and law enforcement communities to find those responsible and to bring them to justice. We will make no distinction between the terrorists who committed these acts and those who harbor them."

10:30 PM

RESCUE WORKERS LOCATE TRAPPED PAPD OFFICERS

Around 10:30 p.m., rescuers locate PAPD Officer William Jimeno and PAPD Sergeant John McLoughlin alive in the debris of the World Trade Center. They free Officer Jimeno after three hours of dangerous tunneling work. Sergeant McLoughlin's rescue will take another eight hours. Workers will extricate the 18th survivor, Port Authority employee Genelle Guzman, on the afternoon of September 12. She will be the last person rescued.

11:30 PM

NEW YORK STATE GOVERNOR GEORGE PATAKI VISITS GROUND ZERO

11:50 PM

FIRST BROADCAST OF FLIGHT 11'S IMPACT

While filming a documentary with the FDNY in lower Manhattan that morning, videographer Jules Naudet captured the impact of hijacked Flight 11 into the North Tower. Just minutes short of midnight, the footage is broadcast on television internationally. It is the first time that the public, other than eyewitnesses, sees the crash.

The number of casualties will be more than any of us can bear, ultimately.

—Rudolph Giuliani, New York City Mayor

LEGACY OF ABSENCE

While not yet fully known, the human toll was estimated to be in the thousands. News outlets disseminated what information was available as piecemeal facts and figures were released by government sources, the airline industry, and companies that had offices in the Twin Towers.

The attack on America had become the lead—and in some cases, the only—news story around the world. In the United States, coverage of the disaster and the emergency response replaced regular programming on almost all television channels. Coverage was uninterrupted by commercial advertising throughout the day and evening. National media began to use the term Ground Zero to describe the World Trade Center site.

As night came, questions swirled about who perpetrated the attacks, what motivated them, and how America would respond. Messages of grief, concern, and anger were left on answering machines and shared over e-mails around the world. In Washington, D.C., the Capitol Building—the seat of the U.S. Congress and presumed target of hijacked Flight 93 that crashed in western Pennsylvania—remained illuminated on the evening of September 11, 2001, signifying the nation's fortitude and resilience.

SALVAGED BICYCLE RACK

Recovered from the World Trade Center site after September 11, 2001
Collection 9/11 Memorial Museum, Courtesy of the Port Authority of New York and New Jersey

Bicycle racks at the site were used primarily by messengers with documents and workers delivering orders from nearby restaurants. After 9/11, only one owner stepped forward to claim his bicycle, locked to this rack located on Vesey Street that was shielded from cascading debris by 5 World Trade Center. The status of other owners and riders is unknown.

"RESURRECTION WITHIN"
REMNANT OF SOUTH TOWER FACADE
Photograph by G.N. Miller

BEFORE 9/11

Having encountered the events of the day in the first part of the historical exhibition, we step further back in time as we enter the second part, which provides historical context for what transpired on September 11, 2001. Differentiated by warmer, brighter lighting and a linear arrangement of galleries, this section of the exhibition tempers the emotional intensity of the first part with a more cognitive journey through the attack's historical antecedents, toward an understanding of who did this, and why.

Opening with a retrospective look at the symbolism of the Twin Towers, the exhibition's second part places a more than seven-foot-tall, original architectural model of the towers at the center of the first room. Revealed below the model is a vestige of the floor slab from the North Tower's lowest level.

A specific question informs this display: Why was the World Trade Center a terrorist target not just once but twice? The answer to this question begins to take shape through a multiplicity of images and memorabilia that speak to the iconic status of the towers as they figured in the public imagination. While a landmark to some, they were a target to others, as evidenced by the first terrorist attack on the complex: the February 26, 1993 bombing of the World Trade Center, in which six people were killed.

Though carried out by different groups of extremists, the attacks of 1993 and 2001 both occurred within the broader context of an emerging radical Islamist ideology. The link between the two attacks is explored in a presentation on how al-Qaeda, the group that perpetrated the 9/11 attacks, came into existence. Tracing the origins of the 9/11 plot and the movements of the hijackers in the months prior to the attacks, the exhibition returns to the early morning hours of September 11, as the hijackers prepared their assault and boarded and took over the four flights. An animation tracks the flight paths and demonstrates the coordinated nature of the attacks. The timeline introduced previously now reappears. Where, in the first part of the historical exhibition, the timeline began at 8:46 a.m. with the impact of the first hijacked plane, here it provides the prequel to the events of the day and ends with an image of that first airplane only seconds from impact into the World Trade Center's North Tower.

The exhibition has come full circle, enabling a transition into the next and final section, chronicling the aftermath of the attacks.

WORLD TRADE CENTER PRESENTATION MODEL, 1971

Collection 9/11 Memorial Museum, Gift of the American Architectural Foundation, Washington, D.C., made in association with Save America's Treasures at the National Trust for Historic Preservation and at the National Endowment for the Arts, Alcoa, Otis Elevator Company, McGraw-Hill Construction, the American Institute of Architects, and Minoru Yamasaki Associates

In 1962, the Port of New York Authority commissioned architect Minoru Yamasaki and his firm to design the World Trade Center. Together, they considered many possibilities before settling on the plan for the buildings that came to be known as the Twin Towers. This architectural presentation model allowed the client to see the way the entire 16-acre complex would look upon completion. It is the only presentation model of its size still in existence. A similar model, housed with the Port Authority on the 88th floor of the North Tower, was destroyed on 9/11.

HIGH-WIRE WALKER PHILIPPE PETIT CROSSES BETWEEN THE TWIN TOWERS, AUGUST 7, 1974
Photograph by Alan Welner, AP Photo

WORLD LEADERS, DECEMBER 7, 1988
Photograph by Scott Applewhite, AP Photo

U.S. President-elect George H. W. Bush, U.S. President Ronald Reagan, and General Secretary Mikhail Gorbachev of the Soviet Union are photographed on Governors Island during the Soviet leader's trip to deliver a historic speech before the United Nations announcing unilateral arms cuts.

PICTURE PERFECT POSTCARD
Photograph by André Souroujon, Here is New York Collection, New-York Historical Society, Gift of Here is New York, date unknown

THE NEW YORKER COVER, JULY 19, 1982
Artwork by Arthur Getz, Cover © 1982, The New Yorker, Used with permission

FASHION SHOOT OF THE NEW YORK CITY SKYLINE, 1995
Photograph by Rodney Smith

LANDMARK AND ICON

Soon after it was built, the World Trade Center, and specifically the Twin Towers, took on iconic status. Although initially criticized for their architecture of "gigantism," the two soaring towers soon became a landmark, looming large in the public imagination as a symbol of New York City's audacity and vitality. They were seen as emblematic of America itself—a place of possibilities and dreams that defied limitation.

THE WORLD TRADE CENTER AS SEEN FROM AN AIRPLANE, SPRING 2001
Photograph by Katie Day Weisberger

THE 1993 WORLD TRADE CENTER BOMBING

While a landmark of New York City, the Twin Towers also became a target for violent extremists. One of them was Sheikh Omar Abdel Rahman, an Egyptian-born cleric. In the early 1990s, from mosques in New Jersey and New York, he condemned U.S. policy in the Middle East and called for the murder of Americans, Jews, and certain political leaders in the Arab world. Known as the Blind Sheikh, he attracted a circle of followers prepared to implement his violent agenda. Among them were the six individuals, led by co-conspirator Ramzi Yousef, who carried out the bombing of the World Trade Center in 1993, the first attack on the complex, eight years before 9/11.

At 12:18 p.m. on Friday, February 26, 1993, terrorists detonated approximately 1,200 pounds of explosives in a rented van parked in the World Trade Center's underground parking garage. The bomb killed six people and injured more than 1,000. More than 1,000 emergency personnel arrived to aid in the evacuation and treat the injured. Meanwhile, most of the 40,000 people who were in the Twin Towers walked down smoke-filled stairways in the dark. The last survivors escaped from the buildings more than 11 hours after the bomb blast.

WALL FRAGMENT FROM THE WORLD TRADE CENTER PARKING GARAGE

Recovered from the World Trade Center site after September 11, 2001
Collection 9/11 Memorial Museum, Courtesy of the Port Authority of New York and New Jersey

After the bombing, the belowground garage, where the truck bomb was detonated, was repaired but never reopened for public parking. The truck had been parked on the B-2 level, one of six belowground levels at the World Trade Center. The soot stains on this fragment of wall from the B-2 level are the result of the fires that burned following the 9/11 attacks.

FRAGMENT OF RENTAL VAN (AT LEFT IN PHOTO)

Courtesy of the U.S. Department of Justice

Investigators recovered fragments of the rented Ford Econoline van that carried the bomb. Two pieces bore the van's Vehicle Identification Number (VIN), a 17-digit code unique to every car and truck sold in the United States. The FBI traced the VIN to the Jersey City, New Jersey, facility where the terrorists had rented the van.

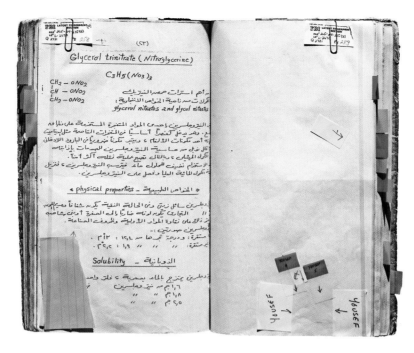

BOMB-MAKING MANUAL

Courtesy of the U.S. Department of Justice

To prepare for an attack, Ramzi Yousef traveled to the U.S. in 1992 with Ahmad Ajaj, who had attended a terrorist training camp in Afghanistan. After presenting his counterfeit passport at customs, Ajaj was arrested, and his luggage was searched. This bomb-making manual was discovered among other suspicious materials during the search.

NYPD OFFICERS ASSIST AN EVACUEE, FEBRUARY 26, 1993

Photograph by Joe Tabacca

GOOD-BYE LETTER

Courtesy of Carl Selinger

Alone and in darkness after the bombing, Carl Selinger, a manager in the Port Authority's aviation department, was trapped inside a North Tower elevator stalled around the 50th floor that was slowly filling with smoke. Fearing that he might die, Selinger wrote a letter to his family. He used the back of a piece of loose-leaf paper he happened to have with him. Rescuers freed Selinger around 5:30 p.m., five hours after the blast.

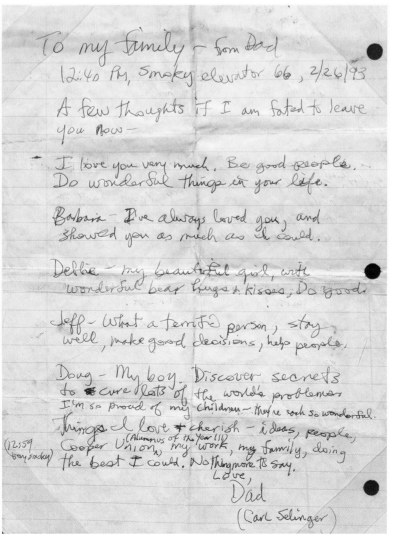

SENTENCING OF WORLD TRADE CENTER BOMBERS, 1994

Courtroom drawing courtesy of the artist, Christine Cornell

Four of the accused were brought to trial in 1994 in federal court in lower Manhattan, blocks from the World Trade Center. A jury found all of them guilty of involvement in the bombing. In 1997, Ramzi Yousef was tried and convicted in federal court for his role as the plot's leader. A sixth conspirator was convicted with Yousef. All six convicted bombers remain in prison in the United States. A seventh conspirator was not apprehended.

JUDGE KEVIN T. DUFFY SENTENCING RAMZI YOUSEF, JANUARY 8, 1998

Courtroom drawing courtesy of the artist, Christine Cornell

Given an opportunity to address the court at his 1997 trial, Ramzi Yousef declared: "Yes, I am a terrorist, and I am proud of it. And I support terrorism so long as it was against the United States government and against Israel."

Fear is another weapon that's used against you. And that's what terrorists are all about . . . what they're trying to do is deny you normalcy and what we must do in this safest and greatest city and state and nation in the world is return as quickly as we can to normalcy.

—Mario Cuomo, Governor of New York, speaking at a news conference on February 27, 1993

REPAIRING AND MEMORIALIZING

With a crew of 2,700 working around the clock to clean and repair the towers, the World Trade Center's South Tower reopened on March 18, 1993, less than a month after the bombing. The North Tower followed on April 1.

In the wake of the bombing, the Port Authority's security team increased emergency preparedness at the World Trade Center. It implemented a fire warden program, staged regular drills, improved stairwell lighting, and coated stairs and handrails with luminescent paint. These changes made it possible for thousands of people in the towers to evacuate safely before the buildings fell on September 11, 2001.

The Port Authority also took action to strengthen security at the World Trade Center. Security improvements transformed it from an open complex into one with access restricted to those conducting business within its confines. Even this was no simple task, as by 2001 more than 500 different companies were tenants of the World Trade Center.

SECURITY BOLLARDS RECOVERED FROM THE WORLD TRADE CENTER SITE AFTER 9/11

Collection 9/11 Memorial Museum, Gift of the New York State Museum

After the attack, the Port Authority eliminated public parking at the World Trade Center and installed bollards and 250 multi-ton planters around the periphery of the complex. These barriers were intended to prevent vehicles from getting close enough to the towers to detonate a bomb that could cause significant damage. At that time, no one could have anticipated that an attack might be launched from above, using airplanes as missiles.

FRAGMENT OF THE 1993 BOMBING MEMORIAL

Recovered from the World Trade Center site after September 11, 2001
Collection 9/11 Memorial Museum, Courtesy of the Port Authority of New York and New Jersey

A memorial fountain was erected on the World Trade Center Plaza in 1995, directly above the site of the explosion. It was designed by New York City–based artist Elyn Zimmerman. Arrayed around the fountain were the names of the six victims: **John DiGiovanni, Robert Kirkpatrick, Stephen A. Knapp, William Macko, Wilfredo Mercado,** and **Monica Rodriguez Smith** and her unborn child.

The memorial was destroyed on 9/11. A fragment, bearing part of the name of bombing victim John DiGiovanni, was the only piece recovered from the wreckage of the World Trade Center.

TWIN TOWERS LIT UP ON THE NIGHT OF FEBRUARY 26, 1993

Photograph by © Allan Tannenbaum. All rights reserved.

ROOTS OF AL-QAEDA

THE RISE OF AL-QAEDA

A short film that plays in this gallery describes the emergence of the terrorist organization that carried out the 9/11 attacks.

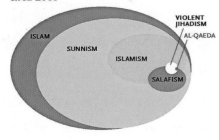

AL-QAEDA IN THE CONTEXT OF SUNNI ISLAM, CIRCA 2000

Adaptation of illustration from Combating Terrorism Center at West Point

AFGHANISTAN, 2003

Photograph by Jean-Marc Giboux, Getty Images

ISLAMISM AND THE EMERGENCE OF AL-QAEDA

The World Trade Center bombing in 1993 and the 9/11 attacks both emerged out of a period of radicalization in the Middle East among some followers of Islam, which is among the world's major religions. During the second half of the 20th century, political groups known as Islamists began to oppose governments they believed were not ruling in accordance with Islamic law, or were being manipulated by foreign ideologies and powers. Their objective was to replace those governments with religious states organized according to their own, strict interpretation of Islamic law.

By the late 1970s, several independent historic events showed these movements becoming increasingly militant. The most violent among them typically represented fringe elements within the greater community of Islam.

Within Islamism, a movement known as Salafism seeks to reform Muslim society by returning to what it considers a more authentic practice of Islam. Salafis are a minority within the broad community of Sunni Muslims, and not all Salafis advocate violence to purify society. Al-Qaeda is one of a number of Salafi groups that did turn toward an active strategy of violent *jihad*, a struggle to defend Islam. Among the *jihadi* leaders who have targeted the West are Osama bin Laden, al-Qaeda's founder; Khalid Sheikh Mohammed, the 9/11 mastermind; and Ramzi Yousef, Mohammed's nephew who orchestrated the 1993 World Trade Center bombing.

THE SOVIET-AFGHAN WAR (1979-1989)

In late December 1979, when indigenous Muslim groups rose up against the communist government of Afghanistan, the Soviet Union sent in armed forces to support the government. The Soviet occupation of Afghanistan inspired militants from around the Muslim world to fight alongside Afghan opposition groups—known as *mujahideen*—to defeat the Soviets.

Among those inspired to defend Afghanistan was Osama bin Laden, the wealthy son of a Saudi Arabian construction magnate. He traveled to Pakistan to support this new effort, which was seen as a *jihad*.

Bin Laden raised funds and used some of his personal wealth to support Arab fighters who would cross the border into Afghanistan. He eventually organized his own force of Arab *mujahideen* to fight the Soviets.

The United States government also supported the Afghan rebellion against its Cold War rival, the Soviet Union. The CIA funneled money and arms through Pakistan's intelligence agency. This funding was directed to native Afghans. Arab fighters had their own resources.

After almost a decade of war, the Soviets started to withdraw from Afghanistan, having lost more than 13,000 troops and having failed to defeat the *mujahideen*.

While Arab fighters had little to do with defeating the Soviets, bin Laden viewed the victory as evidence that a group of true believers could topple a superpower. In 1988, he formed a new organization, "al-Qaeda," which, in Arabic, means "the base."[8] Al-Qaeda would be a mobile army of fighters serving as the base from which armed *jihad* could be waged.

THE PERSIAN GULF WAR (1990–1991)

When Iraq invaded Kuwait on August 2, 1990, bin Laden offered Saudi King Fahd the use of his al-Qaeda fighting force to defend the neighboring Kingdom of Saudi Arabia. Bin Laden's proposal was rejected. King Fahd invited U.S. troops to provide that military presence. This infuriated bin Laden, who believed that Saudi Arabia, as home to Islam's two holiest sites, in Mecca and Medina, should be free of "non-believers."

Six days after Iraq's invasion of Kuwait, U.S. President George H. W. Bush authorized the deployment of American troops to Saudi Arabia. Ultimately, hundreds of thousands of American soldiers were deployed. After Iraqi forces were repelled from Kuwait in February 1991, several thousand American troops remained stationed on bases across the Arabian Peninsula.

Bin Laden's anger now focused on the United States and the Saudi royal family. Going forward, al-Qaeda was dedicated to removing all Western influence from Muslim lands.

THE RISE OF AL-QAEDA

In 1994, the Saudi government revoked bin Laden's citizenship. He had established a base for al-Qaeda operations in Sudan, but was expelled from that country in May of 1996 and returned to Afghanistan. Just three months after returning to Afghanistan, bin Laden openly issued a declaration of war against the United States, demanding that American forces leave Saudi Arabia. Al-Qaeda also hoped to end U.S. support for the State of Israel.

In 1998, bin Laden was joined by Ayman al-Zawahiri, an Egyptian militant he had met in Pakistan during the Soviet-Afghan War. Earlier, Zawahiri had helped plan terrorist attacks aimed at overthrowing the government in Egypt, with the goal of establishing a fundamentalist state governed by Islamic law. He would now play a vital role in determining al-Qaeda's strategy.

Bin Laden and Zawahiri expanded their pronouncements to call for and justify the indiscriminate killing of Americans and their allies. This position marked a turning point for al-Qaeda, and moved it to an even farther fringe of radical Islam.

On February 23, 1998, Osama bin Laden released a declaration from the World Islamic Front, which called for a war of *jihad* against the U.S. and the killing of "Jews and Crusaders." The declaration was also signed by four other leaders of violent Islamist groups. In response to critics who challenged bin Laden's qualifications to issue a religious proclamation, the declaration cited Muslim religious authorities to justify the killing of American civilians. The declaration asserted that American policies constituted a war

OSAMA BIN LADEN (CENTER) WITH OTHER FIGHTERS IN AFGHANISTAN, LATE 1980s
Photograph courtesy of AAR/SIPA

U.S. PRESIDENT RONALD REAGAN (CENTER LEFT) MEETS WITH AFGHAN REBEL LEADERS IN THE WHITE HOUSE, 1983
Photograph courtesy of the Ronald Reagan Archives, University of Texas

SOVIET TANKS WITHDRAW FROM AFGHANISTAN, 1989
Photograph by Gueorgui Pinkhassov, Magnum Photos

CNN JOURNALISTS PETER ARNETT,
PETER BERGEN, AND PETER JOUVENAL
INTERVIEW OSAMA BIN LADEN,
MARCH 1997

Photograph courtesy of Peter Bergen

U.S. EMBASSY, NAIROBI, KENYA,
AUGUST 7, 1998

Photograph by Sayyid Azim, AP Photo

U.S. EMBASSY, DAR ES SALAAM, TANZANIA,
THE DAY AFTER THE ATTACK,
AUGUST 8, 1998

Photograph by Brennan Linsley, AP Photo

against Muslims and that violent opposition to the U.S. was required by Islamic law. The authors claimed that their "ruling to kill the Americans and their allies—civilians and military—is an individual duty for every Muslim who can do it in any country in which it is possible to do it."

JOURNALISTS INTERVIEWING OSAMA BIN LADEN

Bin Laden's threats of violence against the U.S. were broadcast nationally to American audiences.

> *All Americans are our enemies, not just the ones who fight us directly, but also the ones who pay their taxes.*
>
> —Osama bin Laden, January 1999

In an effort to boost al-Qaeda's profile, bin Laden repeatedly invited Western journalists to Afghanistan. In interviews broadcast in the United States on ABC and CNN, he projected himself as the leader of a global movement.

ATTACKS ON U.S. TARGETS BY AL-QAEDA BEFORE 9/11

Al-Qaeda would follow through on its threats by first attacking American targets abroad. On August 7, 1998, the eighth anniversary of the arrival of American troops in Saudi Arabia, al-Qaeda launched a suicide attack, detonating truck bombs outside the American embassies in Nairobi, Kenya, and Dar es Salaam, Tanzania.

Planted hundreds of miles apart, the bombs exploded almost simultaneously, killing 213 people in Kenya, including 12 Americans, and 11 in Tanzania and injuring more than 4,500.

In response to the embassy bombings, the FBI placed bin Laden on its Most Wanted List. Two years later, on October 12, 2000, al-Qaeda suicide bombers turned a fishing boat into a bomb, filling it with explosives. They detonated it next to the American naval destroyer USS *Cole* as the vessel refueled in Aden, Yemen. Seventeen American sailors were killed and more than 40 were injured.

THE ORIGINS OF THE 9/11 PLOT

Osama bin Laden sought to launch an attack on American soil. Bin Laden's agenda was shared by Ramzi Yousef, mastermind of the 1993 World Trade Center bombing, and Yousef's uncle, Khalid Sheikh Mohammed.

Only three years apart in age, Khalid Sheikh Mohammed and Ramzi Yousef grew up together in a suburb of Kuwait City. Both were educated in the West—Khalid Sheikh Mohammed in the United States, Ramzi Yousef in the United Kingdom. Together, they plotted an ambitious attack targeting multiple American passenger jets. Although Yousef was already in American custody by the late 1990s, under Osama bin Laden's influence, this idea evolved into the 9/11 plot.

> *The continuation of tyranny will bring the fight to America,*
> *as Ramzi Yousef and others did.*
>
> —Osama bin Laden, interview broadcast on ABC's *Nightline*, June 10, 1998

**USS *COLE* TOWED FROM YEMEN,
OCTOBER 29, 2000**

*Photograph by Sergeant Don L. Maes,
U.S. Marine Corps*

The 1993 World Trade Center bombing did not accomplish Ramzi Yousef's goal of toppling the Twin Towers. Seeking other means of attacking the United States, Yousef concluded that a small explosion could devastate an airplane, and he began developing plans to target passenger jets.

For two years after the 1993 World Trade Center bombing, Ramzi Yousef, the plot leader, remained at large. Working from the Philippines, Yousef and his uncle, Khalid Sheikh Mohammed, took advantage of computer technology to develop a different plot, known as Bojinka. The plan was to place bombs under seats on 11 American airliners and detonate them over a two-day span.

**LAPTOP COMPUTER AND BOOKING
PHOTOGRAPHS OF RAMZI YOUSEF**

Courtesy of the U.S. Department of Justice

In January 1995, a chemical fire in Yousef's apartment in Manila, Philippines, disrupted the terrorist plot. Yousef escaped, but investigators seized his laptop. On the computer's hard drive, they uncovered the Bojinka plot, a draft of Yousef's claim of responsibility letter, and the names of nearly all involved, including his uncle, who would become the self-professed mastermind of the 9/11 attacks. Yousef was arrested in Pakistan on February 8, 1995, for his role in the World Trade Center bombing and was later indicted for the unfulfilled Bojinka plot.

Yousef's laptop serves as a link between the 1993 and 2001 attacks at the World Trade Center. The plan for a terrorist attack found on the laptop was devised by the leaders of both World Trade Center attacks and marked a step in the evolution of the 9/11 plot.

While hatching a plot to plant bombs on American airplanes that would explode over the Pacific Ocean, Ramzi Yousef and Khalid Sheikh Mohammed brainstormed about other potential terrorist attacks. They determined that a hijacked plane could be used as a missile. This new idea relied on suicide operatives who would fly hijacked planes into buildings. Because he was not allied with a terrorist network, Khalid Sheikh Mohammed did not have access to willing volunteers. He solved that problem by working with Osama bin Laden.

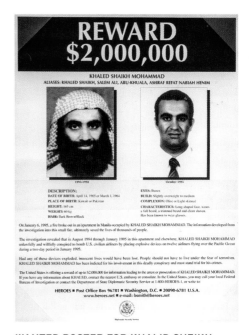

**WANTED POSTER FOR KHALID SHEIKH
MOHAMMED, ISSUED BY THE U.S.
DEPARTMENT OF STATE, 1998**

*Collection 9/11 Memorial Museum,
Gift of Frank Pellegrino*

In his 1996 meeting with Osama bin Laden, Khalid Sheikh Mohammed proposed simultaneously hijacking 10 American airplanes and crashing nine into symbolic targets. He envisioned landing the 10th plane himself as a platform to broadcast his political message.

Eventually, bin Laden agreed to carry out a scaled-down version of Khalid Sheikh Mohammed's plot. Commercial airplanes would hit four symbolic targets inside the United States. At the top of the list was the pair of buildings Ramzi Yousef had failed to bring down in 1993: the Twin Towers.

By 2000, al-Qaeda's plans to take the fight to the American homeland were already underway. The objective was to attack symbols of American military, political, and economic power, killing thousands of innocent civilians. Al-Qaeda believed that such a spectacular attack would lead to the withdrawal of U.S. troops and diminish American influence in Muslim lands, opening the way for the rule of Islamic law in those nations.

THE PLOT COMES TO AMERICA

*The threat could not be
more real . . . do whatever is
necessary to disrupt UBL's
[Osama bin Laden's] plans. . . .*

—George Tenet, Director, CIA, 1999

INTELLIGENCE ACTIVITIES

Prior to 9/11, pieces of information relating to al-Qaeda activities came to the attention of various intelligence services. That information was not connected in a way that clearly revealed the plot under way. The 9/11 attacks highlighted gaps in communication and information sharing between law enforcement and intelligence agencies. Later investigations suggested that the 9/11 attacks might have been prevented if federal agencies had exchanged information more fully. Restrictive federal laws, lack of clarity about the rules, and insular agency cultures inhibited communication and collaboration.

As part of CIA counterterrorism operations abroad, 9/11 hijackers Nawaf al-Hazmi and Khalid al-Mihdhar were photographed at a January 2000 meeting with al-Qaeda associates in Malaysia. Multiple American agencies received information about that meeting. The two men entered the United States undetected days later. In August 2001, the U.S. State Department placed al-Mihdhar and al-Hamzi on a watch list for suspected terrorists attempting to enter the United States, not knowing that both were already in the country. Neither was placed on a domestic "no fly" list, so they were able to travel in the United States freely.

By June 2001, the level of reporting on terrorist threats had increased dramatically, and American intelligence agencies had received information about possible al-Qaeda attacks. None of this "chatter" provided any specific details about likely targets or timing. As a result, the CIA and FBI instructed their agents stationed throughout the world to increase intelligence gathering. U.S. Central Command placed American military forces abroad on high alert. The National Security Council briefed domestic agencies about the potential threats.

Like all modern U.S. presidents, George W. Bush received a daily briefing from the CIA. Informed about al-Qaeda's intent to attack American interests abroad, President Bush asked the CIA to assess the threat posed by Osama bin Laden. The CIA responded with a report presented to the president on August 6, 2001, titled "Bin Ladin Determined to Strike in US."

PREPARATIONS FOR THE ATTACK

Leaders of al-Qaeda selected the hijackers who carried out the 9/11 attacks from a pool of young men who attended terrorist training camps in Afghanistan. They ultimately chose as pilots four individuals who, having lived in the United States and Western Europe, would be unobtrusive while attending a U.S. flight school. Al-Qaeda leaders trained additional recruits as "muscle hijackers" and taught them how to take over a plane by physically subduing passengers and crew. Al-Qaeda leaders characterized selection for a suicide attack as an honor.

In March 2000, al-Qaeda member Mohamed Atta e-mailed 31 U.S. flight schools. A year and a half later, he would hijack American Airlines Flight 11 and fly it into the North Tower of the World Trade Center in New York City.

Bin Ladin Determined To Strike in US

Clandestine, foreign government, and media reports indicate Bin Ladin since 1997 has wanted to conduct terrorist attacks in the US. Bin Ladin implied in US television interviews in 1997 and 1998 that his followers would follow the example of World Trade Center bomber Ramzi Yousef and "bring the fighting to America."

After US missile strikes on his base in Afghanistan in 1998, Bin Ladin told followers he wanted to retaliate in Washington, according to a ██████████████ service.

An Egyptian Islamic Jihad (EIJ) operative told an ██████ service at the same time that Bin Ladin was planning to exploit the operative's access to the US to mount a terrorist strike.

The millennium plotting in Canada in 1999 may have been part of Bin Ladin's first serious attempt to implement a terrorist strike in the US. Convicted plotter Ahmed Ressam has told the FBI that he conceived the idea to attack Los Angeles International Airport himself, but that Bin Ladin lieutenant Abu Zubaydah encouraged him and helped facilitate the operation. Ressam also said that in 1998 Abu Zubaydah was planning his own US attack.

Ressam says Bin Ladin was aware of the Los Angeles operation.

Although Bin Ladin has not succeeded, his attacks against the US Embassies in Kenya and Tanzania in 1998 demonstrate that he prepares operations years in advance and is not deterred by setbacks. Bin Ladin associates surveilled our Embassies in Nairobi and Dar es Salaam as early as 1993, and some members of the Nairobi cell planning the bombings were arrested and deported in 1997.

Al-Qa'ida members—including some who are US citizens—have resided in or traveled to the US for years, and the group apparently maintains a support structure that could aid attacks. Two al-Qa'ida members found guilty in the conspiracy to bomb our Embassies in East Africa were US citizens, and a senior EIJ member lived in California in the mid-1990s.

A clandestine source said in 1998 that a Bin Ladin cell in New York was recruiting Muslim-American youth for attacks.

We have not been able to corroborate some of the more sensational threat reporting, such as that from a ██████████████ *service in 1998 saying that Bin Ladin wanted to hijack a US aircraft to gain the release of "Blind Shaykh" 'Umar 'Abd al-Rahman and other US-held extremists.*

continued

"BIN LADIN DETERMINED TO STRIKE IN US," REPORT DATED AUGUST 6, 2001

Reproduction courtesy of the Central Intelligence Agency

SAN DIEGO TELEPHONE DIRECTORY, 2000

Courtesy of the Ephemera Collection, San Diego
History Center Library

Mohamed Atta's e-mail to the Academy of Lakeland flight school, Florida, later released by the U.S. Department of Justice, read:

> *From: httpd@ithink.net*
> *To: programs@theacademy.net*
> *Date: Wed, Mar. 22, 2000 12:02 PM*
> *Dear Sir,*
> *we are a small group (2-3) of joung men from different arab countries. Now we are living in Germany since a while for study purposes.*
> *We would like to start training for the career of airline professional pilots. In this field we haven't yet any knowledge, but we are ready to undergo an intensive training program (up to ATP and eventually higher).*
> *Concerning this we would like to know which possibelities can be offered to us in Your reputable school/institution.*
> *Please be kind enough to give detailed information about topics like time schedule, total costs, accomodation, visa requirements and eventually financing, . . . etc.*
> *Thank You in advance and remain.*
> *M. Atta*

Nawaf al-Hazmi and Khalid al-Mihdhar resided in San Diego, California, for about a year, taking English classes and flight lessons. Hiding in plain sight, al-Hazmi was listed in the San Diego phone book. He and al-Mihdhar dropped out of flight school because of their difficulties learning English. They were later replaced as the hijacker pilot of Flight 77 by Hani Hanjour, who had some prior flight training. In summer 2000, Mohamed Atta, Marwan al-Shehhi, and Ziad Jarrah arrived in the U.S. and enrolled in flight schools in Florida.

By June 2001, the remaining hijackers, all under the age of 29, had arrived in the United States. Fifteen of the 19 hijackers were from Saudi Arabia. Two were from the United Arab Emirates, one was from Egypt, and one was from Lebanon.

On August 4, 2001, immigration inspectors at Orlando International Airport in Florida denied Mohamed al-Kahtani entry to the United States because he was unable to answer routine questions. Al-Qaeda member Mohamed Atta was waiting outside security to pick up al-Kahtani, who likely would have been the fifth hijacker on board Flight 93.

On August 16, 2001, Zacarias Moussaoui was arrested for violating immigration laws after arousing suspicion at a flight school. The FBI learned about Moussaoui's connection to al-Qaeda after 9/11.

Following the attacks, investigators recovered three copies of a letter titled "The Last Night." This letter provided instructions to the hijackers, describing rituals to be performed on the night before the attacks and during the takeover of the planes. The three copies were found in an abandoned rental car registered to Flight 77 hijacker Nawaf al-Hazmi, in the wreckage of Flight 93 in Somerset County, Pennsylvania, and in the luggage of Mohamed Atta. Atta's luggage had not been loaded onto Flight 11 due to its late arrival from a connecting flight.

"THE LAST NIGHT" LETTER, 2001

Courtesy of the U.S. Department of Justice

FLIGHT 11

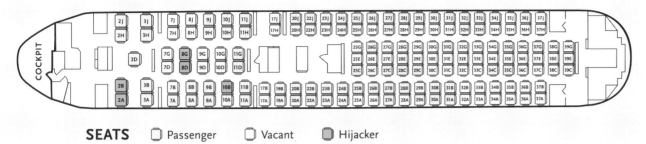

SEATS ☐ Passenger ☐ Vacant ☐ Hijacker

**FLIGHT 11 HIJACKERS
1 WORLD TRADE CENTER,
NEW YORK CITY**

Mohamed Atta, pilot
Abdul Aziz al-Omari
Wail al-Shehri
Waleed al-Shehri
Satam al-Suqami

FLIGHT 175

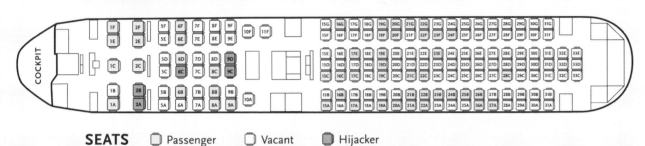

SEATS ☐ Passenger ☐ Vacant ☐ Hijacker

**FLIGHT 175 HIJACKERS
2 WORLD TRADE CENTER,
NEW YORK CITY**

Marwan al-Shehhi, pilot
Fayez Banihammad
Ahmed al-Ghamdi
Hamza al-Ghamdi
Mohand al-Shehri

FLIGHT 77

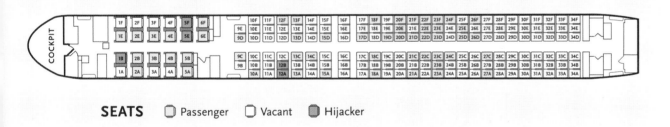

SEATS ☐ Passenger ☐ Vacant ☐ Hijacker

**FLIGHT 77 HIJACKERS
THE PENTAGON,
ARLINGTON, VIRGINIA**

Hani Hanjour, pilot
Nawaf al-Hazmi
Salem al-Hazmi
Khalid al-Mihdhar
Majed Moqed

FLIGHT 93

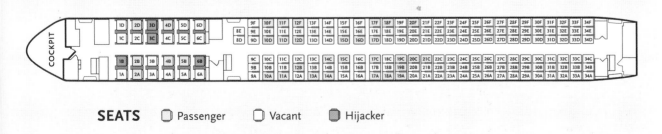

SEATS ☐ Passenger ☐ Vacant ☐ Hijacker

**FLIGHT 93 HIJACKERS
PRESUMED TARGET,
U.S. CAPITOL BUILDING,
WASHINGTON, D.C.
CRASHED IN
SOMERSET COUNTY,
PENNSYLVANIA**

Ziad Jarrah, pilot
Saeed al-Ghamdi
Ahmad al-Haznawi
Ahmed al-Nami

Based on diagrams provided by the U.S. Department of Justice

THE CHALLENGES OF DOCUMENTING HISTORY IN A MEMORIAL MUSEUM
Presenting the Perpetrators

BY CLIFFORD CHANIN

Senior Vice President for Education and Public Programs

From the very start of planning the 9/11 Memorial Museum, team members recognized the need not only to tell the story of the attacks but also to identify the specific individuals who had planned and willfully perpetrated these terrorist acts. But, among some constituents, the agonies of grief did not easily concede a place for the perpetrators.

The Museum's Conversation Series provided a forum for a broad discussion of these participants' views. In a memorial museum built at the site of mass murder, they argued, the presence of the perpetrators amounted to the glorification of their deed. The strongest advocates of this view came from within the community of 9/11 family members. Some worried that, by dint of numbers, the 19 hijackers might end up being more prominent in the Museum than the 2,977 victims of 9/11. In the words of one participant, photographs of the perpetrators would only make matters worse, proffering them a posthumous "victory lap."

However, others maintained that, as painful as the reality was, the 9/11 attacks had been attacks, calculated and deadly. Mass murder was the intention of the plotters. From this perspective, obscuring this part of the history would spare the killers accountability at the scene of the crime.

This debate highlighted the tensions between the commemorative and educational functions of a memorial museum. The mandate to honor and memorialize those killed in the attacks is central to the Museum's mission. Deciding how to portray the killers within the same physical space as the victims was intensely nuanced. From an educational perspective, a 9/11 museum that did not describe the hijackers and their motivations would leave visitors—especially younger visitors, who have no memory of the event—wondering why the attacks had happened.

Strikingly, these disagreements generated little recrimination. All involved understood the twofold nature of the Museum's mission, even if they differed on where the balance should be set. Ultimately, Museum planners decided to include U.S. Department of Justice mug-shot-style photos of the hijackers in the historical exhibition—presenting them clearly as the criminals they were.

The decision to include the perpetrators within the exhibition narrative required that Museum planners tackle three fundamental questions that emerged early in the effort to conceive the historical exhibition: *When does the story of 9/11 begin? Is 9/11 best understood by recounting the details of the plot? And why did al-Qaeda attack the United States?*

The first order of business was to determine the entry point into the 9/11 narrative. Clearly, the story did not begin on that Tuesday morning, when al-Qaeda's years of planning exploded into view. The 9/11 attacks were a second attempt, on a much grander scale, to bring down the Twin Towers. The first, a truck bomb in the underground parking facility on February 26, 1993, killed six people and injured more than a thousand.

The 1993 bombing was not an al-Qaeda attack, though it did have a link to the lead plotter of the 9/11 attack, Khalid Sheikh Mohammed (KSM). KSM is the uncle of Ramzi Yousef, who organized the 1993 bombing and remained at large until February 1995, when he was arrested in Pakistan. During those two years, Yousef, working both with KSM and separately, planned a series of global terror attacks.

How much background would be enough to make the story understandable to Museum visitors, without either overwhelming them or oversimplifying a complex and lengthy history?

Museum staff consulted with a number of subject matter experts, some of whom were affiliated with the Combating Terrorism Center at the U.S. Military Academy at West Point. It was clear that the process of developing this part of the narrative was going to require paring a vast array of facts and interpretations into a precise account of the history that had led to 9/11. Adding complexity to the process was the fact that the experts themselves had not settled on a single explanation of the train of events that had produced the attacks. Quite the contrary. Academic and policy experts differed over the origins of bin Laden's views, and few of them had the experience of presenting the story in a museum setting, where there would be no place for lengthy chapters or footnotes. Visitors would be digesting this material in a limited physical environment—and while they were moving—in addition to everything else the Museum would be presenting.

The challenge did not deter the experts who served as advisers, a role that would span several years and included meetings at the Museum's office and rounds of comments on exhibition designs, text panels, and film scripts. Their expertise was essential, but no more so than their unwavering commitment to making this material accessible and understandable. While they were all professionally acquainted, none of them had worked together on a major project before.[9]

Their initial advice focused on where to begin the 9/11 story. By then, planners had reached an important decision about how the space within the historical exhibition would be allotted. Entry into the exhibition would start with the day of September 11, 2001 (also the formal name of the historical exhibition). The story would unfold from the blue sky of that morning, with the bustle of a mayoral election primary, leading to the first confused reports of events at the World Trade Center. And then, the excruciating succession of attacks, the response, and the death toll. Only after an encounter with the painful reality of the day would visitors come to the second section of the historical exhibition, where the violent radicalism of the perpetrators of both the 9/11 attacks and the 1993 World Trade Center bombing would be explained.

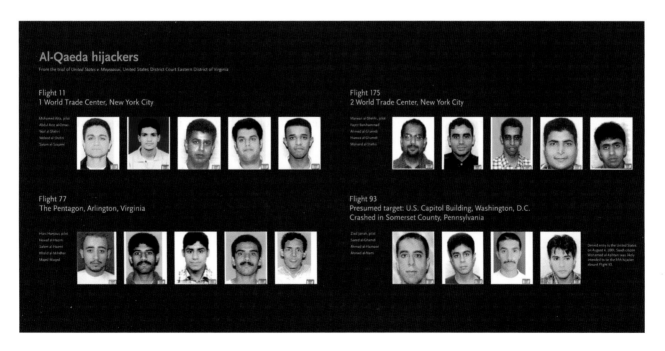

BEARING GOVERNMENT EXHIBIT STICKERS, THESE PHOTOS WERE SELECTED FOR USE AT THE TRIAL
UNITED STATES V. MOUSSAOUI, UNITED STATES DISTRICT COURT FOR THE EASTERN DISTRICT OF VIRGINIA

For this part of the exhibition, there had been some early discussion among staff of a chronology presented in Lawrence Wright's Pulitzer Prize–winning account of 9/11 and its origins, *The Looming Tower*. In his book, Wright follows the development of a particular idea through the 20th-century politics of the Arab world: Islamism, a term for political movements that seek to transform Muslim-majority societies through the application of religious law to all aspects of life. The Muslim Brotherhood, which was founded in Egypt in the 1920s, was the first of these movements to play an important role in modern politics, opposing both the Egyptian government and the colonial influence of Great Britain and other western powers. The inability of the Brotherhood, and the like-minded movements that would come later, to seize control of their societies would produce increasingly radicalized offshoots, each finding justification for violence in order to realize their goals. In Wright's telling, Osama bin Laden and al-Qaeda were the product of this 20th-century brew of frustration and religious fanaticism.

Our advisers raised challenges to this as the starting point for the Museum's narrative about the perpetrators, pointing out that a narrative beginning in Egypt in the 1920s would have to recount decades of complicated, disputed history, all as a prologue to the 9/11 plot. Doing this history justice could likely fill a museum of its own, where 9/11 would be but a subplot in a larger story. At the 9/11 Memorial Museum, this was neither a practical nor appropriate option.

There was a deeper problem with this initial approach. It took the spotlight off the terrorists' decision to commit mass murder. The plotters had been meticulous in their planning and were aware of the enormity of carrying out a coordinated attack on the United States, using civilian aircraft to inflict mass casualties. In explanations of his hostility toward the U.S. and the West, Osama bin Laden, the leader of al-Qaeda, cited different moments in time and different historical circumstances. Examples—U.S. troops in Saudi Arabia, the establishment of the State of Israel, the end of the Ottoman Caliphate, among many others— reflected bin Laden's view that Muslims had repeatedly experienced a succession of calamities. The position of Museum planners was emphatically that there is no justification for committing mass murder. But the question remained whether the starting point for presenting the 9/11 story at the Museum would need to reference one or all of these preceding events, and even whether it should address them within the context of bin Laden's perspective of recurring injustices.

The starting point, our advisers ultimately urged, should be the history of the attackers, not the history of their ideas. A museum dedicated to presenting the consequence of al-Qaeda's choice should focus on the individuals who made it.

Thus, the Museum's story of the roots of the 9/11 plot begins with the emergence of al-Qaeda in Afghanistan, as a small group of mostly Arab volunteers who joined the Afghan fight against the Soviet invasion in 1979. The war had drawn Osama bin Laden from Saudi Arabia and provided him with a rationale for defending Muslims around the world, even after the Afghan war was over and the Soviets had withdrawn. Over time, al-Qaeda became the institutional manifestation of malignant ideas about religion and violence. Most importantly, it was the perpetrator of 9/11, and this would frame the Museum's presentation of the historical context of the attacks.

This framing would include al-Qaeda's own words, its stated justification—and, consequently, its responsibility— for mass murder. This was a difficult choice, because of how much suffering these words had caused. Their inclusion in the Museum, however, meant that the killers would incriminate themselves. Bin Laden is quoted directly on text panels that make clear the strategic vision that guided his leadership of al-Qaeda. A timeline traces the back-and-forth between bin Laden and his American pursuers, including pre-9/11 attacks on American embassies in Kenya and Tanzania (1998) and the USS *Cole* in Aden, Yemen (2000), and a federal indictment as well as the reward for bin Laden's capture issued by U.S. authorities.

The most prominent feature of this part of the exhibition is a nearly seven-minute film, *The Rise of al-Qaeda*, which follows bin Laden from Afghanistan to Saudi Arabia to Sudan and back to Afghanistan in the years before 9/11.

Bin Laden and his associates are seen in still and video images and heard in public statements. Their claims to be acting in accordance with Islamic law on behalf of all Muslims are stated plainly.

Even before the Museum opened, the film was challenged on its presentation of these claims. A group of interfaith advisers (that included Muslim religious leaders, among others), which had provided advice over several years on a number of issues in the Museum's development, rejected the idea that the justification for 9/11 could be found in any interpretation of Islam, no matter what bin Laden said. They were concerned that Muslims were being defamed by bin Laden's false claim, and would be judged complicit in his crimes by the public at large.

This objection highlighted some of the most sensitive issues that Museum staff faced in developing the historical exhibition.

Several principles shaped the exhibition's approach.

- The violent radicalism of al-Qaeda would be placed in its proportionate context within the global Muslim community: a tiny fringe. The Museum rejects any implication of collective responsibility for what this particular group of terrorists did.

- The perpetrators would be portrayed as fully responsible for what they had done. Their stated justifications, many of them rooted in their extreme interpretation of scripture, would be cited.

- The Museum exhibitions would not enter into longstanding and contentious scholarly debates about the appropriate interpretation of religious sanctions for violence.

The resulting exhibition does not provide a comprehensive account of the worldview of al-Qaeda, even while presenting an outline of its main features and providing visitors with cues for further exploration. In this, the 9/11 Memorial Museum is not much different than most other history museums. All face the challenge of converting books, documents, and debate into engaging three-dimensional presentations. All must adapt extensive source materials to limited gallery space.

The 9/11 Memorial Museum does differ from most other history museums in the urgency and immediacy that its visitors feel. Still living in the aftermath of the attacks, they are not simply looking back at history. The emotions triggered by 9/11 remain raw. We all know that something important changed on 9/11, but we don't know the exact shape of this change or when it will be completed. There are more questions than answers.

Years after 9/11, the same ideas that motivated al-Qaeda are proclaimed by even more violent groups to mobilize support and threaten the global community, not just the United States. Though they claim religious sanction for their brutality, their most numerous victims are Muslim.

At a certain moment, perhaps on 9/11 itself, the complexity of history crossed into incomprehensibility. How can we account for a worldview that would inflict suffering universally, including on fellow believers? The 9/11 Memorial Museum presents this worldview and details its awful consequences. We could not know, but had to assume, that 9/11 would not be the end of it. As with so much that has followed 9/11, real clarity may come only when the fighting ends.

**FLIGHT 11 HIJACKERS
PASS THROUGH
SECURITY SCREENING IN
PORTLAND, MAINE**

Hijackers Mohamed Atta and Abdul Aziz al-Omari pass through security at Portland International Jetport in Maine. Atta and al-Omari board a flight to Boston Logan International Airport, where they connect to American Airlines Flight 11.

**MORNING NEWS FORECASTS
CLEAR SKIES**

The forecast for the eastern seaboard of the United States is sunny, with uninterrupted visibility. Such ideal conditions for flying are known as "severe clear" in the aviation industry.

7:59 AM

FLIGHT 11 TAKES OFF

American Airlines Flight 11 takes off from Boston for Los Angeles. Eleven crew members, 76 passengers, and five hijackers are on board.

EARLY MORNING OF SEPTEMBER 11

On the morning of September 11, 2001, four terrorists boarded Flight 93; five boarded each of the other flights. After each plane reached its cruising altitude, the hijackers launched their attacks, using force or the threat of force to take control of the aircraft. On at least three flights, crew members were stabbed and, in at least two instances, passengers were also stabbed. On some of the planes, hijackers sprayed Mace to force passengers and crew to the rear. On at least three flights, they claimed to have a bomb, using the threat of an explosion to deter defensive action.

Hijackers on each plane forced their way into the cockpit, where they killed or incapacitated the pilots. The hijacker with flight training likely assumed control of the aircraft and turned off the transponder or changed its code to prevent air traffic controllers from tracking the plane.

Flight crews aboard the hijacked aircraft were the first to respond to the 9/11 attacks. Facing great personal danger, flight attendants took steps to protect their passengers and themselves.

The crews' quick and decisive actions during the 9/11 hijackings ran counter to the instructions conveyed in their training manuals. Standard procedure at the time directed flight attendants not to challenge hijackers, based on the assumption that hijackers would negotiate the return of passengers and crew and land the plane to achieve their goals.

Passengers and crew members also relayed critical information through telephone calls to officials on the ground about what was occurring aboard the hijacked planes. Based on those communications, together with information gleaned from subsequent investigations, it is clear that the terrorists had followed a shared, predetermined plan.

INSTALLATION SHOWING FLIGHT PATHS OF HIJACKED PLANES

8:24AM

FLIGHT 11 HIJACKER TRANSMITS A MESSAGE

Evidence suggests that the hijacker pilot on each plane attempted to broadcast an announcement to airplane passengers that the plane had been hijacked. Inside Flight 11's cabin, hijacker Mohamed Atta presses the wrong button, broadcasting instead to air traffic control and unwittingly alerting controllers to the attacks. Minutes later, Atta again makes an unintended transmission to ground control.

8:42AM

FLIGHT 93 TAKES OFF

Scheduled to leave Newark International Airport within minutes of the other hijacked flights, United Airlines Flight 93 takes off after a delay due to routine traffic. Seven crew members, 33 passengers, and four hijackers are on board the San Francisco-bound flight.

8:46AM

MOMENT OF IMPACT

By 8:46 a.m. on September 11, 2001, approximately 20,000 people have arrived at work in the World Trade Center. Tens of thousands more are on their way. More than 1,300 are in offices on floors 92 and above, inside the North Tower, when hijacked Flight 11 crashes into the building.

EXCERPT OF PHONE CALL TO AMERICAN AIRLINES BY FLIGHT ATTENDANT BETTY ANN ONG
Collection 9/11 Memorial Museum, Gift of the Ong family

Betty Ong: *I think we're getting hijacked. . . .*

Reservations Operator Winston Sadler: *What is your name?*

Betty Ong: *Okay, my name is Betty Ong. I'm number three on Flight 11.*

Sadler: *Okay.*

Betty Ong: *And the cockpit is not answering their phone. And there's somebody stabbed in business class. And there's, we can't breathe in business class, somebody's got Mace or something. . . . Okay. Our number one is, got stabbed. Our purser's stabbed. Nobody knows who stabbed who, and we can't even get up to business class right now because nobody can breathe. . . .*
And we can't get the cockpit, the door won't open. Hello? . . .

Supervisor Nydia Gonzalez: *This is Operations.*
What flight number are we talking about?

Sadler: *Flight 12.*

Gonzalez: *Flight 12, okay—*

Betty Ong: *No, we're on Flight 11 right now. This is Flight 11. . . . Boston to Los Angeles. . . . Nobody can call the cockpit, we can't even get inside. Is anybody still there?*

Sadler: *Yes, we're still here.*

Betty Ong: *Okay, I'm staying on the line as well.*

RADIO TRANSMISSIONS UNINTENTIONALLY BROADCAST TO AIR TRAFFIC CONTROL BY HIJACKER MOHAMED ATTA
Courtesy of the Federal Aviation Administration

8:24 a.m.: *We have some planes. Just stay quiet, and you'll be okay.*
We are returning to the airport.

Seconds later: *Nobody move. Everything will be okay.*
If you try to make any moves, you'll endanger yourself and the airplane.
Just stay quiet.

8:34 a.m.: *Nobody move please. We are going back to the airport.*
Don't try to make any stupid moves.

7:35 am
Hani Hanjour passes through Washington Dulles International Airport security to board Flight 77

7:35 am
Security camera footage of commuters traveling through the World Trade Center PATH station

FLIGHT 77 HIJACKERS AT DULLES INTERNATIONAL AIRPORT, SEPTEMBER 11, 2001
Courtesy of the U.S. Department of Justice
COMMUTERS AT THE WORLD TRADE CENTER PATH STATION, SEPTEMBER 11, 2001
Courtesy of the Port Authority of New York and New Jersey

The five terrorists who hijacked Flight 77 were videotaped as they passed through Dulles's west checkpoint. Three set off metal detectors, but no weapons were found, and they proceeded to the gate. The hijackers were carrying concealed knives on their person or in their carry-on luggage. Before 9/11, knives were allowed on planes if the blade was less than four inches in length. Simultaneously, tens of thousands of people were passing through the turnstiles at the PATH station below the World Trade Center en route to offices in the complex and elsewhere in lower Manhattan.

8:14 AM

FLIGHT 11 IS HIJACKED
Boston Air Traffic Control Center is alerted to a possible problem aboard Flight 11 when Captain John A. Ogonowski and First Officer Thomas F. McGuinness, Jr., do not respond to a routine radio communication.

FLIGHT 175 TAKES OFF
United Airlines Flight 175 takes off from Boston for Los Angeles. Nine crew members, 51 passengers, and five hijackers are on board.

8:19 AM

FLIGHT ATTENDANT CALLS AMERICAN AIRLINES
Flight crew members aboard hijacked Flight 11 convey critical information to airline personnel on the ground. Veteran flight attendant Betty Ann Ong transmits information to American Airlines reservations employees for about 25 minutes, using an in-flight phone. During the call Ong relays the terrorists' seat numbers, as does flight attendant Madeline Amy Sweeney in a separate call to a manager at Boston Logan International Airport. The calls enabled authorities to identify the perpetrators quickly.

8:20 AM

FLIGHT 77 TAKES OFF
American Airlines Flight 77, en route to Los Angeles, takes off from Washington Dulles International Airport. Six crew members, 53 passengers, and five hijackers are on board.

HIJACKED FLIGHT 11 APPROACHING THE NORTH TOWER, WORLD TRADE CENTER

Video by Jules Naudet and Gédéon Naudet, © Goldfish Pictures, Inc.

AFTER 9/11

With the story of the day coming full circle, the third and final section of the historical exhibition attends to the aftermath of 9/11. Here, we enter into a fractured landscape, defined by disparate though concurrent responses in the immediate days and weeks after the attacks. As the world struggled to take in the massive devastation and the unthinkable toll in human lives, people around the world gathered to express shared grief and solidarity. Heightened anxiety was experienced side by side with resurgent patriotism, evidenced in the proliferation of American flags draped off balconies, affixed to car antennas, pinned to jacket lapels. Meanwhile, in a lower Manhattan blanketed with dust and debris, the desperate search for the missing continued around the clock, even as funerals and memorial services were already being scheduled, and as recovery operations commenced at all three attack sites.

In telling the story of the nine-month recovery at Ground Zero, the exhibition tracks the painstaking search for human remains and ultimate clearing of nearly two million tons of debris from the site. Film footage of bucket brigades that were part of the initial recovery is projected onto a damaged remnant of one of the iconic Twin Tower tridents that were part of the buildings' facades. As we hear the voices of recovery workers recounting their experiences, it is as if the steel is sharing its own memory of witness. The random nature of what was found at the site—a cache of letters, keys, a child's doll, golf balls—attests to the serendipity of survival. The beloved Cross at Ground Zero, a crossbeam that became a locus of spiritual comfort for many of the workers, testifies to the search for meaning and hope amid the destruction. The story of 9/12—the days, weeks, and months following the devastation of 9/11, epitomized by acts of compassion, public service, and volunteerism that significantly contributed to the cleanup and recovery efforts—is shared, as are the personal reflections of ironworkers, first responders, forensic experts, and operators of the enormous excavating equipment required to transform "the pile," a mountain of tangled steel, into a pit before the recovery effort officially ended in late May 2002.

The exhibition's chronological narrative closes with the ceremony of removing the Last Column from the site. But the exhibition itself continues. A final chapter explores issues being negotiated in the open-ended context of the post-9/11 world and poses ongoing questions arising out of 9/11: How do democratic societies effectively balance civil liberties with national security in a world where terrorism is a real and present threat? What are the ongoing physical and mental health effects of 9/11, and what is our obligation as a society to those who suffer from them? How should we memorialize?

As we exit the historical exhibition, we are reminded of the multitude of ways people have turned grief into constructive action by combining remembrance with service, whether it be a quilter providing comfort to strangers through the work of many hands or an educator building a school in Afghanistan. With our pathway illuminated by the *Tribute in Light*—the twin beams of light that shine every September 11 to evoke the memory of the Twin Towers and the brightness of too many lives taken far too soon—we are guided by the final words of the National September 11 Memorial mission statement:

May the lives remembered, the deeds recognized, and the spirit reawakened be eternal beacons, which reaffirm respect for life, strengthen our resolve to preserve freedom, and inspire an end to hatred, ignorance, and intolerance.

GROUND ZERO, SEPTEMBER 2001
Photograph by Heera Kapoor, Here is New York Collection, New-York Historical Society, Gift of Here is New York

MOURNING AND MEMORIALIZATION

The urge to mourn alongside others brought people together throughout New York City and across the country. People gathered in parks and town halls, on college campuses, in places of worship, and elsewhere. Spontaneous memorials appeared in town squares, on roadside billboards, in murals painted on the sides of buildings, and outside firehouses and police stations. Across the nation, flags were flown at half-staff in recognition of the country's loss and candlelight vigils were held in remembrance of the victims and in solidarity against terrorism. The death toll on 9/11 included nearly 3,000 individuals from more than 90 nations and stirred sympathy around the globe.

VIGIL IN UNION SQUARE PARK, NEW YORK CITY, MID-SEPTEMBER 2001

Photograph by Brandon Remler

Just hours after the towers' collapse, New Yorkers congregated in Union Square Park, a historical gathering place at 14th Street in Manhattan. This street marked the southernmost point accessible to the public immediately after the attacks. For more than two weeks, people brought flowers, flags, and candles, and they chanted songs of peace, patriotism, and faith.

"GLOBAL RESPONSE" INSTALLATION IN THE HISTORICAL EXHIBITION

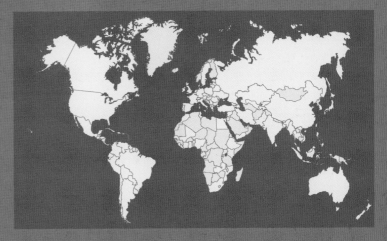

Antigua and Barbuda	Guyana	Sierra Leone
Argentina	Haiti	South Africa
Armenia	Honduras	South Korea
Australia	India	Spain
Austria	Indonesia	Sri Lanka
Azerbaijan	Iran	Sweden
Bangladesh	Ireland	Switzerland
Barbados	Israel	Syria
Belarus	Italy	Taiwan
Belgium	Jamaica	Thailand
Belize	Japan	Togo
Bolivia	Jordan	Trinidad and Tobago
Brazil	Kazakhstan	Turkey
Burma	Kenya	Ukraine
Canada	Lebanon	United Kingdom, including
Chile	Liberia	Bermuda, Montserrat, and
China, including	Lithuania	the British Virgin Islands
Hong Kong	Malaysia	United States of America,
Colombia	Mali	including Guam,
Côte d'Ivoire	Mexico	Puerto Rico, and the
Croatia	Moldova	U.S. Virgin Islands
Cuba	Morocco	Uruguay
Cyprus	Mozambique	Uzbekistan
Czech Republic	Netherlands	Venezuela
Dominica	New Zealand	Vietnam
Dominican Republic	Nigeria	Yemen
Ecuador	Pakistan	Yugoslavia (Serbia and
Egypt	Panama	Montenegro)
El Salvador	Paraguay	Zambia
Ethiopia	Peru	
France	Philippines	This list of countries and
Gambia	Poland	territories is based on
Georgia	Portugal	information provided by
Germany	Romania	victims' next of kin; the NYC
Ghana	Russia	Commission for the United
Greece	Saint Lucia	Nations, Consular Corps and
Grenada	Saint Vincent and the	Protocol; and the National Park
Guatemala	Grenadines	Service. Place names are listed
		as they were known in 2001.

In those early hours and days,
we truly believed he would be found.
—Lindsey Murdock, daughter of **R. Mark Rasweiler**

THE MISSING

Almost immediately, the faces and names of the missing began to appear on flyers created by relatives and friends. Descriptions included details such as height, weight, birthmarks, scars, and tattoos. The flyers were taped to walls outside hospitals, in heavily trafficked locations such as train stations, and on lampposts, bus shelters, telephone booths, and store windows. Internet forums emerged as portals to share information. Family members and friends called hospitals and hotlines established by the airlines and World Trade Center companies, and they waited at home for news. Hoping their loved ones were still alive, relatives showed missing posters to anyone likely to have seen the people in question, as well as to television reporters who could broadcast the images more widely. As the chances for survival faded, the posters themselves became memorials, adorned with messages, flowers, flags, and personal tributes.

PANEL FROM PIER 94 FAMILY ASSISTANCE CENTER

Presented with permission of the City of New York and the New York City Office of Emergency Management, custodian of the property on behalf of unknown persons and donors

The New York City Mayor's Community Assistance Unit set up a temporary center to assist people concerned about loved ones believed to have been at the World Trade Center. First located at a hospital, the center moved to progressively larger spaces until September 17, when a passenger ship terminal at Pier 94 on the Hudson River was transformed into a family assistance center. Staffed by hundreds of workers from more than 50 agencies, the center provided legal, financial, and mental health services to victims' relatives. Missing posters and messages to loved ones lined its walls.

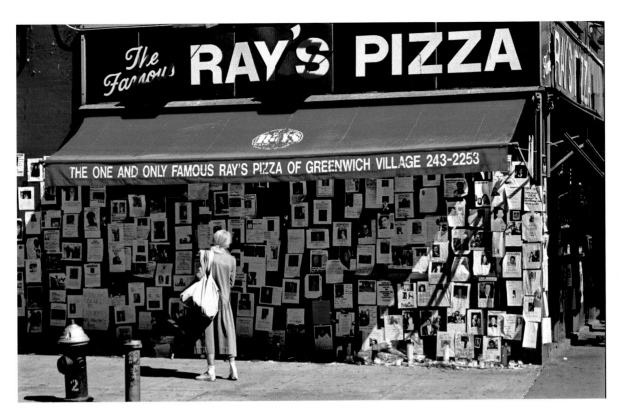

PIZZERIA AT 11TH STREET AND SIXTH AVENUE, NEW YORK CITY, FALL 2001
Photograph by David Turnley, Corbis

FIRST MONTHS AFTER

In the first few months after 9/11, feelings of grief, anger, fear, anxiety, and loss were pervasive. Communities gathered for ceremonies of mourning and remembrance. Newspapers published profiles of those who were killed, bringing names, faces, and lives into focus. Television networks struggled to revise their programming to fit the national mood, and broadcast news reports fixated on the terrorist attacks and their aftermath during the weeks and months following 9/11. Fear of additional terrorist attacks lingered. Government warnings to be prepared for an emergency intensified a sense of vulnerability and uncertainty. The 9/11 attacks also stirred patriotic feelings. Some individuals were inspired to enlist in the U.S. military. Others hung flags at home and work. The reopening of capital markets in New York City less than a week after 9/11 stimulated a sense of confidence and resilience. However, economic uncertainty persisted nationwide. Mayor Rudolph Giuliani called upon New Yorkers to go about their daily lives and support local establishments, and he reassured tourists that New York was a safe destination. Locally and nationally, individually and collectively, America struggled to regain its bearings.

Come here now. . . . Enjoy our thousands of restaurants, the museums and sporting events and shopping and Broadway; but also come to take a stand against terrorism.
—New York City Mayor Rudolph Giuliani

IMMEDIATE AFTERMATH TELEVISED
Courtesy ABCNews VideoSource; CNN Image Source; ITN/Fox News; NBC/NBCU Photo Bank, Getty Images; Robin Hood Foundation

It was so dusty. It looked like a moonscape.
The whole neighborhood, every leaf, everything was covered in dust.

—Kerri Courtney, Battery Park City resident

AERIAL VIEW OF LOWER MANHATTAN AND THE WORLD TRADE CENTER SITE, SEPTEMBER 23, 2001

Photograph courtesy of the National Oceanic and Atmospheric Administration

LOWER MANHATTAN

Immediately following the attacks, emergency personnel and barricades turned lower Manhattan into a "frozen zone." Mail delivery was suspended. Schools, courthouses, and most businesses were closed. Subway service was disrupted and public bus service stopped. Bridges, tunnels, and roadways were barred to all vehicles except those needed in rescue and recovery efforts. Businesses dependent on tourism lost revenue. Proof of residence was required to enter the restricted area, effectively isolating those who still lived there. Within a week, the frozen zone contracted significantly, but access to the area remained limited. Although the frozen zone had geographic boundaries, a distinctive smell of burning drifted far beyond Ground Zero and persisted for months.

CHELSEA JEANS MEMORIAL

Collection 9/11 Memorial Museum, Gift of the New-York Historical Society, Courtesy of David and Sabina Cohen; Photograph by Barbara Alper, Here is New York Collection, New-York Historical Society, Gift of Here is New York

Dust, ash, and debris from the collapsed Twin Towers filled the interior of Chelsea Jeans, a nearby retail store. Store owner David Cohen resolved to capture the moment in time by maintaining part of the store as it appeared after 9/11. This memorial was seen by thousands, including rescue and recovery workers, people returning to work in the area, and those coming to Ground Zero to pay their respects. After a struggle to stay in business, the store closed in October 2002. The New-York Historical Society removed and preserved the memorial as documentary evidence.

INTERIOR OF BROOKS BROTHERS STORE, ONE LIBERTY PLAZA, A COMMERCIAL BUILDING ADJACENT TO THE WORLD TRADE CENTER SITE, SEPTEMBER 12, 2001
Photograph by © Sean Hemmerle, Contact Press Images

AMERICA IN SHOCK

The 2001 terrorist attacks were the deadliest foreign strike on American soil and the first major attack by a foreign entity since the 1941 bombing of Pearl Harbor. It awakened both a new sense of vulnerability and resurgent patriotism. American flags appeared everywhere from lapel pins to automobile antennas. Many feared additional attacks, including the use of chemical and biological weapons. Anxiety about terrorism characterized the "new normal."

The U.S. government initiated a Global War on Terror. Within the first month after 9/11, the U.S. announced the formation of the Office of Homeland Security, declared war on "a radical network of terrorists and every government that supports them," and launched military operations in Afghanistan, thought to be the hiding place of al-Qaeda leader Osama bin Laden. While there was not a public consensus about military action, many Americans supported the nation's armed forces and affirmed patriotic resolve. And while the declaration of war and ensuing military measures were not an accusation of Islam, nonetheless, some Americans remained suspicious of anyone perceived to be Muslim.

"AMERICA IN SHOCK" INSTALLATION IN THE HISTORICAL EXHIBITION

PRESIDENT GEORGE W. BUSH AMID THE WRECKAGE OF THE WORLD TRADE CENTER, NEXT TO RETIRED FIREFIGHTER BOB BECKWITH, WITH NEW YORK GOVERNOR GEORGE PATAKI, SEPTEMBER 14, 2001

Photograph by Eric Draper, George W. Bush Presidential Library and Museum

Standing atop a pile of debris, President Bush addressed the rescue and recovery workers: "I can hear you! The rest of the world hears you! And the people who knocked these buildings down will hear all of us soon!"

VENDOR SELLING SOUVENIRS WITH PATRIOTIC MOTIFS, NEW YORK CITY, FALL 2001

Photograph by Barbara Kirshenblatt-Gimblett, Here is New York Collection, New-York Historical Society, Gift of Here is New York

***THE NEW YORKER* MAGAZINE WITH MEMORIAL COVER FEATURING BLACK-GHOSTED TOWERS, SEPTEMBER 24, 2001**

Collection 9/11 Memorial Museum, Gift of Timothy G. Stickelman, Cover © 2001, The New Yorker, underlying art © 2001 by Art Spiegelman and Françoise Mouly, used with permission

RECOVERY AT THE PENTAGON

A swift and efficient recovery at the Pentagon—a symbol of America's military strength and headquarters of the U.S. Department of Defense—was deemed vital to national security. A high priority was to retrieve files, disks, and hard drives containing sensitive military information from structurally unstable areas. Meanwhile, the search for victims, personal property, and criminal evidence proceeded both inside the building and outside on the west lawn and North Parking Lot. Leading the firefighting and rescue efforts, the Arlington County Fire Department contained the flames by the evening of September 12, 2001. It would take days to extinguish the blaze completely. Still, civilian and military employees, many of whom had survived the attack on 9/11, returned to work at the Pentagon on September 12. The task of recovering human remains and evidence was completed two weeks later. Thousands of mourners attended a memorial service overlooking the attack site on the one-month anniversary. After a seven-day-a-week demolition operation beginning on October 18 and focused on the damaged western side of the Pentagon, workers commenced reconstruction of the building on November 19.

RECOVERY OPERATIONS ON THE PENTAGON'S WEST LAWN, SEPTEMBER 14, 2001
Photograph by Technical Sergeant Cedric H. Rudisill, U.S. Department of Defense

PRAYER CARD RECOVERED FROM THE PENTAGON CRASH SITE

Collection 9/11 Memorial Museum, Gift of the family of Capt. Charles F. Burlingame III

Captain **Charles F. Burlingame III,** a 22-year employee of American Airlines and retired naval aviator previously stationed at the Pentagon, was the pilot of Flight 77. Since his mother's death in November 2000, Captain Burlingame had carried this memorial prayer card in his wallet. It was recovered at the crash scene.

I couldn't believe it was happening here. . . . These people, they had no reason to be in Somerset. They were just flying over it.

—Wallace Miller, Somerset County coroner

RECOVERY NEAR SHANKSVILLE

Within minutes of the crash of hijacked Flight 93 in a field in Somerset County, Pennsylvania, local firefighters and state police arrived on site. Assuming immediate jurisdiction of the crime scene, the Federal Bureau of Investigation was among 74 local, state, and federal agencies participating in the recovery effort. By week's end, both black boxes from the plane were retrieved intact, ultimately verifying that hijackers had reprogrammed the autopilot system for a Washington, D.C., destination and that passengers and crew had resisted. Also recovered were 14 knives, two of the perpetrators' passports, and a document handwritten in Arabic describing their plans. Victims' family members arrived within days, attending memorial services and providing DNA samples. When the FBI closed its field investigation in late September, the Somerset County Coroner assumed control of the site, eventually identifying remains of all passengers and crew members.

TRIBUTE ITEM LEFT AT THE FLIGHT 93 CRASH SITE

Courtesy of the National Park Service, Flight 93 National Memorial

Visitors flocked to the Flight 93 crash site to honor passengers and crew members who had attempted to gain control of the hijacked aircraft. They came to pay respects both to individual victims and to the collective heroic effort. Many brought objects decorated with American flags, religious symbols, and the phrase "Let's roll," attributed to passenger Todd M. Beamer when passengers and crew took action. Members of the military, law enforcement personnel, and representatives of various service organizations left mementos bearing their insignia.

SEARCH TEAMS INVESTIGATE THE CRATER FORMED BY THE CRASH OF FLIGHT 93, SEPTEMBER 12, 2001
Photograph by Tim Shaffer, Reuters

GROUND ZERO, SEPTEMBER 25, 2001

Photograph by Joel Meyerowitz, Courtesy Howard Greenberg Gallery

BUCKET BRIGADES, SEPTEMBER 13, 2001

Photograph by Mario Tama, Getty Images

RECOVERY AT GROUND ZERO

Within hours of the attacks, journalists began referring to the scene of mass destruction at the World Trade Center site as Ground Zero, a term for the epicenter of an explosion. The search for survivors began immediately. The focus later shifted to the search for remains of an unknown number of victims. In less than a week, thousands of rescue personnel, investigators, engineers, laborers, and volunteers had arrived to join the effort. Particles of pulverized concrete, smoke, and omnipresent dust made breathing difficult, while smoldering fires and unstable surfaces created extremely hazardous conditions. Over the next nine months, recovery workers cleared approximately 1.8 million tons of debris, excavating 70 feet belowground. Surrounding the site, American flags and photographs of the missing were visible reminders of the workers' commitment and resolve. In late May 2002, a ceremony marked the close of the recovery effort.

PILGRIMAGE TO GROUND ZERO

Thousands gravitated to Ground Zero to pay their respects to victims of the disaster and witness the devastation firsthand. Although photography was prohibited, many visitors brought cameras to document their pilgrimage and the enormous task of recovery. A temporary ramp and platform allowed visitors a safe and dignified place for reflection. The public viewing platform opened on December 30, 2001, and was accessible with free, timed tickets. Its plywood walls were left bare so that visitors might inscribe their own messages and read those left by others. By the time the platform was disassembled in the summer of 2002, the boards were filled with signatures, inscriptions, memorial cards, and tributes left by tens of thousands of visitors from around the world.

Designated a crime scene, the World Trade Center site was off-limits to civilian photographers. Photographer Joel Meyerowitz convinced New York City officials of the need for a historical record of both the devastation and the recovery. Chronicling its changing landscape over the next eight months, he produced an unparalleled archive of more than 8,000 images that record the challenges faced by workers.

SEARCH AND RESCUE

Search and rescue teams, along with volunteers, immediately converged on Ground Zero. Many offered their expertise to locate survivors trapped in the wreckage. Federal Emergency Management Agency Urban Search and Rescue teams from 14 states supported the work of local police and firefighters. Rescuers used special tools to peer into voids and searched for remnants of stairwells and elevators that might have sheltered survivors. Uniformed responders, building trades workers, and volunteers formed bucket brigades, passing rubble from person to person to tackle the monumental task of clearing debris in search of survivors and victims. Aware that the window for survival was limited, many workers stayed at the site for days. The search continued long after it was realistic to think that anyone would have survived beneath tons of steel and burning debris. Only 18 people were found alive at the site. The last successful rescue occurred midday on September 12.

Even though there [were] two hundred twenty stories of offices, I never saw a computer. I never saw a chair. I never saw a desk. It was either red iron or concrete dust.
—Joseph Bartlett, FEMA Florida Task Force 2

"SEARCH AND RESCUE" INSTALLATION IN THE HISTORICAL EXHIBITION

DOLL FOUND IN RUBBLE AT GROUND ZERO
Collection 9/11 Memorial Museum,
Gift of Brian Van Flandern

**RECOVERY WORKER SEARCHES FOR
REMAINS AT GROUND ZERO, MAY 2002**
*Photograph by Joel Meyerowitz, Courtesy Howard
Greenberg Gallery*

**THE CROSS AT GROUND ZERO
(OPPOSITE PAGE)**
*Recovered from the World Trade Center site after
September 11, 2001*
*Collection 9/11 Memorial Museum, Courtesy of the
Port Authority of New York and New Jersey
and the New York City Building Construction and
Trades Council*

Few recognizable objects survived the collapse of the Twin Towers. Among them were metal keys, random souvenir items, and a large quantity of golf balls, designed to withstand intense pressure. One notable example was a doll found in the rubble. The toy, known as Little Red, did not belong to a victim but was in fact the mascot of the Chances for Children charity, located on the 101st floor of the North Tower.

RECOVERY OF HUMAN REMAINS

In addition to searching for survivors, finding the bodies of victims buried in the ruins of the World Trade Center was a primary goal for those who worked at the site. Using their hands and small tools, rescue and recovery workers dug through debris piled 70 feet high and extending equally far belowground. Spotters scrutinized debris as operating engineers controlling grappler claws lifted loads of steel and all that was entangled in them. Dogs trained to find remains assisted in the search. Following the advocacy of operating engineer Pia Hofmann, civilians' remains were soon afforded the same honor in removal as had been previously reserved for the remains of uniformed responders. A member of the clergy was summoned, an honor guard formed, and the remains were draped with an American flag as they were carried from the site. By the time the site was cleared in spring 2002, nearly 20,000 separate human remains, but few intact bodies, had been recovered. The force of the towers' collapse and the fires that burned for months left no trace of many victims. The New York City Office of Chief Medical Examiner has been responsible for the work of identifying remains. As of the 15th anniversary of 9/11, 40 percent of World Trade Center victims had not been identified, despite the extraordinary efforts to recover and identify them.

FINDING MEANING AT GROUND ZERO

Workers at Ground Zero struggled to come to terms with the horrific circumstances at the site. Some sought to counter the sense of utter destruction by holding on to something recognizable, whether a metal bolt or a shard of glass salvaged from the debris. Others, contending with the absence of survivors and the frequent recovery of human remains, found purpose by forging relationships with relatives of a particular victim, carrying a memorial card or photograph to bolster their resolve. Some workers turned to symbols of patriotism to reinforce a sense of commitment and community, hanging American flags in multiple locations across the site. During breaks, some ironworkers cut symbols and shapes out of discarded steel to give as mementos and tokens of comfort to other workers and victims' relatives.

Recovery workers found an intersecting steel column and crossbeam in the rubble of 6 World Trade Center. Perceived as a religious cross by many who saw it, the steel fragment was relocated to the edge of the site near West Street to increase its visibility and accessibility to workers and victims' family members. Hundreds working on the recovery attended a ceremonial blessing of the cross and weekly services by Father Brian Jordan, a Franciscan priest ministering to the Ground Zero community. Individuals of

THE CROSS AT
GROUND ZERO

Ground Zero was such a tight-knit community, and all that work, all those months, were because we felt like we had to give something back.

—Debora Jackson, Salvation Army volunteer

many faiths and belief systems at the site and around the world saw the cross as a symbol of hope, faith, and healing.

In the aftermath, some people's spiritual convictions were challenged. Clergy members of many faiths were granted access to the World Trade Center site to bless recovered remains and to comfort rescue and recovery workers confronted daily with horrific evidence of death and violence. Many sought comfort in counseling, the solace of ceremonies and rituals, and religious symbols. One firefighter searching for victims at Ground Zero came upon a torn Bible fused to a piece of metal. Open to a passage in Matthew, chapter 5, the fragment's legible text includes the phrase "an eye for an eye," followed by ". . . resist not evil: but whosoever shall smite thee on thy right cheek, turn to him the other also."

DEMOLITION AND EXCAVATION

The New York City Department of Design and Construction managed demolition, excavation, and debris removal operations at Ground Zero, working with other government agencies and coordinating construction workers from numerous building trade unions. They had to dismantle what remained of the Twin Towers and five other buildings at the World Trade Center site in an efficient manner that also facilitated the recovery of victims. The site was divided into quadrants, each assigned to a primary contractor. The endeavor involved creation of access roads and ramps, stabilization of shifting wreckage, and removal of vehicles from the underground parking garages and train stations. As excavation work proceeded, objects recovered from Ground Zero came from the highest and lowest areas of the buildings, from the top floors of the towers to their basement levels. A continuing challenge was how to remove debris without further damaging human remains or creating even more unsafe conditions. The site itself was hazardous. Jagged, razor-sharp steel, subterranean hot spots, and contaminants in the air and in debris posed constant threats. During the nine months of recovery, there were few serious injuries and no fatalities. Nonetheless, the recovery effort at Ground Zero exacted a toll on the health and well-being of the workers.

DEMOGRAPHICS OF GROUND ZERO

By noon on 9/11, the New York City Department of Design and Construction had begun assembling a team of engineers and contractors to assess the damage and implement a strategic response to clearing the wreckage so firefighters and police could search for survivors and victims. Ironworkers and other members of the construction and demolition trades, knowing their skills would be in immediate demand, reported directly to the World Trade Center site or coordinated with building contractors and union leaders to assure the deployment of personnel and equipment to best advantage. Committed to showing the world that the terrorists had not broken the nation's spirit, many worked beyond their assigned shifts in the humanitarian effort to return the remains of victims to their families. This workforce, spanning a breadth of vocations and skills, formed a community that also included volunteers offering food and comfort to the workers and the bereaved who congregated at the site.

PAY TELEPHONE FROM THE 107TH FLOOR SOUTH TOWER OBSERVATION DECK

Courtesy of the AT&T Archives & History Center

SIGNAL FROM THE BELOWGROUND PATH TRAIN STATION

Recovered from the World Trade Center site after September 11, 2001, Collection 9/11 Memorial Museum, Courtesy of the Port Authority of New York and New Jersey

SIGN RECOVERED FROM THE WARNER BROS. STUDIO STORE ON THE CONCOURSE LEVEL OF THE WORLD TRADE CENTER

Recovered from the World Trade Center site after September 11, 2001, Collection 9/11 Memorial Museum, Courtesy of the Port Authority of New York and New Jersey

"DEMOLITION AND EXCAVATION" AND "DEMOGRAPHICS OF GROUND ZERO" INSTALLATIONS IN THE HISTORICAL EXHIBITION (OPPOSITE PAGE)

RELIEF CENTERS

Within days of 9/11, places where rescue and recovery workers could grab a cup of coffee, eat a meal, or simply unwind sprang up near Ground Zero. Some relief centers, like the massive white tent nicknamed the Taj Mahal, evolved as part of disaster response plans of the Salvation Army and American Red Cross. Others were spontaneous initiatives. Restaurateur David Bouley transformed an abandoned storefront into the Green Tarp Café, named for the tarpaulin draped over its broken windows. There, celebrity chefs prepared thousands of hot meals for weeks. The cruise ship *Spirit of New York* and the hospital ship USNS *Comfort* became floating relief centers, providing meals, hot showers, and beds. Nearby restaurants like Nino's and Capsouto Frères offered hospitality away from the site. At St. Paul's Chapel, open around the clock, workers could rest, receive massages, listen to live music, and enjoy letters of support and artwork sent in thanks for their efforts. Many volunteers traveled to lower Manhattan from across the country to provide assistance.

LANYARD WORN BY THERAPY DOG AT GROUND ZERO

Collection 9/11 Memorial Museum, Gift of Frank Shane, K-9 Disaster Relief, in memory of Nikie

Nikie, a golden retriever, worked at Ground Zero with his handler, Frank Shane. Trained by K-9 Disaster Relief, a humanitarian organization that uses dogs to help disaster victims, Nikie received credentials through the American Red Cross. Wearing a work vest, a bandana, and booties to protect his paws, Nikie roamed the site and respite centers with Shane. Offering comfort in a grim place, Nikie provided relief from the emotional stress of recovery work.

ST. PAUL'S CHAPEL, FEBRUARY 18, 2002
Photograph by Larry Racioppo

INVESTIGATORS IN A DEBRIS FIELD AT FRESH KILLS LANDFILL, NOVEMBER 2001
Collection 9/11 Memorial Museum, Gift of the photographer, Michael Falco

THE THREE SHADES, IN THE
OFFICES OF CANTOR FITZGERALD,
CIRCA 1990
Photograph courtesy of Howard W. Lutnick

FRAGMENT OF THE THREE
SHADES, A BRONZE SCULPTURE
BY AUGUSTE RODIN (FRENCH,
1840-1917), 1902-1904 (CAST 1989),
RECOVERED AT FRESH KILLS
*Courtesy of Howard W. Lutnick/
Cantor Fitzgerald*

*I knew that based upon the devastation we saw,
people were not going to be getting many things back. . . .
Everything with an image on it—we had thousands of
ID cards—or anything we felt would have
personal value, like jewelry, we vouchered and safeguarded.*

—James Luongo, Deputy Inspector, NYPD, Fresh Kills Incident Commander

FRESH KILLS LANDFILL

Beginning at daybreak on September 12, and continuing through the end of the recovery, roughly one and a half million tons of World Trade Center wreckage were transported by truck and barge to the newly reopened Fresh Kills Landfill on Staten Island. Meaning "fresh water," its name reflects New York's Dutch colonial past. Vast open space, relative isolation, proximity to lower Manhattan, and accessibility made Fresh Kills the most viable location for conducting the massive human remains and evidence recovery operation. Two dozen federal, state, and city agencies staffed the forensic operation. In total, investigators recovered tens of thousands of pieces of personal property and more than 2,300 human remains, which have been matched with more than 700 victims. Some 9/11 family members objected to the use of a landfill for such a sensitive purpose. Some continued to advocate for a renewed search for remains so that burial could take place.

Cantor Fitzgerald, a bond brokerage firm, maintained offices on floors 101 to 105 of the North Tower and sustained the largest loss of life from one company on 9/11. Its reception areas and conference rooms had displayed works of art, primarily from the collection of the firm's cofounder, B. Gerald Cantor. Fragments of bronze sculptures, including a torso from 19th-century French sculptor Auguste Rodin's *The Three Shades*, were recovered at Fresh Kills. When workers found the figure, they discovered a gaping hole where the heart should be.

THE COMPLEXITIES OF DISPLAYING WORLD TRADE CENTER DUST

BY JAN SEIDLER RAMIREZ

Senior Vice President for Collections and Chief Curator

On September 11, 2001, Roger Hawke fled his 54th-floor law office in the North Tower shortly after hijacked Flight 11 cut its fatal path though the building. His evacuation down the crowded stairwell was, in every sense, arduous. Upon reaching the street, he waded through debris from the fallen South Tower before reorienting himself, and then walked five miles north to his daughter's apartment to shower off the grit covering him. Hawke's safe arrival occasioned intense mutual relief. Loath to track dirt into the apartment, he left his dust-covered shoes at the door.

Among those greeting him was his son-in-law, the writer Colum McCann, who philosophized about Hawke's soiled footwear in an essay published four days later titled "Why does grandpa smell of smoke?" In the wake of the terrorist attacks that obliterated the World Trade Center, McCann observed that a new disquietude had seeped into the cityscape. He would later recall: "The dust on the windowsill, you know, you'd pick the dust up and then you'd wonder what was contained in that dust, whether it be the piece of flying paper that came down; whether it be a concrete girder; whether it be just an ordinary piece of New York dirt, whether it be an eyelash, whether it be, you know, someone's helmet from one of these young firefighters who walked up the stairs." Hawke's shoes seemed to embrace these perplexing possibilities, prompting McCann and his wife, Allison Hawke, to preserve them not only as a memento of Roger's deliverance but also of the inherent ambiguities of the dust pasted on the shoes.

Some years later, when these shoes were transferred to the 9/11 Memorial Museum, Ground Zero dust was no longer a hypothetical substance. It was understood as the elemental by-product of the World Trade Center cataclysm and its complicated legacy. Dust coats our collective memory of the day. This is especially true for those who witnessed the attacks, watched the plumes of smoke rising into the blue September sky, and experienced the otherworldly blizzard they discharged. "Everything was dust," recalled Raymond Thomas, a now retired lieutenant with the FDNY who responded downtown shortly before the collapse of the North Tower. "There was no office furniture; there were no computers; there were no flowerpots. There was nothing but dust, grayish, brownish, burning dust."

When the Twin Towers collapsed, their energy produced seismic waves that registered as two separate earthquakes in four surrounding states. The plumes released by those cascades consisted of unburned or partially burned jet fuel and 220 floors of macerated cement, office furniture, ceiling tiles, wall insulation, carpeting, fluorescent lights, plastics, electronics and cabling wires, sewage lines, air-conditioning and heating conduits, elevator equipment, window glass, and business documents. Asbestos, lead, mercury, silica, fiberglass, polychlorinated biphenyls, benzene, and sundry other contaminants were mixed into that slurry.

The debris clouds pushed outward, fouling anything in their path. Irritants wafted into the air. A ghostly chalk migrated inside banks, boardrooms, bodegas, and bedrooms. (The *Chelsea Jeans Memorial* installed in the Museum,

THE LAST COLUMN, WHICH WOULD BE THE FINAL PIECE OF TWIN TOWER STEEL TO BE REMOVED FROM GROUND ZERO AT THE END OF THE RECOVERY, MAY 20, 2002
Photograph by Joel Meyerowitz, Courtesy Howard Greenberg Gallery

with its racks of pallid merchandise, is a time capsule of that infiltration.) The rubble pile became a bake oven, emitting soot, fumes, and aerosols that stung the eyes and lungs of those in proximity to it.

The dust briefly muted the devastation's reality. With communication systems ruptured or erratic, rescue and recovery personnel scrawled urgent messages and motivational words for one another in the powder blanketing surfaces in the vicinity of the World Trade Center site. Subsequently, huge expense would need to be invested in removing the dust from workplaces, residences, stores, and schools in lower Manhattan. In its ambiguity, dust continued to incite grief, particularly for those victims' families who received no remains of loved ones and were thus denied any sense of closure through proper burial. Conversely, for some, dust acquired sacredness because of its intimate association with vanished loved ones.

The scope and anomaly of this dust resulted in the swift involvement of environmental science and public health experts to investigate its components. One of the first authorities granted clearance to obtain specimens was Dr. Paul J. Lioy of the Robert Wood Johnson Medical School in New Jersey, who first went to lower Manhattan less than a week after 9/11. On that trip, Lioy wondered at the strange, weirdly textured, fluffy, pink and gray powder he found. It bore no resemblance to any material he previously had seen, yet intuitively represented everything familiar "that makes up our workplaces and lives." In time, Lioy's research in collaboration with multiple laboratories and other scientists would map the jumbled chemistry of World Trade Center dust. This included its defining signature, slag wool, a thermal insulation fiber aggravating to the human respiratory system, where its large, coarse particles were never intended to be.

As experts hastened to gather Ground Zero dust samples to expand empirical understanding of its possible adverse effects on public health in the long term, so too were everyday New Yorkers conducting their own fieldwork. They scooped or swept dust into containers ranging from plastic food bags and empty juice bottles to food

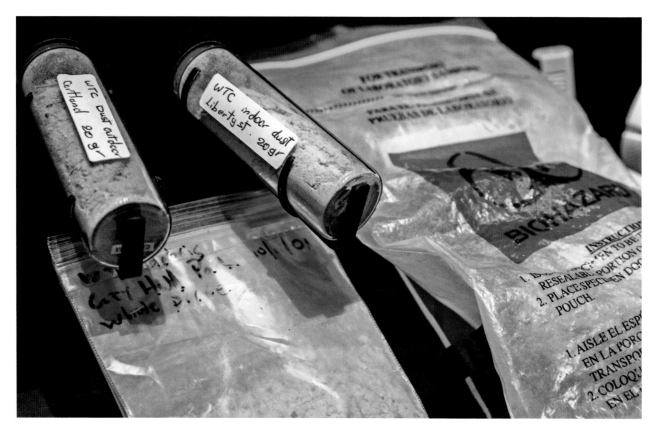

SAMPLES OF WORLD TRADE CENTER DUST AND DEBRIS *Collection 9/11 Memorial Museum, Gift of Dr. Paul J. Lioy, PhD, and Clifford P. Weisel, PhD, Environmental and Occupational Health Sciences Institute (EOHSI), New Jersey; Gift of Skip Blumberg; Recovered from the World Trade Center site after September 11, 2001, Courtesy of the Port Authority of New York and New Jersey*

jars and vacuum cleaner bags. A number of these dust-filled containers were later deposited with the Museum. Some in the downtown community, skeptical of government assurances about safe air quality in the wake of the attacks, commissioned laboratory analyses of the dust they had collected. Detected contaminants in the submitted specimens—including traces of asbestos and shredded glass—bolstered their suspicion that Twin Tower dust was beyond benign, if not conclusively malignant.

Compounding the blow of terrorism, thus, was an environmental disaster set in motion in lower Manhattan, the pernicious impact of which became clear after thousands had fallen sick. Hacking coughs and sinus complaints heard among Ground Zero's emergency workforce heralded those emerging illnesses. In January 2011, President Barack Obama would sign the James Zadroga 9/11 Health and Compensation Act of 2010, providing access to medical treatment to rising numbers of survivors, rescue and recovery personnel, cleanup crews, and local residents with 9/11-related health issues. The law also reopened the September 11th Victim Compensation Fund, dormant since 2004, extending coverage to individuals suffering financial losses due to such issues. As the 10th anniversary of the attacks approached, a belatedly named victim was ruled eligible for inclusion on the National September 11 Memorial, due to open that September. This death, like that of two other victims, occurred sometime after 9/11 and was attributed to complications from pulmonary sarcoidosis, specifically linked to dust from the collapse clouds inhaled while escaping on the day of the attacks.[10]

Disposing of the dust presented its own set of challenges, inextricably linked to the heartbreaking reality of death by incineration and compression on September 11. Through this filter, Ground Zero's ash and sludge cannot simply be reviled as a toxic witches' brew without considering the possibility of its alternate identity as a matrix harboring microscopic human remains. Hundreds of objects infused with dust—mostly personal accessories, garments, and boots—have been offered to the Museum by donors mindful of that latter possibility.

One example is a pair of pants tinged with chalky dust that was donated by an emergency medical technician. He had worn these once navy-colored uniform slacks on 9/11, as he maneuvered through the debris at the World Trade Center site where he remained for several days to help. After finally returning home, instead of laundering or discarding the pants, he sealed them inside a plastic bag with a handwritten note: *"Pants worn 9-11-01 at the WTC. Please do not wash. The ash is the remains of those that died. God bless them!"*

For those developing the 9/11 Memorial Museum, World Trade Center dust posed an extraordinary set of challenges: it was a material requiring sensitive interpretation sufficiently agile to manage its multiple associations, from granules of precious people to menacing pollutant. Yet it also was a substance requiring care and preservation according to professional museum standards.

Preserving dust is not a normative museum function. The American Institute for Conservation of Historic and Artistic Works has long noted its adverse impact on objects and artworks. Dust's properties include abrasiveness, acidity, and bacterial factors that can accelerate staining and corrosion. In most museum display settings, dust is considered unsightly, obscuring surface details and indicating poor gallery maintenance. At the same time, the ethics of historic preservation advocate authenticity as a value paramount for collections held and presented at museums. "Removal of anything that comes with the object, including from its surface, constitutes irremediable alteration if it is subsequently shown that the removed feature was part of the object's integrity," conservators counsel.

In the context of artifacts salvaged from Ground Zero, the dust encrusted on them is comparable to a passport stamp, attesting to their journey through 9/11's torment. As collection curators, conservators, and exhibit planners, our obligation is to safeguard, not sanitize, that evidence of woe. However, with the charge of documenting a still unfolding history came an equal obligation to develop procedures that could ensure the stewardship of dust while facilitating both safe handling and respectful, even reverent, display considerations.

The complexities of associations with World Trade Center dust necessitated a set of curatorial and collections management practices responsive to the sensitivities of key stakeholders and to the security and safety of visitors and staff. For too many bereaved relatives and friends, Ground Zero dust is all that survived of their loved ones.

COMPOSITE *Recovered from the World Trade Center site after September 11, 2001*
Collection 9/11 Memorial Museum, Courtesy of the Port Authority of New York and New Jersey

Accordingly, the Museum ensures that no incoming materials glazed with perceptible dust residues are accessioned into the collection without being inspected by the NYC Office of Chief Medical Examiner, which can elect to test any suspect item for evidence of potential human remains. No such items thus far examined have proved positive.

Similarly, for thousands of responders, recovery workers, survivors, and others disabled by, dead from, or being tracked for illnesses correlated with environmental toxins found in World Trade Center dust, and for a general public understandably wary of environmental pollutants, 9/11's dust residuum is an assumed threat. Out of an abundance of caution, the Museum has taken exceptional steps to seek—and has received—independent guarantees that all dust-blemished artifacts scheduled for display are unassailably safe. Working with hazardous materials consultants, a preemptive protocol is employed for inspecting, handling, screening, mitigating, housing, and, if necessary, hermetically sealing artifacts bearing Ground Zero dust.

Unique to the circumstances of 9/11 at the World Trade Center, multi-ton artifacts known as composites prompted a similar, if more intense, set of concerns as the much smaller items of personal property encrusted with World Trade Center dust.

The composites are amalgamations of building elements produced as a result of the collapse of the Twin Towers. Fused by pressure and heat, they were formed by the pancaking of floor upon floor of the 110-story buildings and then burning at extremely high temperatures. Volcanic in appearance, the composites evidence the consumed, molten interiors of a modern workplace. They consist of striations of mashed rebar, drywall, floor decking, carpeting, cabling, electronics, and improbably, carbonized shreds of business papers, some with type still legible.

Aware of the haunting possibility—and certainly the perception—that traces of unidentified victims might be commingled in this solidified magma, Museum staff conferred with a cross-section of stakeholders as part of its established advisory process, the Museum Planning Conversation Series, to gauge the propriety of presenting one of two salvaged composites in the Museum. The Museum also convened three focus groups: one comprised of lower Manhattan residents, first responders, and recovery workers; one with individuals who lived in the New York City region on 9/11 but with no immediate, personal connection to the disaster; and a third consisting of victims' family members. All were invited to inspect the composites. Without exception, participants believed that one of them needed to be displayed. Acknowledging its potential to disturb, these groups felt that exhibiting a composite would most clearly demonstrate what had actually transpired at the World Trade Center on 9/11.

Still, there remained a minority of voices in the 9/11 community who advocated passionately for burying the composites rather than preserving or displaying them. Given this spectrum of viewpoints, the Museum team pursued more advanced analysis, enlisting forensic specialists from various fields—mass disaster investigators, metallurgists, medical examiners, hazardous materials experts, structural engineers, and detectives from the New York City Police Department—in an effort to confirm or eliminate the presumption of the presence of human remains. Their studies of surfaces, crevices, and interiors of fragments from the composites found no evidence of human remains, and multiple parties concluded that the temperatures required to create the composites exceeded heat levels required for human cremation.

While these examinations delivered a uniform verdict that the presence of identifiable human remains within the composite was virtually impossible, absolute proof would require an interior examination resulting in the composite's destruction. Dedicated to preserving the historical evidence and reassured by these studies, yet cognizant of the concerns and sensibilities of key stakeholders, the Museum team consulted with a panel of museum ethicists in order to reach a final decision about displaying the object.[11] A conclusion was reached. The composite would be presented as a unique, physical testament to the ferocity of the 9/11 attacks, while acknowledging forthrightly our inability to ever comprehend fully the circumstances in which thousands died that day.

Mirroring the ambiguities and multivalent character of World Trade Center dust, a single composite—now reposed in the Museum—concretizes the unknowable.

DETAIL VIEW OF THE COMPOSITE *Photograph by Lane Johnson*

BEYOND THE RECOVERY

In late May 2002, with the ceremonial removal of the Last Column, the major work of cleanup and recovery at the World Trade Center site officially ended. By September, the destroyed portion of the Pentagon was rebuilt, plans to create a national memorial at the Flight 93 crash site near Shanksville, Pennsylvania, were under way, and a process for deciding how to rebuild the World Trade Center site had begun. Though grief was undiminished, the country faced forward. The legacy of the 9/11 attacks would continue to define policy debates, civic discourse, and reflections on public safety, global politics, civil liberties, and finding the right balance between remembering and rebuilding.

RELATIVES OF 9/11 VICTIMS RALLY FOR AN INDEPENDENT COMMISSION TO INVESTIGATE THE 9/11 ATTACKS, WASHINGTON, D.C., JUNE 11, 2002

Photograph by Alex Wong, Getty Images

"BEYOND THE RECOVERY" INSTALLATION IN THE HISTORICAL EXHIBITION

STEEL STUDIED BY NIST AND FOUND TO BE DEFORMED DUE TO COMPRESSION AT THE ONSET OF THE NORTH TOWER'S COLLAPSE AT THE 98TH FLOOR

Recovered from the World Trade Center site after September 11, 2001, Collection 9/11 Memorial Museum, Courtesy of the Port Authority of New York and New Jersey

SIGN TRACKING TIME OSAMA BIN LADEN WAS AT LARGE

Collection 9/11 Memorial Museum, Gift of Cheryl Stewart

MARY FETCHET, MOTHER OF BRADLEY JAMES FETCHET, ADVOCATES FOR THE 9/11 COMMISSION'S RECOMMENDATIONS ALONG WITH OTHER RELATIVES OF VICTIMS AND MEMBERS OF CONGRESS, DECEMBER 1, 2004

Photograph by Mike Segar, Reuters

HOW DO WE KNOW WHAT HAPPENED ON 9/11?

In the wake of the 9/11 attacks, Americans and people from around the world demanded answers. How were 19 men able to hijack four commercial passenger jets for the purpose of using them as missiles? How could U.S. intelligence agencies have failed to detect the plot? What caused the Twin Towers and 7 World Trade Center to collapse?

Government scientists, university researchers, elected officials, counterterrorism experts, and independent analysts studied the causes and consequences of the attacks. Some searched for scientific explanations to facilitate a better understanding of the events and prevent future disasters. For example, the National Institute of Standards and Technology (NIST) studied steel recovered from the World Trade Center site to determine why and how the Twin Towers and 7 World Trade Center collapsed and to recommend improvements in building safety. In 2008, the International Code Council passed 23 building and fire code changes based on NIST's recommendations. Others sought to prove or challenge accounts of what had transpired. Conspiracy theorists have continued to question official narratives.

Some family members of those killed on 9/11 advocated for government investigations. Citizen-driven campaigns advanced various causes including disaster preparedness and skyscraper safety.

WHO SHOULD BE HELD ACCOUNTABLE?

By the afternoon of September 11, 2001, both the Central Intelligence Agency and Federal Bureau of Investigation had surmised that the al-Qaeda terrorist network was responsible for the attacks. Months later, after initially denying culpability, al-Qaeda's leader, Osama bin Laden, asserted his direct involvement. By April 2002, the plot's mastermind, Khalid Sheikh Mohammed, was implicated. Bringing these men and their fellow conspirators to justice became a fundamental goal of the U.S. government and others intent on holding them accountable for 9/11. Osama bin Laden was eventually killed in 2011 by U.S. Navy SEALs in Abbottabad, Pakistan. Like other efforts to thwart al-Qaeda, this mission reflected the work of untold numbers of men and women dedicated to ensuring U.S. and international security.

Some 9/11 family members filed lawsuits against the airline industry. Most eventually dropped their suits and elected to participate in the September 11th Victim Compensation Fund. 9/11 families also advocated for an investigation into weaknesses in the nation's security and intelligence infrastructure. In response, the U.S. Congress established the bipartisan National Commission on Terrorist Attacks Upon the United States. Known as the 9/11 Commission, the panel of former elected and appointed officials interviewed more than 1,200 individuals, held 19 days of hearings, and heard testimony from government officials, survivors, and terrorism experts. Its 2004 public report proposed a major overhaul of America's homeland defense, including 41 recommendations on domestic security, intelligence gathering and sharing, interagency communication, and foreign policy.

HOW CAN AMERICA PROTECT ITS CITIZENS FROM TERRORISM?

A heightened sense of vulnerability after 9/11 prompted calls for new strategies to keep the nation safe. The USA PATRIOT Act—which stands for Uniting and Strengthening America by Providing Appropriate Tools Required to Intercept and Obstruct Terrorism—expanded the government's intelligence-gathering tools and its ability to detain and deport immigrants suspected of terrorism. Many people continue to debate whether the country is safer as a result, and whether the methods employed effectively protect national security interests without compromising civil liberties.

To prevent future attacks, the U.S. government initiated a Global War on Terror, sending troops to Afghanistan and later to Iraq. One of the objectives was to undermine terrorism by enabling open, democratic elections in countries governed by repressive regimes. Many joined the military to defeat supporters of terrorism.

Since 9/11, al-Qaeda, other terrorist groups such as ISIS, and rogue individuals have committed acts of terror around the world. Increased public awareness and improved counterterrorism strategies have thwarted attempted attacks, but threats of new attacks persist. Debates about national security, civil liberties, and military action continue.

WHAT ARE SOME OF THE ONGOING PHYSICAL AND MENTAL HEALTH EFFECTS OF 9/11?

The 9/11 attacks have continued to affect the health and well-being of victims' families and friends, survivors, rescue and recovery workers, cleaning crews, and those living and working in the vicinity of the three crash sites. Some injuries were immediately obvious, requiring hospitalization, surgeries, and lengthy recuperations. Other injuries were less apparent, including emotional scars and later illnesses.

Questions arose about the long-term impact of exposure to the dust clouds that formed when the towers collapsed on 9/11 and the dangers of working at the site during the recovery. Days after the attack, the U.S Environmental Protection Agency declared the air in lower Manhattan safe. Subsequent tests showed that omnipresent dust—made of pulverized building materials, industrial chemicals, and electronics mingled with jet fuel residue—was hazardous.

Survivors, residents, workers, and concerned citizens fought for legal remedies for injuries, treatment expenses, and loss of work. After years of debate, the James Zadroga 9/11 Health and Compensation Act was passed by Congress in 2010 and reauthorized in 2015. The landmark bill provides financial compensation to individuals who suffered physical injury or death as a result of the 9/11 attacks and established a program to monitor and treat those with 9/11-related health conditions.

HOW ARE VICTIMS IDENTIFIED?

Identifying the nearly 3,000 individuals killed in the 9/11 attacks and returning their remains to their families were principal objectives for medical examiners at all three disaster sites.

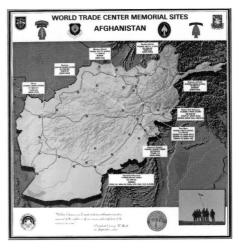

MAP OF AFGHANISTAN SHOWING WHERE WORLD TRADE CENTER STEEL WAS CEREMONIALLY BURIED BY U.S. MILITARY FORCES, NOVEMBER 2001–FEBRUARY 2002
Reproduction, Collection 9/11 Memorial Museum, Gift of 5th Special Forces Group (Airborne)

LAPEL PIN ISSUED BY THE WORLD TRADE CENTER SURVIVORS' NETWORK, A FORUM FOR SURVIVORS TO CONNECT AND SHARE RESOURCES
Collection 9/11 Memorial Museum, Gift of Peter Miller on behalf of the World Trade Center Survivors' Network

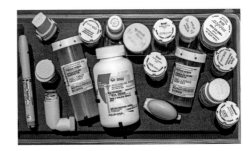

MEDICINE FOR RESPIRATORY AND OTHER AILMENTS BELONGING TO A PARAMEDIC WHO AIDED IN THE RESCUE AND RECOVERY EFFORTS AT GROUND ZERO
Collection 9/11 Memorial Museum, Gift of Freddie Noboa

FLIGHT 93 NATIONAL MEMORIAL, SOMERSET COUNTY, PENNSYLVANIA, OCTOBER 15, 2011

Photograph by Chuck Wagner, Shanksville, PA

PENTAGON MEMORIAL, ARLINGTON, VIRGINIA, SEPTEMBER 11, 2008

Photograph by Jonathan Ernst, Reuters

DANIEL LIBESKIND'S SKETCH PLACING THE MEMORIAL DESIGN INTO THE WORLD TRADE CENTER MASTER PLAN, 2004

Master plan sketch for the 9/11 Memorial by Daniel Libeskind

At the World Trade Center, the force of the towers' collapse and high-temperature fires meant that the bodies of victims were often fragmented, partially incinerated, and commingled with debris and other remains, making identifications particularly challenging.

The New York City Office of Chief Medical Examiner (OCME) launched the most complex forensic investigation in U.S. history, bringing together DNA experts, dentists, anthropologists, and other forensic specialists to maximize the number of positive identifications. The OCME asked victims' relatives for personal possessions that might contain DNA to match DNA extracted from recovered remains. The agency's efforts significantly advanced the technology used to extract usable DNA from minuscule samples, more than doubling the total number of victims identified.

At all three sites, identified remains of the hijackers were segregated from those of the victims. Remains of all Flight 93 victims were recovered, but remains of five Pentagon victims were never identified. Fifteen years after the attacks, remains of 40 percent of World Trade Center victims had not been identified. The commitment to use increasingly precise DNA analysis to identify World Trade Center victims is ongoing. Even with such advances, a large number of remains may elude positive identification.

HOW SHOULD WE REMEMBER?

The selflessness of first responders and many others on and after 9/11, together with the widely experienced impulse to help others in the aftermath of the attacks, forged a connection between 9/11 remembrance and public service. Immediately following the attacks and continuing long after, many people have channeled their grief and anger by volunteering, enlisting in the military, founding charities, contributing to philanthropic causes, or otherwise helping people in need.

Commitments to build permanent memorials at the three attack sites emerged relatively quickly, but took years to realize. The U.S. Congress authorized the Flight 93 National Memorial in September 2002. The first phase of the memorial, including marble walls engraved with the names of Flight 93's seven crew members and 33 passengers, opened on the 10th anniversary of 9/11. An interpretive center opened four years later in 2015.

The U.S. Department of Defense announced the Pentagon Memorial design in March 2003. The Pentagon Memorial was dedicated on the seventh anniversary of the terrorist attacks in 2008, featuring benches and reflecting pools that honor the 184 people killed at the military headquarters and on hijacked Flight 77.

In New York, Ground Zero was, for many, sacred ground and an unintended burial site, which made it particularly challenging to find the right balance between commemoration and redevelopment. Established in 2001 after the attacks, the Lower Manhattan Development Corporation (LMDC) received $2.8 billion in federal funding to support plans for revitalizing downtown, including rebuilding the World Trade Center site. The LMDC held hundreds of public hearings and consulted with the 9/11 community as plans for the site developed. In 2003, through a process led by New York State Governor George Pataki and New York City Mayor Michael R.

Bloomberg, the LMDC selected Studio Daniel Libeskind to create a master plan for the new World Trade Center. Libeskind's *Memory Foundations* site plan included a spiral of towers—the tallest rising 1,776 feet—encircling a memorial that preserved the towers' footprints. A portion of the foundation slurry wall would also remain. In 2003, an open competition for the memorial design received 5,201 entries from 63 countries. The design for the 9/11 Memorial was selected by a jury that included architects, artists, curators, government officials, scholars, and a 9/11 family member. The winning selection, *Reflecting Absence*, was submitted by the architect Michael Arad and completed with Peter Walker Partners.

On the 10th anniversary of the attacks, First Lady Michelle and President Barack Obama and former First Lady Laura and President George W. Bush joined family members of 9/11 victims at the Memorial dedication, officiated by New York City Mayor Michael R. Bloomberg. The 9/11 Memorial Museum opened in 2014.

> This great spirit of community and charity and selflessness
> that helped rebuild this city and this country in
> the aftermath of 9/11—if we can somehow bottle that
> and keep that going . . . then the terrorists don't
> win, and future generations learn not just about the attacks
> but how good people of the world responded.
>
> —Jay Winuk, cofounder of My Good Deed and brother of Glenn J. Winuk

SERVICE AND REMEMBRANCE

Many people channeled their grief into acts of public service and charitable efforts established in memory of 9/11 victims, as well as to honor those who survived and those who responded. New York City public school principal Ada Rosario Dolch helped to open a school built by the World Transformation Center in Afghanistan in memory of her sister, **Wendy Alice Rosario Wakeford**. Retired PAPD lieutenant William Keegan founded H.E.A.R.T. 9/11, which stands for Healing Emergency Aid Response Team, that dispatches rescue and recovery workers, 9/11 family members, and others to help communities and individuals recover from disasters. The parents of **Peter C. Alderman** established a foundation that trains caregivers in post-conflict regions to treat the psychological wounds of terrorism and mass violence. These are but a few of the many expressions of remembrance realized through service.

It may not be possible to ever fully prevent terrorism or forestall heinous acts by individuals intent on doing evil, but we do have control over how we respond. As witnesses to events unfolding in our time, how we choose to respond—participating in a charity run, enlisting in the military to serve the nation, rebuilding communities devastated by a natural disaster, training caregivers to assist victims of mass violence—demonstrates the best of our human nature rather than the worst.

U.S. PRESIDENTS AND FIRST LADIES AT THE NATIONAL SEPTEMBER 11 MEMORIAL DEDICATION, SEPTEMBER 11, 2011
Photograph by Pablo Martinez Monsivais, AP Photo

NEW YORK CITY MAYOR MICHAEL R. BLOOMBERG AT THE DEDICATION OF THE NATIONAL SEPTEMBER 11 MEMORIAL, SEPTEMBER 11, 2011
Photograph by Stan Honda/AFP, Getty Images

PROVIDING EDUCATIONAL OPPORTUNITIES, HERAT, AFGHANISTAN, JULY 2006
Photograph courtesy of Steve Smith

REBUILDING AFTER THE 2010 EARTHQUAKE WITH H.E.A.R.T. 9/11, HAITI, APRIL 5, 2011
Photograph by Robert Kolodny/House of Nod, Inc., Courtesy of H.E.A.R.T. 9/11

To remember and to reflect. But above all, to reaffirm the true spirit of 9/11—love, compassion, sacrifice—and to enshrine it forever in the heart of our nation.

—U.S. President Barack Obama

TRIBUTE IN LIGHT, SEPTEMBER 11, 2012
Photograph by Jin S. Lee

Tribute in Light is a commemorative public art installation first presented six months after 9/11 and then every year thereafter, from dusk to dawn, on the night of September 11. Visible as far as 60 miles from lower Manhattan and reaching up to four miles into the sky, the twin beams were conceived by several artists and designers who were then brought together under the auspices of the Municipal Art Society and Creative Time: John Bennett, Gustavo Bonevardi, Richard Nash Gould, Julian LaVerdiere, and Paul Myoda, with lighting consultant Paul Marantz.

*Life and love cannot be extinguished by blind,
anonymous murder. And neither can the
best of our country. That when someone does
this, all the good things about life and love
and country can be killed, but only with the
permission of the victims who are left behind.
If we do not give that permission, if we build
a sensible response to this, but one which still
reflects what we loved about the people we lost
and what we loved about the country that was
attacked, no matter how bad it is they can't
take the good away.*

—Bill Clinton, 42nd President of the United States,
1993-2001; Founder, Clinton Foundation
[Recorded in 2013]

SEBASTIAN JUNGER
AUTHOR AND JOURNALIST;
COVERED AFGHANISTAN
BEFORE AND AFTER 9/11

CHRISTINE QUINN
SPEAKER OF THE
NEW YORK CITY COUNCIL, 2006–13

CHARLES SCHUMER
U.S. SENATOR (NY) SINCE 1999

REFLECTING ON 9/11

The attacks of September 11, 2001 continue to shape lives and influence public discourse. The enduring impact of the attacks is experienced daily in heightened airport security measures, continuing debates over how to protect civil liberties while ensuring national security, and questions about the extent of military intervention required to root out terrorism. In *Reflecting on 9/11*, visitors contribute their own thoughts about these and other timely issues and hear from others, including prominent political leaders, historians, and journalists, who have contributed the same. The video interviews presented in this gallery are drawn from a vast archive and demonstrate that responses to 9/11 are as varied as the countless individuals whose lives have been, and still are, affected by the attacks. Visitors can record their own stories, memories, and opinions in three adjacent recording booths. Selections from their recordings are regularly integrated into the media programs. In *Reflecting on 9/11*, everyone has a voice.

**SELECTED PARTICIPANTS IN
"REFLECTING ON 9/11" INSTALLATION**

ERIC HOLDER
U.S. ATTORNEY GENERAL, 2009–15

MARJORIE MILLER
WIFE OF JOEL MILLER ✈ (WTC);
FORMER FAMILY OUTREACH COORDINATOR,
WTC FAMILY CENTER

ANTHONY D. ROMERO
EXECUTIVE DIRECTOR,
AMERICAN CIVIL LIBERTIES UNION

DAVID L. BEAMER
FATHER OF TODD BEAMER ✈ (FLIGHT 93)

FARAH PANDITH
SPECIAL REPRESENTATIVE TO
MUSLIM COMMUNITIES,
U.S. STATE DEPT., 2009–14

TOM RIDGE
FIRST SECRETARY, U.S. DEPARTMENT
OF HOMELAND SECURITY, 2003–05

NORTH TOWER EXCAVATION

Like its counterpart at the South Tower footprint, the North Tower Excavation reinforces the archaeological context of the Museum and reveals the underpinnings of what remains of exterior structural columns that once formed the facades of the Twin Towers. Where the South Tower Excavation frames the story of World Trade Center construction, here along the northern edge of the North Tower footprint the excavation of column remnants provides a setting for documentary photographs taken during the earliest days of the rescue and recovery effort at the site.

A walkway that dips down to accentuate the depth of the column footings brings visitors to a spot that aligns with the point of impact, approximately 1,200 feet above, where hijackers crashed American Airlines Flight 11 into the North Tower, tearing a gash in the building more than 150 feet wide. At this place, the building's history—from construction to destruction to recovery—is connected physically, visually, and thematically, intensifying the authenticity of the experience.

WITNESS AT GROUND ZERO

September 12–16, 2001
Photographs by Stephane Sednaoui

In 2001, French photographer and video director Stephane Sednaoui was living on Great Jones Street in lower Manhattan. On the morning of September 11, he witnessed and filmed the events at the World Trade Center from the roof of his building. Over the next few days, Sednaoui volunteered in the urgent rescue efforts underway at what was already being called Ground Zero. This exhibition draws on an archive of more than 500 pictures he captured over three nights between September 12 and 16 and during breaks from the grueling work of digging through the wreckage.

FOUNDATION HALL

With ceiling heights ranging more than 50 feet tall and nearly 17,500 square feet of floor space, Foundation Hall offers a place of reflection for a community of memory. In this dramatic space, U.S. President Barack Obama dedicated the Museum in May 2014, and here, too, in September 2015, Pope Francis led a multi-religious meeting for peace.

Here, visitors encounter the more than 36-foot-high Last Column, the very last piece of Twin Tower steel to be removed from the World Trade Center site at the end of the recovery period in May 2002. Covered with messages, prayer cards, and memorabilia, this totem of the recovery was driven out of the site on a flatbed truck, draped with an American flag, escorted by an honor guard. Here it stands tall, again.

Two touchscreen stations enable exploration of all areas of the column. On the reverse sides of each, a Scroll of Honor recognizes the rescue and recovery workers' dedication and determination, listing the names of thousands of individuals who participated in the recovery efforts at all three crash sites and Fresh Kills Landfill on Staten Island, whether as ironworkers, representatives of other trades, first responders, or volunteers. Visitors see themselves and the Last Column reflected in the mirrored surface on which these names appear. It is a subtle reminder that the task of recovery and rebuilding is within the reach of all of us.

Other elements in Foundation Hall, such as a dynamic timeline and artifact cases, focus on the ongoing relevance of 9/11 in our communities and our lives. Continually growing registries track the experiences of witnesses and survivors of the attacks, the contributions of rescue and recovery workers, and 9/11 memorials around the world.

Providing a dramatic backdrop to Foundation Hall is a monumental portion of the original slurry wall, the retaining wall built to hold back the Hudson River when the World Trade Center was under construction. On 9/11, as approximately 1.8 million tons of debris crashed to earth, piling up across the site, the slurry wall was challenged. Within a month, recovery workers discovered a crack; had the wall breached, the disaster in lower Manhattan would have been even more unimaginable. But it held. And, in holding, the slurry wall has become a symbol of the strength, fortitude, and endurance of our values and our nation. Here in the Museum, it is both a literal foundation of what was once here and a metaphoric foundation for what we now can build.

THE SLURRY WALL

The proximity of the Hudson River posed a significant challenge to the original excavation and construction of the World Trade Center, which began in 1966. River water threatened to seep into or flood the site. The slurry wall technique, not previously employed on such a vast scale, presented a novel solution that led to the construction of a watertight enclosure known as the bathtub, only this bathtub kept water out, not in.

THE LAST COLUMN (OPPOSITE PAGE)

Recovered from the World Trade Center site after September 11, 2001
Collection 9/11 Memorial Museum, Courtesy of the Port Authority of New York
and New Jersey
The preservation of this artifact was made possible in part by the Institute of Museum
and Library Services via Save America's Treasures

The Last Column, a 58-ton, 36-foot-tall piece of welded plate steel, was one of 47 columns that supported the inner core of the South Tower. When the South Tower collapsed, this remnant remained anchored in bedrock, buried beneath the wreckage. Toward the end of the recovery period, the Last Column assumed symbolic status among recovery workers and observers. Individuals marked the column with their names and agencies, messages, photographs, and other memorial tributes.

On the evening of May 28, 2002, the Last Column was cut down by recovery workers and lowered onto a flatbed truck while bagpipers played "Amazing Grace." The column was then shrouded in black and draped with an American flag. Two days later, it was removed from Ground Zero.

SOUTH TOWER GLASS

Recovered from the World Trade Center site after September 11, 2001
Collection 9/11 Memorial Museum, Courtesy of the Port Authority of New York
and New Jersey

Almost all of the more than 40,000 windows in the Twin Towers shattered on September 11, 2001. Only one windowpane, from the 82nd floor of the South Tower, is known to have survived intact. Jan Szumanski, superintendent for Tully Construction at Ground Zero, discovered the unbroken pane of glass still set within a fragment of the South Tower facade that penetrated Church Street. He extricated the glass and was aided in its preservation by Joseph Carsky, Tully's chief engineer.

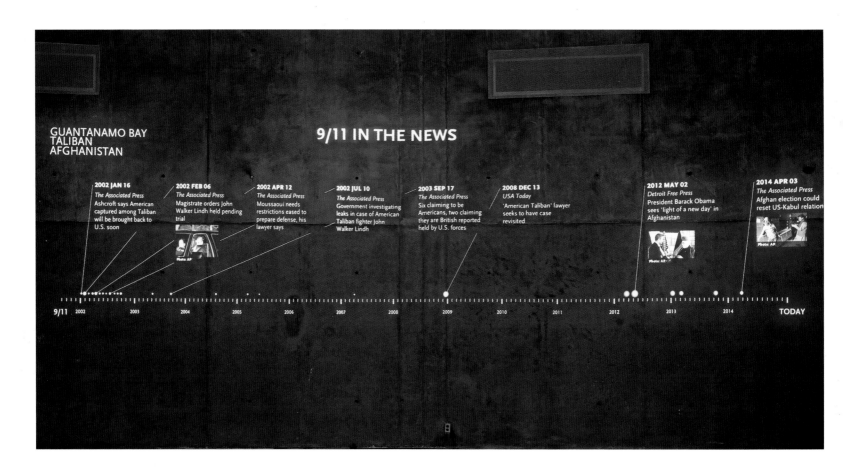

9/11 IN THE NEWS

GUANTANAMO BAY
TALIBAN
AFGHANISTAN

2002 JAN 16
The Associated Press
Ashcroft says American captured among Taliban will be brought back to U.S. soon

2002 FEB 06
The Associated Press
Magistrate orders John Walker Lindh held pending trial

2002 APR 12
The Associated Press
Moussaoui needs restrictions eased to prepare defense, his lawyer says

2002 JUL 10
The Associated Press
Government investigating leaks in case of American Taliban fighter John Walker Lindh

2003 SEP 17
The Associated Press
Six claiming to be Americans, two claiming they are British reported held by U.S. forces

2008 DEC 13
USA Today
'American Taliban' lawyer seeks to have case revisited

2012 MAY 02
Detroit Free Press
President Barack Obama sees 'light of a new day' in Afghanistan

2014 APR 03
The Associated Press
Afghan election could reset US-Kabul relation

9/11   2002   2003   2004   2005   2006   2007   2008   2009   2010   2011   2012   2013   2014   TODAY

TIMESCAPE

Designed by Local Projects with Mark Hansen, Ben Rubin, and Jer Thorp

Timescape is a digital media installation that highlights the ongoing significance of the 9/11 terrorist attacks. It uses a computer algorithm that searches an always-growing database of millions of news articles and finds key terms that frequently appear with references to 9/11. Articles with common themes are identified, grouped together, and displayed on a timeline. In this way, *Timescape* highlights events reported in the news over time that connect back to 9/11. An additional feature tracks stories in the news each day that relate to the attacks and their legacy, reinforcing the idea that 9/11's impact continues to the present moment.

THE HUNT FOR OSAMA BIN LADEN (OPPOSITE PAGE)

In a televised speech from the White House on May 1, 2011, U.S. President Barack Obama delivered the news that Osama bin Laden, the al-Qaeda leader responsible for the 9/11 attacks, had been killed in a targeted military strike carried out by U.S. Navy SEALs. Assuring 9/11 victims' families and the nation that "justice has been done," the President also asserted that the fight against al-Qaeda would continue. Throughout New York City and Washington, D.C., the streets filled with scenes of people gathering to mark the successful raid. Many were concerned about what bin Laden's death would mean for global security and world events. These concerns remain today, as al-Qaeda and other terrorist networks continue to plot violent attacks and counterterrorism experts and civilians approach the global threat with vigilance.

Shirt worn by U.S. Navy SEAL Team Six member during raid on Osama bin Laden's house

Intended for wear under body armor, this camouflage shirt was worn by one of the U.S. Navy SEAL Team Six members who was present when Osama bin Laden was killed during the May 1, 2011 (EDT), nighttime raid on his hideout in Abbottabad, Pakistan. Referencing bin Laden by his codename, the assault team radioed members of the joint Special Operations Command, "For God and country—Geronimo, Geronimo, Geronimo. Geronimo E.K.I.A. [enemy killed in action]."

The success of that high-risk mission, known as Operation Neptune Spear, ended a global manhunt—that started before 9/11—for the ringleader of the al-Qaeda terrorist network.

The American flag patch on the shirt is rendered in black and brown to blend in with the camouflage pattern. The flag is backwards, a symbolic gesture referencing the era when the flag-bearer led soldiers behind him on the charge to battle.

9/11 in the News: The Hunt for Osama bin Laden

In a televised speech from the White House on May 1, 2011, U.S. President Barack Obama delivered the news that Osama bin Laden, the al-Qaeda leader responsible for the 9/11 attacks, had been killed in a targeted military strike carried out by U.S. Navy SEALs. Assuring 9/11 victims' families and the nation that "justice has been done," the President also asserted that the fight against al-Qaeda would continue.

Throughout New York City and Washington, D.C., the streets filled with scenes of people gathering to mark the successful raid. Many remained concerned about what bin Laden's death would mean for global security and world events. These concerns remain current today, as al-Qaeda and other terrorist networks continue to plot violent attacks and counterterrorism experts and civilians remain vigilant to threats around the globe.

U.S. President Barack Obama, along with members of the national security team, monitors the mission in the Situation Room of the White House, May 1, 2011 (EDT)
Photograph by Pete Souza, The White House

Operation Neptune Spear commemorative coins

Brick from Osama bin Laden's house in Abbottabad, Pakistan

Eluding capture, al-Qaeda leader Osama bin Laden and his family had been living in a "safe house" in Pakistan for several years before he was killed in 2011. Local authorities razed the compound in February 2012. Before the complex was completely demolished, journalist Domenic Di Natale obtained a brick from the house's foundation as a souvenir. A correspondent with Fox News then based in the capital city of Islamabad, Di Natale had been reporting on the War on Terror and the international manhunt for bin Laden.

At the start of Kindergarten I
Witnessed + remem

This is a
story of

As a child I grew
up in Brooklyn
I worked at a...
late dinny college
I will never forget
this ultimate
is open
Kindergarten the NYC public school.
3 of us were left at the end of
the

We will

Sending a prayer to
all those who lost
their live Steph Ebony

In memory of the
victimes an

God Bless You All
Loven Prayers
IBEW 716

SAN FRANCISCO
P.D.

Co. G - NEVER FORGET

G.

We were mere kids when this
happened. Now as adults we
understand the impact of this
tragic event and respect all
who lost their lives & th

AND HE WILL WIPE OUT EVERY
TEAR FROM THEIR EYES AND
DEATH WILL BE NO MORE.
REVELATIONS 21:4

GOD BLESS AME!

PROL

Kevin M
Kubler - A man
Who is a hero, brave,
+ A true Amer.

Nasze serca biją
W tym samym żalu.
b

STÖRST AV ALL
Ar

WE SHALL NOT
FORGET THIS DAY.
PEA

We'll Never
Forget!!!

Ruth + Vanard Mendinghall
We Will n

l'Italia
NON d

VLAI

8th Grade Science class
is when I got the news. I remember

Stai

SIGNING STEEL

Recovered from the World Trade Center site after September 11, 2001
Collection 9/11 Memorial Museum, Courtesy of the Port Authority
of New York and New Jersey

As we move toward the escalator that will take us up from bedrock, we make one final stop alongside a dramatic remnant of World Trade Center steel. This column once stood in the core of the South Tower, probably between floors 30 and 33. During the tower's collapse, extreme stresses caused this multi-ton piece of steel to fold over onto itself.

At kiosks next to this column we can sign our names, make an observation, or voice a promise. Soon, the words we write appear on a map projected onto the adjacent area of the slurry wall, appearing geographically in the vicinity of each of our home cities and nations.

The map on which these words appear is similar to the map we saw at the head of the Ramp—the global map that fractured on the morning of 9/11. Now the map is coherent and whole, once again. And what is holding it together are all of us and the promises we make.

We came in as individuals. And we'll walk out together.

—Joe Bradley, operating engineer and recovery worker at Ground Zero, May 2002

ANNIVERSARY CEREMONY AT THE WORLD TRADE CENTER SITE, SEPTEMBER 11, 2002

Photograph by Mike Segar, Getty Images

EXIT FROM BELOWGROUND MUSEUM BACK UP TO MEMORIAL PLAZA

AFTERWORD

BY JAMES E. YOUNG

Distinguished University Professor of English and Judaic Studies,

University of Massachusetts, Amherst;

Jury Member, 9/11 Memorial Design Competition;

Adviser, 9/11 Memorial Museum

Our memorial culture has come a long way over the last few decades. Once upon a time, the aim of a nation's monuments and museums was to cast memory in stone, to establish a fixed and unyielding narrative of past events for the ages. A national monument or museum's life in the communal mind would thus grow as hard and polished as its exterior form, its historical meaning and significance as fixed as its place in the landscape.

National monuments and museums have long sought to provide a naturalizing locus for memory, in which a state's victories and defeats are commemorated as preternaturally ordained. By suggesting themselves as kin to the landscape's geological outcroppings, monuments and museums would cast a nation's ideals and founding myths as naturally true as the landscape in which they stand. These are the traditional monument's sustaining illusions, the principles of its seeming longevity and power. But as a generation of new memorial artists and museum designers and architects have made clear, neither these national monuments and museums nor the meanings they assign to memory are really everlasting. Both are constructed in particular times and places, as conditioned by and subject to the same forces of history as we are.

Beginning sometime after World War I and continuing through the commemorative art and architecture of World War II and the Holocaust, these traditional aims of national monuments and museums began to seem not just archaic but also part of the dangerously blinkered 19th-century imperial mindset that fomented such catastrophic wars. A new generation of memorial makers would now harbor a deep distrust for traditionally static forms of the monument, which in their eyes had been wholly discredited by their consort with the last century's most egregiously dictatorial regimes. The didactic logic of monuments and national museums—their demagogical rigidity and certainty of history—continued to recall too closely traits associated with totalitarian regimes like Nazi Germany and the former Soviet Union. A new generation of memorial artists would now rise up against the traditionally didactic function of monuments and museums, against their tendency to displace the past they would have us contemplate—and finally against the authoritarian propensity in monumental spaces that reduces visitors to passive spectators.

Perhaps no single national "monument" has changed the way we experience and remember the past and our fallen soldiers as profoundly as Maya Lin's 1982 Vietnam Veterans Memorial. Carved into the ground, a black wound in the landscape and an explicit counterpoint to Washington's prevailing white, neoclassical obelisk and statuary, Lin's design articulated loss without redemption and formalized a national ambivalence surrounding the memory of American soldiers sent to fight and die in a war the country now abhorred. In Maya Lin's words, she "imagined taking a knife and cutting into the earth, opening it up, an initial violence and pain that in time would heal." She opened a space in the landscape that would open a space within us for memory. "I never looked at the memorial as a wall, an object," Lin has written, "but as an edge to the earth, an opened side." Instead of a positive V-form (like a jutting elbow, or a spear tip, or a flying wedge military formation), she opened up the V's obverse space, a negative space to be filled by those who come to remember within its embrace. Moreover, as Lin described it in her original proposal, "The memorial is composed not as an unchanging monument, but as a moving composition to be understood as we move into and out of it." Where a traditional monument is fixed and static, her memorial would be defined by our movement through its space, memory by means of perambulation and walking through.

No longer content to allow our monuments and museums to remain fixed icons of remembrance, contemporary memorial and museum designers now ask these spaces to be animated by our visits, our walk-throughs, our questions about how these memorials and museums came to be in the first place. As the nation's monuments have changed from self-certain, overweening monoliths telling people what and how to remember, so too have national museums evolved, building into themselves the capacity to accommodate every new generation's reasons for coming to visit in the first place.

Rather than continuing to insist that national memorial museums establish and fix a particular national narrative and a singular self-aggrandizing interpretation of events, I've long believed that the best way to save a memorial museum from itself is to enlarge its life and texture to include its genesis in historical time, the activity and considered decisions that brought the museum into being. Rather than hiding the debates surrounding its origins, its production, its reception, its life in the mind, the best contemporary museums make these, too, part of their story. That is to say, rather than seeing polemics as a by-product of a memorial museum, I would make the polemics surrounding a museum's existence one of its central, animating features. In fact, I believe that a memorial museum succeeds only insofar as it allows itself full expression of the debates, arguments, and tensions generated in the noisy give-and-take among competing constituencies driving its very creation. In this view, both the history and memory of 9/11 as represented in a memorial museum might also be regarded as a never-to-be-completed process, animated (not disabled) by the forces of history bringing it into being.

The National September 11 Memorial Museum at the World Trade Center in New York City has been designed and curated with this contemporary, double-sided credo in mind: it aims to show and tell both what happened on that fateful day in 2001 and how what happened gets passed down to the next generation. By making the coming into being of this museum and its exhibits so palpably transparent, this publication serves to "unfix" its history and meaning, and thereby animate it. The Museum is constantly coming into being, animated by every visitor's experience. By opening to public view the excruciatingly complex issues of how to present disturbing images and artifacts, how to show or not show the perpetrators, and how to tell both the events leading up to 9/11 and its aftermath, this museum becomes a living, breathing archive of its own coming into being, its own decision making. This book invites readers as well as Museum visitors to work through them together to find answers. It's the arriving at and the working through of these design decisions where some of the most difficult memory work occurs.

This Museum lives because it makes room in its story for the visitors' stories, their memories of the day, their reminiscences of lost loved ones, even their experiences in the Museum itself. This Museum recognizes that the history and memory of 9/11 necessarily include histories and memories of the visitors themselves. The Museum's historical exhibition both documents the facts and the way these facts are now being presented, how they are being understood over time.

WHAT IS A MEMORIAL MUSEUM?

What does it mean to commemorate an event and to tell its history at the same time and in the same space?

The 9/11 Memorial Museum was built on a foundation of transparency and self-reflexive process, what we might even call a self-generating process that continues to carry the Museum forward in time. Rather than telling everyone what to think, the Museum mostly presents the material, stories, faces, and life stories of the victims and offers the time and space for visitors to figure out what to think, what to feel, what to do, and perhaps how to describe the ways they have been changed inwardly by their experiences of the Memorial and Museum.

As memorials have begun to open spaces in the landscape that might now open spaces within ourselves for memory, this museum similarly opens a portal, a way into understanding, into how it came to be in the first place. Its process has been transparent, with constant debate and negotiation as it came into being. Virtually every step of every conceptual and practical decision was vetted among a wide group of reviewers, and periodically major moves were also discussed with an advisory committee composed of museum professionals, historians, and cultural critics. This would become the first of what we might call a transparently self-critical and self-correcting museum, premised not on finding a single, self-certain, and self-serving narrative to tell but rather an opening of space for inquiry, debate, and discussion of what the events of that day mean to us now. And what they meant to us then, and what they may mean to us in 10, 20, or 30 years.

To my mind, this is a sea change in the very premises of a national museum of any kind. It is a space in which we strive to arrive at a national understanding of these events, even as we mourn the very specific losses of loved ones and their rescuers. It is a place for both civic and personal grieving. It is a space that encourages us to distinguish between national memory (defined by reciprocal give-and-take and constant reinterpretation) and nationalist memory (defined by a singular, fixed and self-serving national narrative). As noted in Museum Director Alice Greenwald's essay on page 15, the National September 11 Memorial Museum is, in Harold Skramstad's prophetic words, a place that does "not tell visitors what to think, but rather, what to think about."

In the early planning and design process, I found that the Museum's constant self-reflection was also a way of making the Museum. I found that in the staff's constant questioning and probing of every issue in a totally self-reflexive way, they were unwittingly creating a template for a new kind of contemporary museum. This Museum would not be a space for fixed stories, histories, and interpretations of that day in 2001 but a space for transparent inquiry, debate, and movement through the past into a constantly unfolding present moment. The emphasis of this Museum would be more on presenting than interpreting that day, the life stories of those killed, and the objects, artifacts, and remnants that connect us to the history.

That said, of course, any curated presentation of 9/11 is also an interpretation of events, an invitation to conflate the tactile materiality of artifacts with the meanings we attach to them. But by including the process by which these objects found their places in the permanent exhibition here, the Museum invites what I might call "interpretive circumspection," reminding visitors to be as self-conscious of their need for absolute meanings as the Museum is in constructing such meaning.

As described so vividly in this book by Alice Greenwald, in its open and transparent design process and constant reality checking with advisers and stakeholders, this Museum and its exhibitions became self-correcting. It confronted every possible issue head-on, addressed each one in depth, and arrived each time at a rationale for going forward, one step at a time. This is not an efficient process, obviously, but it was an incredibly effective process in arriving at the best possible design based on the clearest, most compelling conceptual foundation. Indeed, this Museum has already had a huge effect on how other nations are beginning to shape and tell their own painful histories of terror, as evidenced by Norway's national July 22 memorial process, which sought and then welcomed the advice and expertise of representatives of the 9/11 Memorial Museum, among other expert consultants.

This Museum leaves open the possibility for many stories to be told, including those of victims and survivors, first responders and their families, even stories of those around the world who watched the attacks and destruction of the towers on live television, as if they "were there." There will be competing stories, not all of them welcome, not all of them compelling or sympathetic. But the point is that this is not a place of didactic insistence on one meaning, or one lesson, or on one kind of experience on that day. It is not meant to "teach us" one thing about the 9/11 attacks on America but to leave room for visitors to figure out and arrive at their own understanding of that day, how it may have changed them inwardly and why, and how we understand the present moment in light of that terrible day.

Museum and exhibition designers set out on a daunting task when they asked themselves to show and tell about these events in their unfolding continuum, attempting to recall how the events of 9/11 were being grasped in real time. How to do this retrospectively is almost impossible, of course, since we all now know what happened that day. How to capture the uncertainty, the confusion, the inchoate imagery of the moment without turning it into a polished, seemingly foreordained story? Yet, somehow I believe the Museum has accomplished just this feat.

THE INTERPENETRATION OF MEMORY AND HISTORY IN A MEMORIAL MUSEUM

Where does memory end and history begin? As so brilliantly conceived by exhibition designer Dagmar von Wilcken, the Place of Information (really a small museum) underpinning Germany's national Memorial to the Murdered Jews of Europe in Berlin allows commemorative and historical dimensions to interpenetrate and become whole, in which neither history nor memory can stand without the other. As one descends the stairs from the midst of the Peter Eisenman-designed field of waving stelae into the underground Place of Information, it becomes clear just how crucial the underground historical exhibition is to the commemorative field of pillars above. By seeming to allow the aboveground stelae to sink into and thereby impose themselves physically into the underground exhibition space, the "Place of Information" audaciously illustrates both that commemoration is "rooted" in historical information and that the historical presentation is necessarily "shaped" formally by the commemorative space above it. Here we have a "place of memory" literally undergirded by a "place of history," which is in turn inversely shaped by commemoration, and we are asked to navigate the spaces between memory and history for our knowledge of events. Such a design makes palpable the yin and yang of history and memory. While remaining distinct in their respective functions, however, these two sides of the memorial are also formally linked and interpenetrating.

In post-9/11 New York, our memorial questions were very different: how to commemorate and articulate the loss of nearly 3,000 lives at the hands of terrorists and, at the same time, how to create a memorial site for ongoing life and regeneration? By necessity, the 9/11 Memorial and Museum would have to do both. This is why we, the memorial jurors, chose a design that had the capacity for both remembrance and reconstruction, space for both memory of past destruction and for present life and its regeneration. It had to be an integrative design, a complex that would mesh memory with life, embed memory in life, and balance our need for memory with the present needs of the living. It could not be allowed to disable life or take its place, but rather inspire life, regenerate it, and provide for it. It would have to be a design that animates and reinvigorates this site, but does not paralyze it, with memory.

In Michael Arad and Peter Walker's design for *Reflecting Absence*, we found both the stark expressions of irreparable loss in the voids and the consoling, regenerative forms of life in the pools of water and surrounding trees. The cascading waterfalls simultaneously recall the source of life and the fall of the towers, even as they flow into a further unreplenishable abyss at their centers to suggest irreparable loss and absence. The fuller and taller the trees grow, the deeper the volumes of the voids become. The taller the surrounding skyscrapers of the World Trade Center grow, the deeper the open commemorative space at their center becomes. In the National September 11 Memorial, the expressions of loss and regeneration are now built into each other, each helping to define the other. The Memorial plaza and names of the victims have been brought to grade, stitched back into the grid and fiber of the city streets of lower Manhattan. And finally, as the abstract *Denkmal* of stelae in Berlin is anchored in the hard historical facts of the Holocaust in the Place of Information below, the abstract 9/11 Memorial at street level is anchored by the underground 9/11 Memorial Museum built beneath it, which tells the hard history of that day, as well as the life stories of those who were lost in the terrorist attacks on September 11, 2001. Abstract memory is thus anchored in a place of history, both memory and history now dependent on the other for meaning. In effect, the aboveground voids reflecting absence and loss of the victims literally rest atop an exhibition space that fills this absence back in with the victims' life stories and the history of the day that took these people from us.

WHAT ROLE DOES SUCH A PUBLICATION PLAY?

What is it that you now hold in your hands, this exquisitely produced volume for the National September 11 Memorial Museum? Is it merely a "book version" of your visit to the Museum, or is it an extension of your visit?

Just as the Memorial and Museum are not substitutes for or replications of the terrible events of that day, but are deliberately opened-up spaces for contemplation and memory of that day, this book cannot be a substitute for the visitor's experience in the Museum itself. Rather, it is meant to open space in the visitor's mind for further contemplation, almost as if it were a spatial extension of the Museum. This book should be a trigger to further memory and historical inquiry and understanding, not a fixed answer to what happened that day and why we remember it now. Just as every visitor comes for his or her own reasons, readers will read for their own reasons.

As the Memorial's beautifully abstract and symbolically powerful voids aboveground are anchored in the hard historical narrative and artifacts housed in the Museum below, so too might the visitors' memory of their experience at the Memorial and Museum find its historical foundation in this volume.

Memory by means of perambulation through the wrenching exhibits below and the roaring waterfalls above now becomes memory by means of sitting still and reading. It is a physical pausing to contemplate what it all means, sitting in a quiet setting away from the crowds of tourists, the downtown bustle, the cacophony of horns and sirens, to listen to one's own private thoughts in the company of essays and reflections by others who also sat quietly somewhere to meditate on what these things mean to those who visit this Memorial and Museum. This afterword is not the last word, or the "end" of the book, but just another transitional stage in the Museum's ongoing afterlife in the mind of the visitor.

REFERENCE NOTES

1. See staff listing on page 224 for the names of the exhibition team leaders.

2. The Program Committee included Paula Grant Berry (co-chair), Howard W. Lutnick (co-chair), Debra Burlingame, Robert De Niro, Monica Iken, Anthoula Katsimatides, Kate D. Levin, Emily K. Rafferty, Tom Rogér, Jane Rosenthal, and Seth Waugh.

3. Advisers on the site-specific installation in Memorial Hall included Anita Contini, Susan K. Freedman, Kate D. Levin, Nancy Rosen, and Lowery Stokes Sims.

4. Members of the "kitchen cabinet" included Paula Grant Berry, David Blight, Scott Eberle, Barbara Kirshenblatt-Gimblett, Kate D. Levin, Mitchell Moss, John Rockwell, Jane Rosenthal, Deborah Schwartz, and James E. Young.

5. The audio recording extracted from Flight 93's cockpit voice recorder was placed under seal in the 2006 trial *United States v. Zacarias Moussaoui*. A transcript of the recording was also entered into evidence and subsequently released to the public. Several transmissions made by hijacker pilots—including two from Flight 93—were intended for passengers but instead were broadcast to and recorded by the Federal Aviation Commission (FAA). The FAA declassified and released these recordings in 2010.

6. Hijacker pilot Ziad Jarrah attempted to speak to passengers inside Flight 93's cabin, but mistakenly broadcast the announcement over an open frequency. It is heard instead by air traffic control and pilots on other planes.

7. The two audio clips used in the Museum's Flight 93 alcove program were the only transmissions that Ziad Jarrah or his fellow Flight 93 hijackers made that were broadcast to the ground (i.e., recorded by the FAA and subsequently released to the public). The rest of that particular cockpit recording remains under seal, available in transcript only.

8. There is no universally accepted way to transliterate Arabic words and names into English. While scholars and intelligence agencies may use different spellings, the 9/11 Memorial Museum largely follows the transliterations used by the 9/11 Commission, the Council on Foreign Relations, and the Combating Terrorism Center at West Point.

9. The academic advisers for the exhibition presentation on al-Qaeda and antecedents to the 9/11 attacks included Ahmad Dallal, at that time associate professor of Arab and Islamic Studies and chair of the department of Arab and Islamic Studies at Georgetown University; Bernard Haykel, professor of Near Eastern Studies at Princeton University; and Bruce Hoffman, professor of security studies and director of the Center for Security Studies at Georgetown University.

10. The three 9/11 victims whose deaths were attributed to lung complications from dust inhaled during the collapse of the towers and whose names appear on the Memorial are **Jerry J. Borg**, **Felicia Gail Dunn-Jones**, and **Leon Bernard Heyward MC Sundance**.

11. Members of the Museum Ethics Advisory Group included Elizabeth Greenspan, Janet Marstine, Michael Pickering, and Paul H. Williams.

ACKNOWLEDGMENTS

Under any circumstances, it would be a rare opportunity to contribute to the planning of a major civic enterprise and entirely new cultural facility. But to participate in the creation of a museum whose purpose is to commemorate the lives of nearly 3,000 individuals and honor those who toiled selflessly through the recovery; to document an event of profound historical significance for our nation and the world community; and to enshrine the very place where an atrocity occurred so that the alchemy of remembrance might transform tragedy into hope—this is a privilege like none other.

The journey that led to opening the 9/11 Memorial Museum was filled with untold challenges and uncharted territory; it was guided by imagination, creativity, ambition, and sheer persistence. This was a journey of shared dreams and aspirations, setbacks and satisfactions, arguments and resolutions and compromises. While there were moments when we agreed to disagree, those charged with this sacred responsibility demonstrated a relentless pursuit of excellence and a steadfast commitment to delivering a world-class museum that would educate, inspire, and touch the hearts of millions.

What was achieved could never have happened without a legion of participants, each contributing their best and giving their all, in spite of pressures and deadlines and, at times, delays and disappointments. Perseverance was key, as was a sense that this project in its entirety was far greater than the sum of its many parts. I want to express heartfelt thanks for the partnership of so many in this process, and for their devotion, dedication, extraordinary work ethic, profound empathy, sheer stubbornness, and highest standards of professionalism. I remain awed by their talents and humbled by the gift of their participation.

There are far too many people to thank by name; many (but not all of you) are listed in the pages that follow. I want to acknowledge, first and foremost, the family members of the victims for the generosity of their faith in our ability to honor—appropriately and with dignity—the precious lives of their loved ones. Heartfelt thanks go to representatives of other key constituencies who participated in the planning of the Museum, including survivors of the attacks, first responders, former recovery workers, and lower Manhattan residents and business owners, who graciously shared insights, perspectives, life stories, and personal effects. This project was blessed with extraordinary professional expertise—from the architects and landmark preservationists to the curators, oral historians, and conservators; educators, exhibition developers, design and construction managers, and exhibition designers and fabricators; the media producers, systems consultants, and integrators; and the owners' representatives, who together wove an array of imperatives and expectations into a fully realized experience of exceptional power.

We benefited from the wisdom of our advisers and the guidance and confidence of enlightened leaders willing to take a chance on an unconventional vision for a 21st-century memorial museum. In this respect, I must recognize the members of the Memorial's former Program Committee who steered the content development process through unimaginably rocky shoals: co-chairs Paula Grant Berry and Howard W. Lutnick, Debra Burlingame, Monica Iken, Anthoula Katsimatides, Kate D. Levin, Emily K. Rafferty, Thomas H. Rogér, and Seth Waugh.

No project of this scale and complexity could be realized without exceptional leadership at the helm. President and CEO Joe Daniels was a hands-on advocate and indefatigable champion of the project's goals and aspirations. Stalwart in their dedication to the Museum's realization, the Board of Directors generously shared expertise and provided much needed encouragement. Patricia E. Harris, in particular, provided thoughtful and visionary guidance throughout the project. Ultimately, it was the pragmatism, clarity of focus, and courageous decision-making of our Chairman, Michael R. Bloomberg, that were crucial factors in seeing this project through to completion.

This book was conceived as both a companion to a Museum visit and a faithful reflection of the experience of the Museum for those who have not yet had the opportunity to visit. In 2006, a small group of dedicated museum professionals formed the nascent core of what would become a full-fledged museum staff. This Museum would not be what it is, nor this book, without the sustained involvement of Clifford Chanin, Jan Ramirez, and Amy Weisser. The profoundly moving exhibitions and evocative visitor experience mirrored in the pages of this book owe a debt of gratitude to Michael Shulan. The expressive and engaging descriptions of artifacts presented in this book are based on an extensive exhibition script whose first draft—a prodigious effort and remarkable achievement—was entirely written by Amy Weinstein. Reviewed and vetted by multiple readers, that script and its adaptation for this book were subjected to rigorous fact-checking by Liz Mazucci and Kathy Fleming. Allison Blais, Michael Frazier, Shelby Prichard, and Alexandra Rhue provided thoughtful and exceedingly helpful comments. Key members of our Chairman's staff—including Kate D. Levin, Howard Wolfson, Nancy Cutler, Kim Molstre, and Jenny Ruvolo—offered invaluable guidance throughout the process of both building the Museum and producing this book. Finally, this book reflects the diligent and dedicated efforts of Amy Dreher, Ian Kerrigan, and Hicks Wogan, as well as Shanell Bryan, Samantha Cortez, Amanda Lynn Granek, Noelle Lilien, Natalie Pinkerton, Bethany Romanowski, and Christine Valentine; the photographic artistry of Jin Lee; the able assistance of Jaymie Van Valkenburgh; the inspired design of Yo Cuomo in close partnership with Bonnie Briant; and the supportive partnership of Rizzoli's Charles Miers and Jim Muschett. I thank each and every one of you.

The best of what we produce is also informed by those who are no longer here. Never a day went by that we didn't feel the obligation and the privilege of serving those whose lives were so senselessly taken on September 11, 2001 and February 26, 1993. In creating this Museum and this book, I wish to honor personally those who have taught me. What I've learned about museums as catalysts for moral reckoning, I owe to my mentor from the United States Holocaust Memorial Museum, the irrepressible and ingenious Shaike Weinberg. And what I know of memory, I owe to my parents and my sister. May all of their memories be a blessing, always.

At its core, the 9/11 Memorial Museum is a testament to love. We listen to the final words spoken by passengers and crew aboard doomed flights, by people who went to work one morning and got caught in a vortex of unthinkable horror. At that moment, they all spoke the same three words: "I love you." What has truly informed this effort is love. I have often quoted the trenchant observation that memorials are promises we make to the future about the past. What I know of love and its own promises to the future, I owe to my children and grandson. May this Museum, planted in the heart of lower Manhattan, grow in strength and beauty of purpose, and long remind us of the power of memory and of love to heal and transform us.

—Alice M. Greenwald, April 2016

U.S. PRESIDENT BARACK OBAMA AT THE DEDICATION OF THE NATIONAL SEPTEMBER 11 MEMORIAL MUSEUM, MAY 15, 2014
Photograph by Jin S. Lee

ACE CHARITABLE FOUNDATION

THE CAYRE AND CHERA FAMILIES

JON S. CORZINE

THE CROWN FAMILY

BRIAN CURY, EARTHCAM, INC.

FIONA & STANLEY DRUCKENMILLER

THE LEONA M. AND HARRY B. HELMSLEY
    CHARITABLE TRUST

PETER G. PETERSON

PITNEY BOWES INC.

THE PRUDENTIAL FOUNDATION

SANDLER O'NEILL & PARTNERS L.P.

BERNARD & ANNE SPITZER

TIME WARNER FOUNDATION

THE TISCH FAMILIES

DAN & SHERYL TISHMAN FAMILY FOUNDATION, INC.

UNITEDHEALTHCARE

VORNADO REALTY TRUST

THE WESTFIELD GROUP

ACCENTURE

AEA INVESTORS LP

ELIZABETH AND LEE AINSLIE

ANHEUSER-BUSCH INBEV &
    THE ANHEUSER-BUSCH FOUNDATION

AON

THE ASSOCIATED PRESS

AT&T

LOUIS AND GABRIELLE BACON

CABLEVISION SYSTEMS CORPORATION &
    THE MADISON SQUARE GARDEN CO.

CLEAR CHANNEL COMMUNICATIONS, INC.

THE COCA-COLA FOUNDATION

DALIO FAMILY FOUNDATION

DELOITTE

DELTA AIR LINES

THE DURST ORGANIZATION

EDELMAN

ERNST & YOUNG LLP

CHRISTINE A. FERER, IN MEMORY OF NEIL D. LEVIN

FORD FOUNDATION

FRANKLIN TEMPLETON INVESTMENTS AND
    FIDUCIARY TRUST COMPANY INTERNATIONAL

FRED ALGER MANAGEMENT, INC.

SOL & LILLIAN & JOYCE & IRVING GOLDMAN FAMILIES

THE MARC HAAS FOUNDATION –
    STANLEY S. SHUMAN, ROBERT H. HAINES

WILLIAM RANDOLPH HEARST FOUNDATION

HSBC

IRON WORKERS INTL UNION & CONTRACTORS THROUGH IMPACT

JETBLUE AIRWAYS

ROBERT WOOD JOHNSON 1962 CHARITABLE TRUST

THE THOMAS S. JOHNSON FAMILY IN MEMORY OF SCOTT M. JOHNSON

JULIA AND DAVID H. KOCH AND FAMILY

KPMG LLP

THE LEFRAK FAMILY

LEHMAN BROTHERS

STEVE AND SUE MANDEL

THE J. WILLARD & ALICE S. MARRIOTT FOUNDATION

MARSH & MCLENNAN COMPANIES

MCDONALD'S OWNER/OPERATOR ASSOCIATION OF NY/NJ/CT

THE MLB-MLBPA DISASTER RELIEF FUND &
    THE BASEBALL TOMORROW FUND

THE MOODY'S FOUNDATION

SUZANNE AND TOM MURPHY AND FAMILY

SAMUEL I. NEWHOUSE FOUNDATION

NEW YORK METS

NEW YORK YANKEES

STAVROS NIARCHOS FOUNDATION

INDRA AND RAJ NOOYI

OPPENHEIMERFUNDS

PEPSICO FOUNDATION

PRICEWATERHOUSECOOPERS LLP

INGEBORG AND IRA LEON RENNERT

JULIAN, JOSIE, SPENCER, JAY & ALEX ROBERTSON

EDWARD JOHN AND PATRICIA ROSENWALD FOUNDATION

JACK AND SUSAN RUDIN AND THE RUDIN FAMILY

RXR REALTY

STEPHEN AND CHRISTINE SCHWARZMAN

THE SCOTTS MIRACLE-GRO COMPANY

SL GREEN REALTY CORP.

ALFRED P. SLOAN FOUNDATION

STARR INTERNATIONAL FOUNDATION

TISHMAN SPEYER

UNION SQUARE HOSPITALITY GROUP

VIACOM AND PARAMOUNT PICTURES

THE WACHTELL, LIPTON, ROSEN & KATZ FOUNDATION

WEIL, GOTSHAL & MANGES LLP

JOAN AND SANFORD I. WEILL AND THE WEILL FAMILY FOUNDATION

THE WENDY'S COMPANY – NELSON PELTZ, PETER MAY

JOHN C. WHITEHEAD

WILLKIE FARR & GALLAGHER LLP

PUBLIC FUNDING PARTNERS

LOWER MANHATTAN DEVELOPMENT CORPORATION

U.S. DEPARTMENT OF HOUSING AND URBAN DEVELOPMENT

EMPIRE STATE DEVELOPMENT CORPORATION

THE PORT AUTHORITY OF NEW YORK AND NEW JERSEY

CITY OF NEW YORK

EXHIBITS, ARTIFACTS, AND PROGRAM AREA SPONSORS

TRIBUTE WALK (page 68) is dedicated in honor of the victims, survivors, and first responders of September 11, 2001, with generous support from BANK OF AMERICA

The **EDUCATION CENTER** and **CLASSROOM C** (page 72) promote learning about the past to ensure a better future, with generous support from NEW YORK LIFE

The **FAMILY ROOM** has been made possible through the generosity of FRED ALGER MANAGEMENT, INC.

The **MUSEUM STORE** has been made possible through the generosity of PAUL J. NAPOLI & MARK J. BERN, NAPOLI BERN LLP

The **RECORDING STUDIO** has been made possible with support from NEW YORK METS, STAVROS NIARCHOS FOUNDATION, ALFRED P. SLOAN FOUNDATION, TIME WARNER FOUNDATION

SOUTH TOWER EXCAVATION (page 75) has been made possible through the generosity of KEEFE, BRUYETTE & WOODS, with additional support from LOUIS AND GABRIELLE BACON

Presentation of the display on the **1993 WORLD TRADE CENTER BOMBING** (page 142) has been made possible with support from MORGAN STANLEY

Presentation of the remnant of the **ANTENNA FROM THE NORTH TOWER** (page 84) has been made possible with support from AEA INVESTORS LP

Presentation of the **BENT STEEL COLUMN** has been made possible with support from PRICEWATERHOUSECOOPERS LLP, VORNADO REALTY TRUST

Presentation of the **DEAR HERO COLLECTION** has been made possible with support from DELTA AIR LINES

Presentation of the **ELEVATOR MOTOR** (page 85) has been made possible with support from THE MOINIAN GROUP

Presentation of the **EVENTS OF THE DAY AUDIO ALCOVES** have been made possible with support from VERIZON

Presentation of the piece of **EXTERIOR STEEL FROM THE TWIN TOWERS** has been made possible with support from THE STARR FOUNDATION

Presentation of the **FDNY AMBULANCE** (page 132) has been made possible with support from THE CROWN FAMILY, JACK AND SUSAN RUDIN AND THE RUDIN FAMILY, UNITEDHEALTHCARE

Presentation of the **FDNY ENGINE COMPANY 21 TRUCK** (pages 113 and 128) has been made possible with support from ANHEUSER-BUSCH INBEV & THE ANHEUSER-BUSCH FOUNDATION

Presentation of the **FDNY LADDER COMPANY 3 TRUCK** (pages 86–88) has been made possible by PAUL & MARIE NAPOLI AND MARC & CATHY BERN, with additional support from ELIZABETH AND LEE AINSLIE, BARCLAYS, JON S. CORZINE, GE, SHARP ELECTRONICS CORPORATION, JOHN C. WHITEHEAD

Presentation of the **GLASS WINDOWPANE FROM THE SOUTH TOWER** (page 205) has been made possible with support from AON, METLIFE FOUNDATION, THE SCOTTS MIRACLE GRO-COMPANY

Presentation of the **JOEL MEYEROWITZ PHOTOGRAPHS** (page 174) has been made possible with support from DELOITTE, INGEBORG AND IRA LEON RENNERT, KPMG LLP, THE MOODY'S FOUNDATION, WILLKIE FARR & GALLAGHER LLP

Presentation of the **LAST COLUMN** (pages 204–205) has been made possible with support from
IRON WORKERS INTL UNION & CONTRACTORS THROUGH IMPACT

Presentation of the **NEW YORK MARRIOTT WORLD TRADE CENTER HOTEL FLAG** has been made possible with support from THE J. WILLARD & ALICE S. MARRIOTT FOUNDATION

Presentation of the **ORAL HISTORY LISTENING STATIONS** has been made possible with support from AT&T

Presentation of the World Trade Center **PLAZA BENCHES** has been made possible with support from LEONARD LITWIN

Presentation of **REBIRTH AT GROUND ZERO** (pages 80–81) has been made possible with support from POLARIS CAPITAL MANAGEMENT, LLC, WITH THANKS TO PROJECT REBIRTH, with support for production from THE AON FOUNDATION, OPPENHEIMERFUNDS, INC., AND LOWER MANHATTAN DEVELOPMENT CORPORATION

Presentation of **REFLECTING ON 9/11** (pages 196–197) has been made possible with support from ACCENTURE

Presentation of the **STEEL FACADE SECTION FROM THE 93RD THROUGH 96TH FLOORS OF THE NORTH TOWER** (pages 76–77) has been made possible with support from FRANKLIN TEMPLETON INVESTMENTS AND FIDUCIARY TRUST COMPANY INTERNATIONAL, PITNEY BOWES INC., ROBERT WOOD JOHNSON 1962 CHARITABLE TRUST, SL GREEN REALTY CORP., VIACOM AND PARAMOUNT PICTURES

Presentation of the **STEEL FACADE SECTION FROM THE 96TH THROUGH 99TH FLOORS OF THE NORTH TOWER** (pages 50 and 88–89) has been made possible with support from INDRA AND RAJ NOOYI, RELATED COMPANIES, TISHMAN SPEYER, THE WENDY'S COMPANY—NELSON PELTZ AND PETER MAY

Presentation of the **SURVIVORS' STAIRS** (pages 56–57) has been made possible with support from AMERICAN EXPRESS, BNY MELLON

Presentation of **TIMESCAPE** (page 206) has been made possible with support from CREDIT SUISSE, ERNST & YOUNG LLP, FORD FOUNDATION, STARR INTERNATIONAL FOUNDATION

Presentation of **TRIBUTE ART** in the historical exhibition exit lobby has been made possible with support from THE MLB-MLBPA DISASTER RELIEF FUND & THE BASEBALL TOMORROW FUND, PEPSICO FOUNDATION, THE WALT DISNEY COMPANY FOUNDATION

Presentation of **TRIBUTE ART IN TRIBUTE WALK** (pages 70–71) has been made possible with support from CON EDISON

Presentation of the **TRIDENTS** (pages 10, 33–35) has been made possible with support from DEUTSCHE BANK

Presentation of the **TRIDENT FRAGMENT AND VIDEO OF THE RECOVERY AT GROUND ZERO** (page 175) has been made possible with support from HOWARD P. MILSTEIN/EMIGRANT BANK

Presentation of Spencer Finch's artwork **TRYING TO REMEMBER THE COLOR OF THE SKY ON THAT SEPTEMBER MORNING** (pages 22, 52–55, and 62–63) has been made possible by AGNES GUND

Presentation of the display of **VIGILS IN THE AFTERMATH OF 9/11** (page 170) has been made possible with support from THE THOMAS S. JOHNSON FAMILY IN MEMORY OF SCOTT M. JOHNSON

Presentation of **WE REMEMBER** (pages 40–42) has been made possible with support from CITI

Presentation of the display on the **WORLD TRADE CENTER IN THE POPULAR IMAGINATION** (pages 139–141) has been made possible with support from THE MARC HASS FOUNDATION—STANLEY S. SHUMAN AND ROBERT H. HAINES, HSBC, SANDLER O'NEILL & PARTNERS L.P., DAN & SHERYL TISHMAN FAMILY FOUNDATION, JOAN AND SANFORD I. WEILL AND THE WEILL FAMILY FOUNDATION, UBS

9/11 MEMORIAL & MUSEUM SENIOR STAFF

Joe Daniels President and CEO

Alice M. Greenwald Executive Vice President for Exhibitions, Collections & Education, Memorial Museum Director

Allison Blais Chief Operating Officer

Cathy Blaney Executive Vice President, Institutional Advancement

Ernie Blundell Executive Vice President, Operations

Marc Cima Chief Technology Officer

Michael Frazier Executive Vice President, Communications & Marketing

Heidi Hayden Chief People Officer

Noelle Lilien General Counsel

Irene Math Chief Financial Officer

Lou Mendes Executive Vice President, Facilities, Design & Construction

Shelby Prichard Chief of Staff

Jay Weinkam Senior Vice President, Government & Community Affairs

EXHIBITION TEAM LEADERS FOR MUSEUM OPENING

Amy S. Weisser Senior Vice President for Exhibitions

Jan Seidler Ramirez Senior Vice President for Collections and Chief Curator

Michael Shulan Creative Director for Museum Planning

Ian Kerrigan Director of Exhibitions

Amy Weinstein Director of Collections and Senior Oral Historian

Emily Cramer Exhibition Production Manager

Liz Mazucci Director of Research

Clifford Chanin Senior Vice President for Education and Public Programs

Edward Sidor Vice President for Facilities, Design & Construction

EXHIBITION DESIGN AND FABRICATION FOR MUSEUM OPENING

Lead Exhibition Design for the Memorial Museum Thinc Design with Local Projects

Introductory Exhibits, Memorial Exhibition, and Exhibition Level Design Thinc Design

Introductory Exhibits, Memorial Exhibition, and Exhibition Level Fabrication Hadley Exhibits, Inc.

Historical Exhibition Design Layman Design

Historical Exhibition Fabrication Design and Production Incorporated

Media Production Local Projects

Media Integration Electrosonic

Audiovisual System Design PPI Consulting

Lighting Design Fisher Marantz Stone, Layman Design, and Renfro Design Group, Inc.

Acoustic Design Jaffe Holden

Conservation Art Preservation Services

Owner Representation Zubatkin Owner Representation, LLC

Museum Architect Davis Brody Bond, LLP

Pavilion Architect Snøhetta

Construction Manager Lend Lease

SPECIAL THANKS

Acoustiguide, R. Baker & Son, C&G Partners, CDM Sound Studios, Patricia Edmonds, Howard + Revis Design Services, Infusion, Institute for Human Centered Design, KC Fabrications, Libby Kreutz, Lord Cultural Resources, Management Resources, Object Mounts, Christine Valentine

PHOTOGRAPHY CREDITS

All installation and architectural photographs of the Museum by Jin S. Lee, except as noted. Installation photographs on pages 46, 80, 82, and 209 by Amy Dreher. Installation photograph on page 90 by Barry Rustin, courtesy of Layman Design.

Metal fragment on page 96 courtesy of the New-York Historical Society. Lamppost segment on page 106 courtesy of the New York State Museum, Albany. Plane part to left on page 107 courtesy of the Smithsonian National Air and Space Museum, Washington, D.C. Plane parts and clock on page 116 courtesy of the American Airlines C.R. Smith Museum. Burnt television on page 116 courtesy of Curator Branch, Naval History and Heritage Command. Urn on page 164 courtesy of the NYC Department of Records/Municipal Archives. Plaque on page 164 courtesy of the George W. Bush Presidential Library and Museum, National Archives, Washington, D.C. Crystal flag on page 164 courtesy of the Port Authority of New York and New Jersey, Public Safety Department. Steel cut in shape of heart on page 177 courtesy of the Rev. Diane Reiners. Steel cut in shape of Star of David on page 177 courtesy of Alan Reiss. Baseballs on page 177 courtesy of the Williams family. Fragment of *Bent Propeller* sculpture by artist Alexander Calder on pages 177 and 179 recovered from the World Trade Center site after September 11, 2001, Collection 9/11 Memorial Museum, courtesy of the Port Authority of New York and New Jersey, © 2016 Calder Foundation, New York / Artists Rights Society (ARS), New York.

MEMORIAL EXHIBITION ACKNOWLEDGMENTS

In Memoriam was created with resources contributed by family members and friends of those killed in the attacks. Content was also provided through the Voices of September 11th's 9/11 Living Memorial project, originally conceived by September's Mission; the StoryCorps September 11th Initiative, with support from the Lower Manhattan Development Corporation; the 9/11 Tribute Center; the New York City Fire Department Family Assistance Unit; the New York City Police Department; the Port Authority Police Department; the *New York Times*; the Pentagon Memorial Fund; the Cantor Fitzgerald Relief Fund; and the U.S. Department of Justice. The National September 11 Memorial Museum acknowledges with gratitude the participation of family members in providing guidance about their loved one's representation in the memorial exhibition installation.

First published in the United States of America in 2016 by

Skira Rizzoli Publications, Inc.
300 Park Avenue South
New York, NY 10010
www.rizzoliusa.com

© 2016 National September 11 Memorial & Museum

2016 2017 2018 2019 / 10 9 8 7 6 5 4 3 2 1

Printed in the United States of America

ISBN-13: 978-0-8478-4947-5 (hardcover)
ISBN-13: 978-0-8478-4948-2 (paperback)

Library of Congress Catalog Control Number: 2016939352

No Day Shall Erase You
The Story of 9/11 as Told at the National September 11 Memorial Museum
Alice M. Greenwald

For Skira Rizzoli Publications, Inc.
Margaret Rennolds Chace, Associate Publisher
James O. Muschett, Associate Publisher and Project Editor

Book Design by Yolanda Cuomo, NYC
Yolanda Cuomo, Art Director
Bonnie Briant, Associate Designer
Bobbie Richardson and Jonno Rattman, Assistant Designer